Mean Streets

Migration, Xenophobia and Informality in South Africa

Published by the Southern African Migration Programme (SAMP), the African Centre for Cities (ACC) and the International Development Research Centre (IDRC)

Southern African Migration Programme, International Migration Research Centre Balsillie School of International Affairs, 67 Erb Street West, Waterloo, Ontario N2L 6C2, Canada

African Centre for Cities, University of Cape Town, Environmental & Geographical Science Building, Upper Campus, Rondebosch, 7701, South Africa

International Development Research Centre, 160 Kent St, Ottawa, Canada K1P 0B2 and Eaton Place, 3rd floor, United Nations Crescent, Gigiri, Nairobi, Kenya

ISBN 978-1-920596-11-8

© SAMP 2015

First published 2015

Production, including editing, design and layout, by Bronwen Dachs Muller

Cover by Michiel Botha

Cover photograph by Alon Skuy/The Times. The photograph shows Soweto residents looting a migrant-owned shop in a January 2015 spate of attacks in South Africa

Index by Ethné Clarke

Printed by MegaDigital, Cape Town

Mean Streets

Migration, Xenophobia and Informality in South Africa

Edited by
Jonathan Crush
Abel Chikanda
Caroline Skinner

Acknowledgements

The editors would like to acknowledge the financial and programming support of the International Development Research Centre (IDRC), which funded the research of the Growing Informal Cities Project and the Workshop on Urban Informality and Migrant Entrepreneurship in Southern African Cities hosted by SAMP and the African Centre for Cities in Cape Town in February 2014. Many of the chapters in this volume were first presented at this workshop. We would like to extend particular thanks to Paul Okwi, Edgard Rodriguez, Luc Mougeot, and Rosemary Ngigi of IDRC for their assistance. Others deserving thanks for their help with the workshop and the preparation of this volume include Bronwen Dachs, Edgar Pieterse, Gordon Pirie, Maria Salamone, Saskia Greyling, and Ithra Najaar.

Contents

Page

List of Tables

List of Figures

List of Contributors

Roni Amit — Senior Researcher, African Centre for Migration & Society, University of the Witwatersrand, Johannesburg, South Africa

Eugene Campbell — Independent Researcher, Gaborone, Botswana

Andrew Charman — Director, Sustainable Livelihoods Foundation, Cape Town, South Africa

Abel Chikanda — Assistant Professor of Geography and African & African American Studies, University of Kansas, Lawrence, Kansas, United States

Jonathan Crush — Professor and CIGI Chair in Global Migration and Development, Balsillie School of International Affairs, Waterloo, Canada, and Honorary Professor at the University of Cape Town

Belinda Dodson — Associate Professor, Department of Geography, University of Western Ontario, London, Ontario, Canada

Vanya Gastrow — PhD Student, African Centre for Migration & Society, University of the Witwatersrand, Johannesburg, South Africa

Thuso Green — General Secretary, Titi G Foundation, Maseru, Lesotho

Trynos Gumbo — Senior Lecturer, Town and Regional Planning Department, University of Johannesburg, Johannesburg, South Africa

Pranitha Maharaj — Associate Professor, Population Studies and Development Studies, University of KwaZulu-Natal, Durban, South Africa

Madeleine Northcote — MA Student, Department of Geography, University of Western Ontario, London, Ontario, Canada

Sally Peberdy — Senior Researcher, Gauteng City-Region Observatory, Johannesburg, South Africa

Leif Petersen — Managing Director, Sustainable Livelihoods Foundation, Cape Town, South Africa

Ines Raimundo — Associate Professor, Faculty of Arts and Social Sciences, Eduardo Mondlane University, Maputo, Mozambique

Sujata Ramachandran   Research Associate, Southern African Migration Programme, International Migration Research Centre, Waterloo, Canada

Christian M. Rogerson   Professor, School of Tourism and Hospitality, University of Johannesburg, Johannesburg, South Africa

Caroline Skinner   Senior Researcher, African Centre for Cities, and Urban Research Director for Women in Informal Employment: Globalizing and Organizing, Cape Town, South Africa

Akwa Tafuh   Population Studies and Development Studies, University of KwaZulu-Natal, Durban, South Africa

Godfrey Tawodzera   Senior Lecturer, Department of Geography and Environmental Sciences, University of Limpopo, Polokwane, South Africa

Robertson K. Tengeh   Senior Lecturer, Department of Entrepreneurship & Business Management, Cape Peninsula University of Technology, Cape Town, South Africa

Daniel Tevera   Professor, Department of Geography, Environmental Studies and Tourism, University of the Western Cape, Cape Town, South Africa

Vusilizwe Thebe   Lecturer, Department of Development Studies, National University of Lesotho, Roma, Lesotho

Lodene Willemse   Analyst, Centre for Urban and Regional Innovation and Statistical Exploration, Stellenbosch University, Stellenbosch, South Africa

Tanya Zack   Researcher, Centre for Urbanism and Built Environment Studies, School of Architecture and Planning, University of the Witwatersrand, Johannesburg, South Africa

Nomsa Zindela   Lecturer, Department of English Studies, University of South Africa, Pretoria, South Africa

List of Acronyms

ACC	African Centre for Cities
CBD	Central Business District
CID	City Improvement District
CJP	Central Johannesburg Partnership
CoJ	City of Johannesburg
COMESA	Common Market for Eastern and Southern Africa
DSBD	Department of Small Business Development
DTI	Department of Trade and Industry
EMU	Eduardo Mondlane University
ESAP	Economic Structural Adjustment Programme
GCRO	Gauteng City-Region Observatory
HDS	Human Development Strategy
IBUF	Informal Business Upliftment Facility
ICBT	Informal Sector Cross-Border Trade
IMRC	International Migration Research Centre
JDA	Johannesburg Development Agency
JMPD	Johannesburg Metropolitan Police Department
MEC	Member of the Executive Council
NIBDS	National Informal Business Development Strategy
NIBUS	National Informal Business Upliftment Strategy
NSBAC	National Small Business Advisory Council
O&D	Origin and Destination
SAMP	Southern African Migration Programme
SAPS	South African Police Services
SARS	South African Revenue Service
SEDA	Small Enterprise Development Agency
SMMEs	Small, Medium and Micro Enterprises
SPSS	Statistical Package for the Social Sciences
SSA	Statistics South Africa
VAT	Value-Added Tax
ZDP	Zimbabwe Documentation Project

"No matter how much you tried to be one of them, you'd never belong, they wouldn't let you. Maybe they couldn't. Maybe they didn't belong themselves." – Piri Thomas, *Down These Mean Streets*, 1967

Chapter One

Migrant Entrepreneurship and Informality in South African Cities

Jonathan Crush, Abel Chikanda and Caroline Skinner

INTRODUCTION

In 2012, the police in Limpopo launched an aggressive military-style campaign to apprehend criminals and tackle illicit activities in the province. In practice, this crusade, dubbed "Operation Hardstick", targeted small informal businesses run by migrants and refugees. The police closed over 600 businesses, detained owners, confiscated their stock, imposed fines for trading without permits, and showered them with verbal abuse (Supreme Court, 2014). The business owners were informed that "foreigners" were not allowed to operate in South Africa, that their asylum-seeker and refugee permits did not entitle them to run a business, and that they should leave the area. Thirty displaced migrants from Ethiopia were forced to flee when the house they had taken refuge in was fire-bombed. Despite its label as a crime-fighting initiative, Operation Hardstick was selectively enforced, affecting only migrant entrepreneurs and not South African businesses in the same locations.

An affidavit before the Supreme Court in the landmark 2014 case of *Somali Association of South Africa and Others v Limpopo Department of Economic Development, Environment and Tourism and Others* claimed that the police actions "tell a story of the most naked form of xenophobic discrimination and of the utter desperation experienced by the victims of that discrimination" (Supreme Court, 2014: 6-7). The Supreme Court judgment observed that "one is left with the uneasy feeling that the stance adopted by the authorities in relation to the licensing of spaza shops and tuck-shops was in order to induce foreign nationals who were destitute to leave our shores" (Supreme Court, 2014: 25). Opposing the appeal were all three tiers of government: national, provincial and municipal. Among them were the Limpopo Member of the Executive Council (MEC) for Safety, Security and Liaison; the Provincial Commissioner of Police; the National Police Commissioner; the Standing Committee on Refugee Affairs; the Ministers of Police, Labour and Home Affairs; and two municipalities.

In its judgment in favour of the appellants and against the state, the Supreme Court found that "the manner in which the respondents conducted the litigation in this matter (is) disconcerting. In the main they avoided dealing with any of the specific allegations of maltreatment and abuse raised by the appellants" (Supreme Court, 2014:12). Their main argument was simply that "foreigners" had no constitutional or legal right to self-employment in South Africa. While the case represents a significant victory for refugees and asylum seekers, the Hardstick affair is symptomatic of an endemic problem: that is, the myriad regulatory and legal obstacles and the culture of police and official impunity that confront small migrant businesses not just in Limpopo province but throughout South Africa. In late 2013, for example, the Johannesburg City Council violently removed and confiscated the inventory of an estimated 6,000 inner-city street traders, many of them migrants. A group of traders took the City to court and, in April 2014, the Constitutional Court ruled in their favour with Acting Chief Justice Moseneke noting that the so-called Operation Cleansweep was an act of "humiliation and degradation" and that the attitude of the City "may well border on the cynical" (Constitutional Court, 2014).

In other contexts, international migrants are lauded for their enterprise, hard work and business acumen in successfully establishing and growing small enterprises in countries of settlement (Waldinger et al., 1990; Rath, 2000; Kloosterman and Rath, 2001; Ensign and Robinson, 2011). Although these "unsung heroes" (Kloosterman and Rath, 2003: 1) face considerable economic and social challenges, they make a vital contribution to economic growth, job creation and social cohesion. Increasingly, they are also seen as playing an important role in the development of their countries of origin, through remittances, investments and skills transfer. Not so in South Africa, where migrant entrepreneurs are more often vilified than seen as heroic. Since the advent of democracy in South Africa in 1994, migrant entrepreneurs have been consistently portrayed by government and the media as unwanted parasites, as driving South African small businesses to the wall, as taking jobs from citizens and as engaged in nefarious business practices.

Official disdain from above is accompanied by, and licenses, hostility from below. Murderous attacks and looting of migrant-owned small businesses have become a daily occurrence up and down the country, most recently in Johannesburg and Durban in early 2015. Organized police operations to try to eradicate informal enterprise are also commonplace. Unsurprisingly, then, many migrant entrepreneurs complain that they receive little police protection when their business premises or lives are in danger and that they are even the victims of police extortion (Abdi, 2011; Charman and Piper, 2012; Gastrow, 2013). There were even recent press reports that police were coordinating the orderly looting of migrant-owned businesses in Soweto (City Press, 2015).

Against the backdrop of ongoing hostility towards migrant entrepreneurs in the corridors of power and on the streets of major cities, the partners in the Growing Informal Cities Project convened a policy workshop on migrant entrepreneurship in South Africa, Mozambique and Zimbabwe in February 2014 in Cape Town. The primary objective of the workshop was to examine the role of migrant entrepreneurs in the regional urban informal economy, to test the myths and stereotypes around migrant economic activity with hard evidence, and to initiate a conversation about the positive contribution that migrant entrepreneurs make to South Africa. This volume includes a selection of papers presented at the workshop. The book focuses on the South African informal economy and the role of informal migrant entrepreneurship in South Africa. Other project publications will present a more regional perspective and discuss the results of research with migrant entrepreneurs and informal traders conducted during 2014.

ENTREPRENEURIAL MOBILITIES

Within urban areas, mobility is essential to the operation and dynamism of the urban informal economy and a vital component of the business strategies of informal operatives who work spaces with niche markets or a relative absence of the formal sector. While some businesses operate from fixed sites others are extremely mobile, conducting business in different parts of the city on different days or at different times of a single day. Many of the participants in the informal economy are internal or international migrants, often in competition with one another for market share. Although the numbers of international migrants are frequently exaggerated, it is clear that they have played an increasingly important role in the informal economies of South African cities over the last two decades and have reshaped the nature of informality and informal entrepreneurship in the region. Yet the importance of that role is underestimated, invisible to researchers and denigrated by policy-makers (Peberdy and Rogerson, 2003; Visser, 2010; Wafer, 2011).

In the 1990s and early 2000s, most aspirant migrant entrepreneurs in South Africa settled in large cities such as Johannesburg, Cape Town and Durban (Morris, 1998; Peberdy and Rogerson, 2002). These cities continue to be the major sites of informal migrant enterprise. However, one of the distinctive features of migrant entrepreneurship is its diffusion throughout the country and down the urban hierarchy to many intermediate and smaller cities. A growing number of studies attest to the increase in business activity of migrant entrepreneurs in other South African urban centres (Pauw and Petrus, 2003; Masonganye, 2009; Park and Chen, 2009; Hikam, 2011; Gebre et al., 2011; Fatoki and Patswawairi, 2012; Garg and Phayane, 2014; Mthombeni et al., 2014). This is a direct response to the search for new markets and the fact that the policing of informality and immigration is more relaxed in smaller centres. There is also evidence of a growing diversification of migrant source countries. Most migrants are still from neighbouring countries but there are increasing numbers from many other African countries as well as farther afield, including Bangladesh, Pakistan and China (Huynh et al., 2010; Govender, 2012; Harrison et al., 2012; McNamee, 2012; Munshi, 2013; Lin, 2014; Willemse, 2014).

According to Census data, rates of unemployment among migrants in South Africa are generally lower than among South Africans, varying from a low of six per cent in the case of Indian migrants to a high of 30 per cent in the case of migrants from Lesotho (South Africans have an unemployment rate of 31 per cent). Only 18 per cent of Zimbabwean and 24 per cent of Mozambican migrants were unemployed in 2011 (Budlender, 2013). The key question is how many migrants either work in or are self-employed in the informal economy. A 2010 SAMP survey of recent Zimbabwean migrants in Johannesburg and Cape Town found that 20 per cent were involved in the informal sector (Crush et al., 2013). Studies of other migrant groups such as Somalis suggest even higher rates of informal economy participation (Jinnah, 2010; Gastrow and Amit, 2013). Asylum seekers and refugees from various countries are largely excluded from the formal labour market and show high levels of enterprise and innovation in the informal economy (Maqanda, 2012). The 2012 South African Quarterly Labour Force Survey (Q3) showed clear differences between South Africans and international migrants (Budlender, 2014). Twenty-one per cent of international migrants were classified as self-employed compared with seven per cent of internal migrants and nine per cent of non-migrants. However, only 13 per cent of the self-employed were international migrants compared with 15 per cent of internal migrants and 71 per cent of non-migrants.

The common perception that migrants are far more successful entrepreneurs than South Africans in the informal economy has prompted a new focus on migrant entrepreneurial motivation and comparisons with South African entrepreneurship (Fatoki and Patswawairi, 2012; Lapah and Tengeh, 2013). One study of 500 SMMEs in the retail sector in Gauteng found no significant difference between South Africans and migrants in terms of their motivation to start a business (Radipere and Dhliwayo, 2014). Another study of the entrepreneurial orientation of South African and non-South African street traders in inner-city Johannesburg actually found that South Africans were more innovative than international migrants (Callaghan and Venter, 2011). However, South Africans were associated with lower levels of the entrepreneurial qualities of "proactiveness" and "competitive aggression" and, overall, South African nationality was "negatively and significantly associated with total entrepreneurial orientation" (Callaghan, 2009). A third study of the spaza shop sector in Khayelitsha, Cape Town, found that migrants scored higher on four separate indicators of entrepreneurial orientation: achievement, innovation, personal initiative and autonomy (Basardien et al., 2014).

Other aspects of migrant entrepreneurial motivation have been examined in various case studies. One, for example, analyzed the "competitive intelligence" of migrant-owned businesses in Johannesburg and found that competition information-seeking is performed by the majority of owners and their employees, especially to monitor the prices of their competitors (Fatoki, 2014a). This enables them to undercut their competition and attract more customers. The study also examined the growth expectations of migrant entrepreneurs and found a high degree of optimism (Fatoki, 2013a). Education, managerial experience, related experience, motivation and networking were all significant predictors of positive growth expectations. At the firm level, innovation and adequate access to finance were significant predictors of growth expectations.

In terms of the economic challenges confronting informal-sector entrepreneurs, a major issue is the lack of access to financial services including start-up capital and ongoing credit. Formal financial institutions are extremely reluctant to do business with migrant informal entrepreneurs. These entrepreneurs "have limited access to debt finance from commercial banks as they have problems in opening bank accounts, and acquiring visas and permits. In addition, most…have never applied for credit, despite the need for credit and may thus be classified as discouraged borrowers" (Fatoki, 2013b: 92-3, see also Fatoki, 2012). The study of migrant entrepreneurs in inner-city Johannesburg, cited above, found that less than a third had applied for credit and only a third of these were successful (Fatoki, 2014b). Another study of Cape Town entrepreneurs from 19 African countries found that only 9 per cent had acquired a bank loan as start-up capital (Khosa, 2014).

As a result of the lack of credit, many migrant entrepreneurs rely on various "boot-strapping" methods to minimize their capital outlay and running costs. The most common methods include obtaining loans from family and friends, sharing business premises, buying on consignment, cash discounts, and delaying payments to suppliers (Fatoki, 2013, 2014b). Migrant entrepreneurs also have small mark-ups and long working hours, resulting in increased gross earnings (Callaghan, 2012). Many are using mobile phones and other technology that allows for increased interaction with suppliers and customers while reducing the need to travel (Hyde-Clarke, 2013). Some also make use of social media by, for instance, advertising their services on Facebook. However, a large number still lack access to computers, which means records continue to be kept manually (Fatoki, 2014c). It has been suggested that the success of some migrant businesses-owners in South Africa is also due to superior educational qualifications and there is certainly some empirical support for this contention (Morris and Pitt, 1995; Kalitanyi and Visser, 2010; Callaghan, 2013).

A central premise of the hostility towards "foreigners" in South Africa is that they "steal" jobs from South Africans. A SAMP survey in 2010 found that 60 per cent of South Africans believe that migrants take jobs and only 27 per cent that they create them (Crush et al., 2013). Furthermore, nearly 60 per cent felt that reasons for the xenophobic violence of 2008 included that migrants take jobs from South Africans and that they do not belong in the country. At the same time, only 16 per cent of South Africans claimed that they had personally been denied a job because it was given to a foreign national. Studies in Johannesburg in the late 1990s suggested that migrant-owned businesses actually created jobs for South Africans through direct hire (Rogerson, 1997). This finding was widely cited but was based on a small sample in a localized area of the city. More recent research has consistently corroborated that migrant entrepreneurs generate employment for other migrants and for South Africans (Kalitanyi and Visser, 2010).

One study of migrant entrepreneurs from Cameroon, Ethiopia, Ghana, Senegal and Somalia in Cape Town found that 52 per cent had paid employees and that, of these, 48 per cent employed South Africans (Tengeh, 2012). Another study of migrant entrepreneurs from Somalia, Nigeria and Senegal, also in Cape Town, found that 96 per cent employed South Africans (Kalitanyi, 2007). A different picture emerged in a comparative study of South African-owned and migrant-owned small, medium and micro enterprises (SMMEs) in Tshwane and Johannesburg (Radipere, 2012). Two-thirds of the South African enterprises employed other South Africans and only 5 per cent employed non-South Africans. Nearly 30 per cent employed both. Only 12 per cent of the migrant-owned enterprises employed only South Africans but almost half employed South Africans and non-South Africans. These positive findings about job creation were confirmed by a Growing Informal Cities study in Cape Town and Johannesburg in 2014, whose results will be published in the SAMP Migration Policy Series.

Migrants are often more entrepreneurial than most, yet the constraints they face in establishing and growing their businesses are considerable. Their general contribution to employment creation and inclusive growth is undervalued and often misrepresented as a threat. Migrants in the South African informal economy do have considerable entrepreneurial ambition but are severely hampered in growing their enterprises by a range of obstacles (Rogerson, 1997; Peberdy and Rogerson, 2002, 2003; Moyo and Gumbo, 2014; Grant and Thompson, 2015). These include: lack of access to financial services (refugees and asylum seekers are commonly refused bank accounts and loans); national immigration and refugee policies, which determine the terms and conditions of entry and the ability to move along migration corridors between countries; documentation, which determines the degree of access to social, financial and support services; immigration enforcement, with the ever-present threat of arrest and deportation disrupting business activity; municipal regulations, which are generally unfriendly to the informal sector; and hostile and xenophobic local attitudes (Hunter and Skinner, 2003; Skinner, 2006; Maharaj, 2009; Crush and Ramachandran, 2010).

This volume builds on previous research by offering new insights and nuance on the nature and contribution of migrant entrepreneurship to the South African economy. It draws on empirical work conducted in Johannesburg, Cape Town and Durban but also on cross-border trade. Work has been done in different settlement types (informal settlements, township and suburban settings as well as the inner city). Trade is the dominant activity in South Africa's informal economy and much of the content reflects on migrants' role in this activity. Some chapters focus on migrants from particular countries including China, Cameroon and Somalia, while others focus on migrants in particular localities or types of activity. Research methods range from area censuses to large-scale regional surveys to area surveys of smaller samples of migrant entrepreneurs. Some chapters involve more detailed ethnographic work or a combination of both survey material and ethnographic interviews.

HOSTILITY AND XENOPHOBIA

In the next chapter, Jonathan Crush and Sujata Ramachandran provide a backdrop to the main themes of the volume by detailing the pattern of collective violence against migrant-owned businesses in South Africa. Drawing on the SAMP database of media coverage they find that from 1994 to August of 2014 (and excluding the nation-wide xenophobic attacks in May 2008), there were at least 228 documented episodes of collective violence against migrants and refugee businesses in various locations around the country. They point out that the actual tally is likely to be even higher since not all events reach the attention of the media and monitoring organizations. They identify an upswing of incidents from 2006 onwards, with the sharpest growth occurring after 2008. The five years with the largest number of incidents were from 2010 to 2014. Their data suggests that while the Western Cape and Gauteng have experienced particularly high levels of violence, since 2009 the majority of provinces have witnessed repeated incidents.

From this it is clear that many migrant entrepreneurs face constant belligerence and abuse. These actions include written or verbal threats and insults, extortion for protection by local leaders, police and residents, public intimidation through protests or marches and damage to the physical structure of shops, especially through arson. What is striking is the numerous cases of looting, the direct physical violence towards migrant store own-ers or their employees and the temporary or permanent forced displacement of migrant entrepreneurs and their families. Crush and Ramachandran cite numerous cases that illus-trate the nature and intensity of collective violence. South African politicians and senior officials at national, provincial and municipal levels are quick to label collective violence against migrants and refugees as "opportunistic crimes," committed by "criminal elements." In many of these episodes of violence targeting foreign-owned businesses, migrants have reported that police are passive and there have been very few convictions of perpetrators. As they note, weak or lack of effective punishment for the perpetrators of violence sends "permissive signals."

A recurrent theme throughout the volume is the extent to which migrant entrepreneurs experience violence and live in constant fear. South African business competitors, both individuals but increasingly organized in groups (for example, the Greater Gauteng Business Forum and Zanokhanyo Retailers' Association in Khayelitsha, Cape Town) are identified by a number of authors as playing a role in animating or inciting collective violence against migrant entrepreneurs. Madeleine Northcote and Belinda Dodson's study of refugees and asylum seekers working in a range of different sectors in Cape Town describes the violence that many experience as "an extremely common theme" in interviews. This was particularly acute in township settings. Their more ethnographic methods also highlight the violence that refugees experienced in their home countries that drove them to seek protection in South Africa.

Cameroonian informal entrepreneurs interviewed in Akwa Tafuh and Pranitha Maharaj's study reported that the hostility they face from South Africans is a "major challenge" affecting how they conduct their businesses. Somali spaza shop owners interviewed in Vanya Gastrow and Roni Amit's study expressed little interest in purchasing immovable property due to insecurity. They reported worrying about being run out of the area in the event of xenophobic attacks and also feared a local backlash if they tried to buy houses in the townships. Trynos Gumbo describes the phenomenon of "small screen counters and hidden doors" among migrant spaza shop owners in Soweto. He explains how, against the backdrop of "criminality, resentment and disapproval of their business activities by local spaza owners," migrants have had to devise ways of securing their goods including having small windows that are used as counters and reinforced burglar bars.

Another dominant strain of hostility emanates from the state itself. Tanya Zack provides a detailed account of how Operation Cleansweep impacted on informal traders working in the Ethiopian quarter in the Johannesburg inner-city. Traders reported the confiscation of all their goods, and losses related to the monies they had paid for trading infrastructure and upfront rentals. Many reported "losing everything." One interviewee noted that there was no warning when their goods were confiscated and that "it's as if the police are loot-ing." As noted above, the traders took the council to court and won the case. However, the impact was still very negative. As the judge concluded after reviewing the evidence, "the undisputed evidence showed that the applicants and their families' livelihood depended on their trading in the inner city. They have been rendered destitute and unable to provide for their families" (Constitutional Court, 2014).

Other studies reveal ongoing attempts by state officials to extort monies from migrant entrepreneurs. Chinese entrepreneurs in Lodene Willemse's study reported regular attempts by officials to extort bribes from them. When asked to identify the factors that influenced day-to-day business operations police corruption was the most cited factor. Cross-border traders seem particularly vulnerable to extortion. Vusilezwi Thebe's interviews with those transporting remittances and people between South Africa and Zimbabwe found that on average they were paying between ZAR2,000 and ZAR5,000 in bribes on a single journey.

Too little attention has been paid to how developments in the formal economy shape what happens in the informal. For example, there has been much negative focus on migrant penetration of the spaza market as a core source of tension and conflict. This conveniently overlooks the fact that the biggest challenge to South African spaza owners comes not from migrants but from South Africa's own formal supermarket chains, which have now estab-lished themselves in townships throughout the country (Battersby and Peyton, 2014).

THE NATURE AND CONTRIBUTION OF MIGRANT BUSINESSES

Despite the hardships frequently faced by migrant entrepreneurs, several chapters in this book paint a picture of significant economic contributions. In their chapter, Andrew Char-man and Leif Petersen, for example, outline how migrants have transformed the relatively new township settlement of Ivory Park in Johannesburg. They argue that migrants have introduced "a diverse range of products, business activities and opportunities, and brought scarce manufacturing skills into the township economy" and conclude that they have "indeed enhanced the Ivory Park economy." Gumbo's study of migrant spaza entrepreneurs in Soweto echoes these findings by demonstrating the innovations they have introduced, while Zack describes the many hundreds of street traders and micro retailers in Jeppe in inner city Johannesburg as comprising a "booming agglomeration economy." She argues that this intense trade is a manifestation of low-end globalization, "where the transnational flows of people and goods are oiled not by high finance but by small amounts of capital and through informal transactions."

Thebe's study of the informal transnational movement of remittances and people on the route between Gauteng and the rural hinterlands of Zimbabwe draws attention to the particular niches or gaps in the market that migrants often identify and fill. His analysis spans the period from the late 1980s, when the industry first emerged, to the present and shows how it has adapted to changing circumstances, especially developments in the Zimbabwean economy and South African migration regulatory regime. Key beneficiaries are poorer consumers who can access cheap goods often in appropriate quantities, at places and times of day that are convenient, or have their niche demands met like the transport of people and money to areas not serviced by the formal economy.

Another aspect of the contribution of migrant entrepreneurs is the payment of rentals to South African landlords. The amounts cited are significant. Gumbo's survey of 120 migrant spaza shops in Soweto, for example, found that 96 per cent paid more than ZAR1,500 a month to their South African landlords, while 22 per cent paid between ZAR2,500 and ZAR3,000. In the Johannesburg inner city, Zack found that landlords and leaseholders charge extremely high rentals for shops. In addition, she found that the informal property market in this area operates according to a practice of "key money." This is a non-refundable advance payment made to secure the property.

Crucially, and contrary to xenophobic "wisdom" that all migrants take jobs from South Africans, migrant entrepreneurs do generate employment. The evidence on whether these employees are South African or foreign is mixed. For example, the majority of paid employees in Robertson Tengeh's study of Cape Town migrant entrepreneurs from multiple countries found that there was a strong preference for employing South Africans when migrants established their businesses – 70 per cent of the 135 migrants interviewed cited a preference for South Africans during the start-up phase. But he also found that as migrants became more established, they gained confidence to employ people from their home country. Willemse notes that Chinese entrepreneurs in Johannesburg employed local residents and Tafu and Maharaj found that Cameroonians in Durban employed both South Africans and fellow migrants. In contrast, Soweto migrant spaza shop owners interviewed by Gumbo mainly employed either their relatives or someone from their country of origin. Charman and Petersen had similar findings, noting that "migrant businesses in Ivory Park almost exclusively employ members of the same ethnic group, usually family members, friends or friends of friends or at minimum members of the same clan." Given these variations, further research is clearly needed on the employment generating capacity and practices of migrant entrepreneurs.

Taken together, these studies show that rather than being disconnected from the formal economy, migrant entrepreneurs, like their non-migrant counterparts, are integrally linked into the formal economy and contribute to it significantly. All of the studies that interrogated where migrants sourced their goods found that large formal retailers and wholesalers – Shoprite, Makro, Metro Cash & Carry among others – are key players. Plastow (2015), a retail industry insider, assesses the contribution of spaza shop sales to Massmart at approximately half of group sales in 2010. He notes that American giant Walmart purchased a 51 per cent stake in Massmart for USD2 billion and concludes that "one the largest direct foreign investments in the country since democracy was underpinned by the buying power of immigrant spaza store sector" (Plastow, 2015).

Sally Peberdy et al's study of informal cross-border trade between South Africa and neighbouring countries provides further evidence of the importance of informal entrepreneurship – in this case informal trade – to South African retailers and wholesalers. At the Beitbridge border post with Zimbabwe, to cite one example, 84 per cent of traders had goods valued between ZAR1,000 and ZAR5,000 and 16 per cent had goods valued at over ZAR5,000. Collectively, given the sheer volume of trade, this represents a significant contribution to South Africa's exports to the region. In addition, the multiple purchases made by migrant entrepreneurs through the formal economy are subject to value-added tax (VAT). Cross-border traders who have invoices are entitled to claim back the VAT they have paid but only a very small minority actually did so.

MIGRANT BUSINESS STRATEGIES

A core curiosity in the research and policy arena is the nature of migrant business strategies. This is particularly the case in the spaza market where migrants are especially active and seem to be doing slightly better than their South African counterparts. Three chapters in this volume provide critical insights into the spaza sector – Gumbo's work on migrant spaza shops in Soweto; Charman and Petersen's piece on the migrant economy in Ivory Park and Gastrow and Amit's analysis of Somali spazas in Cape Town. Together the evidence suggests that migrants' competitive edge stems from hard work (long hours), careful attention to sourcing of products and servicing customer needs. The business model suggested by all three studies is one of low mark ups and reliance on high turnover.

They also suggest that migrants tend to stock a greater variety of goods. Petersen and Charman describe this as the emergence of "mini-markets" (large shops akin to small supermarkets.) In addition, goods are offered in flexible quantities (such as a single egg rather than a box of eggs, or a small plastic pouch of sugar as opposed to a whole kilogram). This is particularly important for servicing the needs of poorer consumers. Gastrow and Amit found that Somali spaza operators had introduced innovations like selling hampers of goods at a discount, end-of-month sales and special offers to draw customers in. All three studies observed that migrant entrepreneurs offered credit. Gumbo found that migrant spaza operators in Soweto sell goods on credit especially where the customer is short of cash. Gastrow and Amit report that Somali traders offered credit to pensioners who pay for their purchases at the end of the month when their pension payments come through. Offering credit builds customer loyalty. A final component of the business model appears to be a culture of thrift.

There is conflicting evidence on the sourcing strategies of migrant businesses. Charman and Petersen suggest that migrants engage in collective buying and Gumbo reports the existence of bulk purchasing, while Gastrow and Amit found evidence of neither. Their respondents reported that they carefully compared the prices of competing wholesalers from advertising leaflets and information obtained from other traders. Traders noted that they generally divide their purchases among a number of wholesalers and do not make bulk purchases at one wholesaler. All the traders in their Cape Town sample purchased goods individually. They did report, however, that they often shared transport to reduce costs, which might give rise to the mistaken perception of collective bulk buying. This is an issue that requires further investigation since it has important policy implications. One policy response to conflict in the spaza market has been to suggest that South Africans need to learn from migrants' business strategies including collective purchasing (Magubane, 2015). Gastrow and Amit's work suggests that focusing simply on collective buying and bulk purchasing might be misplaced.

Together, the chapters in this volume show that rather than adopting underhand and secretive strategies, migrant retailers are simply employing many of the strategies adopted by their formal sector counterparts. Plastow (2015) describes this business model as "providing what your shopper wants, reducing margins and selling more, whilst cutting your overheads to the bone." He adds that this is no different to the model that made household names out of Raymond Ackerman and Whitey Basson (founders of the formal sector retail giants Pick n Pay and Shoprite respectively).

Another important element of migrant business strategies mentioned by numerous authors is the role of networks and kinship ties in facilitating and supporting business. This issue is a particular preoccupation of Tengeh's study of African migrants in Cape Town. He finds that while the decision to migrate and then establish an informal business (rather than formal employment) is largely an individual one, once taken, "social networks play an extremely important role in the ongoing running of the business and therefore to its success." He notes that ethnic and friendship networks, which often overlap, are relied upon by the vast majority of migrants for financial and other support. In her chapter, Willemse highlights the role played by networks among Chinese entrepreneurs. She notes that the Chinese even have a term – *guanxi* – that refers to the networks that facilitate business activity. *Guanxi* is defined as personal relationships in which "long term mutual benefits are more important than short term individual gains." She finds that these networks give entrepreneurs a competitive advantage due to sharing business information (about suppliers, cost and labour), joint training initiatives, and finance through credit or investment associations. In Thebe's research on the informal transport of monies and people (including children and even babies), neighbourhood and kinship ties emerge as a central feature of this aspect of the informal economy. In the Somali spaza market, Amit and Gastrow show that there is concurrent competition and cooperation among Somali shop owners – they compete to get the best price through individual purchasing and bargaining with wholesalers while cooperating in sharing transport and jointly investing in shops. Northcote and Dodson point out that family networks can be both an asset and a liability – while family often supply start-up capital this comes with the pressure to remit money that might otherwise be saved or reinvested in the business.

The gendered nature of migrant entrepreneurship emerges in the chapter by Dodson and Northcote. They outline the specificity of migrant women entrepreneurs' experiences and contributions and show how certain migrant occupations are heavily gendered, such as women in hair braiding and men in craft production and sales, or construction work for males and domestic service for females engaged in casual labour. Within trading and hawking activities, the women in this study were engaged in more marginal and less secure forms of trade, such as itinerant selling or roadside stalls, whereas it was men who ran spaza shops. Gender, they argue, is a critical element of whether or not migrants succeed in business.

POST-APARTHEID POLICY RESPONSES

The informal economy in the post-apartheid period has at best been ignored, and at worst actively discouraged. In his chapter, Christian Rogerson provides a detailed account of national government policy and institutional support to the informal economy during the post-apartheid period. He concludes that from 1994 to 2011, government made a set of "rhetorical commitments" to supporting informal business but few initiatives were actually launched. The active discouragement of informality is particularly evident at a city level, as is evident from Zack's account of Operation Cleansweep in Johannesburg. Despite lip service to the positive role of the informal economy in general and street traders in particular, the city has a history of ambiguous practices. Wafer's (2011, 2014) detailed analysis shows how the City of Johannesburg has long been ambivalent to the informal economy.

Although less draconian, Cape Town's approach has elements of systematic exclusion of critical aspects of the informal economy (Crush et al., 2015). Consider for example street trading. Recent research on Cape Town found that the City had allocated only 410 street-trading bays in the whole inner city (Bukasa, 2014; Mwasinga, 2013). There is also evidence of ongoing harassment of traders throughout the city (IOL, 2012; Weiss, 2013). Although the policy environment varies in different parts of the city, and between different segments within the informal economy, the modernist vision of the "world-class city" with its associated antipathy towards informality and the pathologizing of informal space and activity seems to predominate.

Two recent policy developments – the 2013 draft Licensing of Businesses Bill and the 2014 National Informal Business Upliftment Strategy (NIBUS) are significant as they are the first post-apartheid national initiatives on the informal economy but also because both aim to curtail migrant participation in that economy. While Rogerson analyses these developments in detail, key elements are worth reiterating. The draft Bill specified that any person involved in business activities – no matter how small – would be required to have a licence and that licences would only be given to non-citizens who have first acquired a business permit under the Immigration Act or a refugee permit under the Refugees Act (RSA, 2013). Business permits have to be applied for in the country of origin and are only granted if the applicant can demonstrate that he or she has ZAR2.5 million to invest in South Africa. Few, if any, cross-border traders and migrant entrepreneurs currently operating in the South African informal economy would qualify. It also suggests that enforcement of the Bill would be delegated to community-based organizations, non-governmental organizations and others in collaboration with the licensing authorities. The implication here is that South Africans would assist the police in identifying and "rooting out" foreign traders, a particularly unfortunate scenario in light of the well-documented hostility of local business bodies towards migrants.

The final version of NIBUS echoes the anti-foreign sentiment of the draft Bill, identifying foreign trading as an "express challenge" and asserting there are "no regulatory restrictions in controlling the influx of foreigners" and that there is "no synergy between the DTI and Home Affairs in devising strategies and policies to control foreign business activities" (DTI, 2014: 22). As precedent, NIBUS approvingly cites the 2013 Ghana Investment Promotion Centre Act, which has reserved the sale of any goods in a market, petty trading and hawking, and the operation of metered taxis, car hire services, beauty salons and barber shops to nationals only (DTI, 2014: 22). However, simply because another African country adopts a xenophobic policy does not make it right for South Africa. Nor does NIBUS reference the many other African countries that do not discriminate against migrants in this way.

The draft Licensing of Businesses Bill would result in large-scale criminalization of current informal activities both South African and migrant-owned. The sections of NIBUS that focus on regulation echo similar sentiments of needing to regulate and control in an attempt to tackle "the foreign trader challenge." This focus is counter to all good policy practice of management and support of the informal economy both in South Africa and globally (Chen, 2012). Ironically, this would be destructive for South African and migrant informal operators alike. The focus on curtailing migrant entrepreneurship diverts attention from what Crush and Ramachandran identify as "the real, urgent need to support and enhance opportunities for all small entrepreneurs."

The courts are playing an increasing important role in securing the livelihoods of informal economy operators in general and migrant entrepreneurs in particular. The Constitutional Court challenge to Johannesburg's Operation Cleansweep was complemented by the February 2015 Durban High Court ruling challenging the legality of the Durban's city council's relentless confiscation of street traders' goods (Broughton, 2015). For refugees and asylum seekers, the 2014 Supreme Court of Appeal's ruling that they had a right to self-employment is of particular significance. Litigation has been one of the only sources of support to migrant entrepreneurs and points to the core contradiction between, on the one hand, the rights enshrined in the South African Constitution and South Africa's relatively progressive refugee regime and, on the other, the policies and actions of key government departments and officials. Protecting these rights relies on a cohort of legal non-governmental organizations (such as the Socio Economic Rights Institute, the Legal Resources Centre and Lawyers for Human Rights) continuing to see this issue as a priority and being willing and able to pursue time-consuming and costly litigation.

CONCLUSION

What this volume powerfully demonstrates is that some of the most dedicated and resourceful entrepreneurs in the South African informal economy are migrants to the country. Under any other circumstances they would probably be lauded by government as exemplars of small-scale and micro entrepreneurship. However, the state (and many citizens) view their activities as undesirable simply because of their national origins. Harassment, extortion and bribery of officialdom are some of the daily costs of doing business in South Africa. Many entrepreneurs, especially in informal settlements and townships, face constant security threats and enjoy minimal protection from the police. This is in addition to all the constraints they face simply due to operating informally – lack of infrastructure (both basic and business related), hostile municipal regulations, and no access to skills training and financial services. Informal cross-border traders face another set of obstacles (Lefko-Everett, 2007). These include harassment by police and border guards, demands for inflated customs duties, transportation problems for goods, personal safety and security. As a result, migrant entrepreneurs are unable to utilize their entrepreneurial skills and experience fully and grow their businesses, and thus contribute to the economy in an optimal fashion.

In an analysis of the relationship between migration and inclusive growth, de Haan (2011) draws a parallel between outdated conceptions of the informal economy and migration that see both as transitional. He notes that as with "the concept of informal sector, so with migrants there is a risk that the assumption of transitional existence may hinder creative thinking about ways in which migrants can be supported" (de Haan, 2011: 20). There is certainly a dearth of creative policy thinking in South Africa on the informal economy in general and migrants' role in particular. There needs to be an acceptance by the South African state and the public at large that neither the informal economy nor migrants will go away. Draconian attempts to remove either will simply force their activities underground, but only for a period, generating significant hardship in the process.

There is a critical and urgent need to tackle collective violence against migrant-owned shops and businesses. As Crush and Ramachandran note, the violence will not stop until there are robust sanctions against perpetrators through hate crime legislation and other measures, criminal charges are laid and convictions secured. This is a matter of the South African state respecting basic human rights. This needs to be combined with much stronger statements from national and local leaders, politicians and bureaucrats condemning violence perpetrated against migrants. The claims of police complicity need to be investigated and firmly dealt with. A number of the authors in this volume point to the need for facilitated processes of engagement between migrant entrepreneurs and their South African counterparts. Rogerson, for example, argues that the policy lens "must be re-directed away from xenophobia per se to produce spaces of integration where locals and migrants can interact and coexist in more meaningful ways." Misago et al's (2009) study of the 2008 nationwide xenophobic attacks points to the critical role played by local community leaders in inciting violence as well as in preventing it in the areas that were unaffected. This suggests that they need to be key players in these processes.

There is a critical need to interrogate and address the constraints to growth in the informal economy in general and to shift the register of policy response from restriction to support. The restrictions suggested in the draft Licensing of Businesses Bill and implied in NIBUS would be harmful to South African and migrant entrepreneurs alike. Gastrow and Amit cite a study of spazas in Khayelitsha, Cape Town, which found that 90 per cent of migrant spaza owners kept business records (compared to only 28 per cent of South Africans). This example of the stark skills deficit among South African spazas is a reminder of the extent to which small business support measures bypass the informal economy (Devey et al., 2003, 2006, 2007; Rogerson, 2004). There is an urgent need to address the gap in small business support, not only to dissipate tensions between migrant and South African entrepreneurs but to realize the full potential benefit of informal entrepreneurship for local economic growth. The business problems identified by migrants in this volume – lack of access to financial services, hostile municipal officials and regulations, cash flow management and sourcing issues – are similar to those reported by South African informal operators and it is these issues that need addressing. Skills transfers between South African and migrant entrepreneurs could be a component of this engagement. And the Somali community in Cape Town has already demonstrated a willingness to share its knowledge and practices (Washinyira, 2015).

REFERENCES

Abdi, C. (2011) Moving beyond xenophobia: Structural violence, conflict and encounters with the 'other' Africans. *Development Southern Africa*, 28: 691-704.

Basardien, F., Parker, H., Bayat, M., Friedrich C. and Sulaiman, A. (2014) Entrepreneurial orientation of spaza shop entrepreneurs: Evidence from a study of South African and Somali-owned spaza shop entrepreneurs in Khayelitsha. *Singaporean Journal of Business Economics and Management Studies*, 2: 45-61.

Battersby, J. and Peyton, S. (2014) The geography of supermarkets in Cape Town: Supermarket expansion and food access. *Urban Forum*, 25: 153–164

Broughton, T. (2015) Court victory for informal trader. *The Mercury*, 18 February.

Budlender, D. (2013) Improving the quality of available statistics on foreign labour in South Africa: Existing data sets. MiWORC Report No.2, African Centre for Migration & Society, University of the Witwatersrand, Johannesburg.

Budlender, D. (2014) Migration and employment in South Africa: Statistical analysis of the migration module in the Quarterly Labour Force Survey, Third Quarter 2012. MiWORC Report, African Centre for Migration & Society, University of the Witwatersrand, Johannesburg.

Bukasa, A. (2014) Securing sustainable livelihoods: A critical assessment of the City of Cape Town's approach to inner city street trading. MA Thesis, University of Cape Town.

Callaghan, C. (2009) Entrepreneurial orientation and entrepreneurial performance of Central Johannesburg informal sector street traders. M. Comm. Thesis, University of the Witwatersrand.

Callaghan, C. (2012) Values malleability or the potentially harmful effects of exposure to street trading? *Journal of Business Management*, 6: 8362-8377.

Callaghan, C. (2013) Individual values and economic performance of inner-city street traders. *Journal of Economics*, 4: 145-56.

Callaghan, C. and Venter, R. (2011) An investigation of the entrepreneurial orientation, context and entrepreneurial performance of inner-city Johannesburg street traders. *Southern African Business Review*, 15: 28-48.

Charman, A. and Piper, L. (2012) Xenophobia, criminality and violent entrepreneurship: Violence against Somali shopkeepers in Delft South, Cape Town, South Africa. *South African Review of Sociology*, 43: 81-105.

Chen, M. (2012) The informal economy: Definitions, theories and policies. WIEGO Working Paper No. 1, Cambridge, MA.

City Press (2015) Cops told us to loot. 25 January.

Constitutional Court (2014) South African Informal Traders Forum and Others v City of Johannesburg and Others; South African National Traders Retail Association v City of Johannesburg and Others (CCT 173/13 ; CCT 174/14) [2014] ZACC 8; 2014 (6) BCLR 726 (CC); 2014 (4) SA 371 (CC) (4 April)

Crush, J. and Ramachandran, S. (2010) Xenophobia, international migration and development. *Journal of Human Development and Capabilities,* 11: 209-228.

Crush, J., Chikanda, A. and Skinner, C. (2015) Informal migrant entrepreneurship and inclusive growth in South Africa, Zimbabwe and Mozambique. SAMP Migration Policy Series No. 68, Cape Town and Waterloo.

Crush, J., Chikanda, A. and Tawodzera, G. (2013) The third wave: Mixed migration from Zimbabwe to South Africa. SAMP Migration Policy Series No. 59, Cape Town.

Crush, J., Ramachandran, S. and Pendleton, W. (2013) Soft targets: Xenophobia, public violence and changing attitudes to migrants in South Africa after May 2008. SAMP Migration Policy Series No. 64, Cape Town.

de Haan, A. (2011) Inclusive growth? Labour migration and poverty in India. Working Paper No. 513, Institute of Social Studies, The Hague.

DTI (Department of Trade and Industry) (2014) *The National Informal Business Upliftment Strategy (NIBUS).* Pretoria.

Devey, R., Lebani, L., Skinner, C. and Valodia, I. (2007) The informal economy. In A. Kraak and K. Press (eds.), *Human Resources Development Review 2008: Education, Employment and Skills in South Africa* (pp. 111-133). Cape Town: HSRC Press.

Devey, R., Skinner, C. and Valodia I. (2003) Human resource development in the informal economy. In A. Kraak and H. Perold (eds.), *Human Resources Development Review 2003: Education, Employment and Skills in South Africa* (pp. 142-163). Cape Town: HSRC Press.

Devey, R., Skinner, C. and Valodia, I. (2006) The state of the informal economy. In S. Buhlungu, J. Daniel, R. Southall and J. Lutchman (eds.), *The State of the Nation, 2005-2006* (pp. 223-246). Cape Town: HSRC Press.

Ensign, P. and Robinson N. (2011) Entrepreneurs because they are immigrants or immigrants because they are entrepreneurs: A critical examination of the relationship between the newcomers and the establishment. *Journal of Entrepreneurship,* 20: 33-53.

Fatoki, O. (2012) The impact of entrepreneurial orientation on access to debt finance and performance of small and medium enterprises in South Africa. *Journal of Social Sciences,* 32: 121-131.

Fatoki, O. (2013a) The determinants of immigrant entrepreneurs growth expectations in South Africa. *Journal of Social Sciences*, 37: 209-216.

Fatoki, O. (2013b) An investigation into the financial bootstrapping methods used by immigrant entrepreneurs in South Africa. *Journal of Economics*, 4(2): 89-96.

Fatoki, O. (2014a) The competitive intelligence activity of immigrant entrepreneurs in South Africa. *Journal of Social Sciences*, 38: 1-8.

Fatoki, O. (2014b) The financial bootstrapping methods employed by new micro enterprises in the retail sector in South Africa. *Mediterranean Journal of Social Sciences*, 5: 72-80.

Fatoki, O. (2014c) Working capital management practices of immigrant entrepreneurs in South Africa. *Mediterranean Journal of Social Sciences*, 5: 52-57.

Fatoki, O. and Patswawairi, T. (2012) The motivations and obstacles to immigrant entrepreneurship. *Journal of Social Sciences*, 32: 133-142.

Garg, A. and Phayane, N. (2014) Impact of small businesses owned by immigrant entrepreneurs on the local community of Brits. *Journal of Small Business and Entrepreneurship Development*, 2: 57-85.

Gastrow, V. (2013) Business robbery, the foreign trader and the small shop: How business robberies affect Somali traders in the Western Cape. *SA Crime Quarterly*, 43: 5-15.

Gastrow, V. and Amit, R. (2013). Somalinomics: A case study on the economic dimensions of Somali informal trade in the Western Cape. African Centre for Migration & Society, University of the Witwatersrand, Johannesburg.

Gebre, I., Maharaj, P. and Pillay, N. (2011) The experiences of immigrants in South Africa: A case study of Ethiopians in Durban, South Africa. *Urban Forum*, 22: 23-35.

Govender, S. (2012) The socio-economic participation of Chinese migrant traders in the City of Durban. M.Soc.Sci. Thesis, University of Kwazulu-Natal, Durban.

Grant, R. and Thompson, D. (2015) City on edge: Immigrant businesses and the right to urban space in inner-city Johannesburg. *Urban Studies*, 36: 181-200.

Harrison, P., Moyo, K. and Yang, Y. (2012) Strategy and tactics: Chinese immigrants and diasporic spaces in Johannesburg, South Africa. *Journal of Southern African Studies*, 38: 899-924.

Hikam, A. (2011) An exploratory study on the Somali immigrants involvement in the informal economy of Nelson Mandela Bay. M.Dev.Stud. Thesis, Nelson Mandela University, Port Elizabeth.

Hunter, N. and Skinner, C. (2003) Foreign street traders working in inner city Durban: Local government policy challenges. *Urban Forum*, 14: 301-319.

Huynh, T., Park Y. and Chen, A. (2010) Faces of China: New Chinese migrants in South Africa, 1980s to present. *African and Asian Studies*, 9: 286-306.

Hyde-Clarke, N. (2013) The impact of mobile technology on economic growth among 'survivalists' in the informal sector in the Johannesburg CBD, South Africa. *International Journal of Business and Social Science*, 4: 149-156.

IOL (2012) Hawkers challenge Cape Town's swoop. *IOL News Online,* 21 May.

Jinnah, Z. (2010) Making home in a hostile land: Understanding Somali identity, integration, livelihood and risks in Johannesburg. *Journal of Sociology and Social Anthropology,* 1: 91-99.

Kalitanyi, V. (2007) Evaluation of employment creation by African immigrant entrepreneurs for unemployed South Africans in Cape Town. M.Comm. Thesis, University of Western Cape.

Kalitanyi, V. and Visser, K. (2010) African immigrants in South Africa: Job takers or job creators? *South African Journal of Economic and Management Sciences,* 13: 376-390.

Khosa, R. (2014) An analysis of challenges in running micro-enterprises: A case of African foreign entrepreneurs in Cape Town, Western Cape. M.Tech. Thesis, Cape Peninsula University of Technology, Cape Town.

Kloosterman, R. and Rath, J. (2001) Immigrant entrepreneurs in advanced economies: Mixed embeddedness further explored. *Journal of Migration and Ethnic Studies,* 27: 189-202.

Kloosterman, R. and Rath, J. (eds.) (2003) *Immigrant entrepreneurs: Venturing abroad in the age of globalization.* Oxford: Berg.

Lapah, C. and Tengeh, R. (2013) The migratory trajectories of the post-1994 generation of African immigrants to South Africa: An empirical study of street vendors in the Cape Town Metropolitan Area. *Mediterranean Journal of Social Sciences,* 4: 181-195.

Lefko-Everett, K. (2007) Voices from the margins: Migrant women's experiences in Southern Africa. SAMP Migration Policy Series No. 46, Cape Town.

Lin, E. (2014) 'Big fish in a small pond': Chinese migrant shopkeepers in South Africa. *International Migration Review,* 48: 181-215.

Magubane, K. (2015) Reveal trade secrets, minister tells foreigners. *Business Day,* 28 January.

Maharaj, B. (2009) Migrants and urban rights: Politics of xenophobia in South African cities. *L'Espace Politique,* 8, DOI: 10.4000/espacepolitique.1402.

Maqanda, V. (2012) Competitiveness of small businesses owned by Asians and expatriate Africans in South Africa compared to those owned by indigenous citizens. M.Com.Thesis, University of South Africa, Pretoria.

Masonganye, N. (2009) Street trading in Tshwane Metropolitan Municipality: Realities and challenge. Urban Landmark Report, Pretoria.

McNamee, T. (2012) Africa in their words: A study of Chinese traders in South Africa, Lesotho, Botswana, Zambia and Angola. Discussion Paper 2013/3, Brenthurst Foundation, Johannesburg.

Misago J., Landau, L. and Monson, T. (2009) Towards tolerance, law, and dignity: Addressing violence against foreign nationals in South Africa. International Organisation for Migration, Pretoria.

Morris, A. (1998) 'Our fellow Africans make our lives hell': The lives of Congolese and Nigerians living in Johannesburg. *Ethnic and Racial Studies,* 21: 1116-1136.

Morris, M. and Pitt, L. (1995) Informal sector activity as entrepreneurship: Insights from a South African township. *Journal of Small Business Management,* 33: 78-86.

Moyo, I. and Gumbo, T. (2014) On the edge of malfeasance: Informal African immigrant traders in the Johannesburg inner city, South Africa. *Sociology Study,* 4: 323-333.

Mthombeni, D., Anim, F. and Nkonki-Mandleni, B. (2014) Factors that contribute to vegetable sales by hawkers in the Limpopo Province of South Africa. *Journal of Agricultural Science,* 6: 197-204.

Munshi, N. (2013) Lived experiences and local spaces: Bangladeshi migrants in post-apartheid South Africa. *New Contree,* 67: 119-137.

Mwasinga, B. (2013) Assessing the implications of local governance on street trading: A case of Cape Town's inner city. M.City & Regional Planning Thesis, University of Cape Town.

Park, Y. and Chen, A. (2009) Recent Chinese migrants in small towns of post-apartheid South Africa. *Revue Européenne des Migrations Internationales,* 25: 25-44.

Pauw, H. and Petrus, T. (2003) Xenophobia and informal trading in Port Elizabeth. *Anthropology Southern Africa,* 26: 172-180.

Peberdy, S. and Rogerson, C. (2002) Transnationalism and non-South African entrepreneurs in South Africa's small, medium and micro-enterprise (SMME) economy. In J. Crush and D. McDonald (eds.), *Transnationalism and New African Immigration to South Africa* (pp. 20-40). Kingston and Toronto: SAMP and CAAS.

Peberdy, S. and Rogerson, C. (2003) South Africa: Creating new spaces? R. Kloosterman and J. Rath (eds.), (2003) *Immigrant entrepreneurs: Venturing abroad in the age of globalization* (pp. 79-100). Oxford: Berg.

Plastow, A. (2015) Spaza shops, xenophobia and their impact on the South African consumer. *Daily Maverick,* 20 April.

Radipere, N. (2012) An analysis of local and immigrant entrepreneurship in the South African small enterprise sector (Gauteng Province). PhD Thesis, UNISA, Pretoria.

Radipere, S. and Dhliwayo, S. (2014) An analysis of local and immigrant entrepreneurs in South Africa's SME sector. *Mediterranean Journal of Social Sciences,* 5: 189-198.

Rath, J. (2000) Introduction: Immigrant businesses and their economic, politico-institutional and social environment. In J. Rath (ed.), *Immigrant Businesses: The Economic, Politico-Institutional and Social Environment* (pp. 1-19). Basingstoke: Macmillan.

Rogerson, C. (1997) International migration, immigrant entrepreneurs and South Africa's small enterprise economy. SAMP Migration Policy Series No. 3, Cape Town.

Rogerson, C. (2004) The impact of the South African Government's SMME programme: A ten year review (1994-2003). *Development Southern Africa,* 21(5): 765-784.

RSA (Republic of South Africa) (2013) Licensing of Businesses Bill Notice 231 of 2013. Government Gazette No. 36265, 18 March.

Skinner, C. (2006) Falling though the policy gaps? Evidence from the informal economy in Durban, South Africa. *Urban Forum,* 17: 125-48.

Supreme Court of Appeal (2014) Somali Association of South Africa and Others v Limpopo Department of Economic Development Environment and Tourism and Others (48/2014) [2014] ZASCA 143; 2015 (1) SA 151 (SCA); [2014] 4 All SA 600 (SCA) (26 September).

Tengeh, R. (2012) A business framework for the effective start-up and operation of African immigrant-owned businesses in the Cape Town Metropolitan Area, South Africa. PhD Thesis, Cape Peninsula University of Technology, Cape Town.

Visser, A. (2010) Race, poverty, and state intervention in the informal economy: Evidence from South Africa. PhD Thesis, New School University, New York.

Wafer, A. (2011) Informality, infrastructure and the state in post-apartheid Johannesburg. PhD Thesis, Open University.

Wafer, A. (2014) Informality and the spaces of civil society in post-apartheid Johannesburg. In C. Death and C. Gabay (eds.), *Critical Perspectives on African Politics: Liberal Interventions, State-Building and Civil Society* (pp. 129-146). London: Routledge.

Waldinger, R., Aldrich, H. and Ward, R. (eds.) (1990) *Ethnic Entrepreneurs: Immigrant Business in Industrial Societies.* Newbury Park: Sage Publications.

Washinyira, T. (2015) Somali businessmen share their acumen with locals. *Ground Up,* 20 February.

Weiss, E. (2013) Railway security guards accused of burning down hawkers goods. *SA Breaking News,* 10 May.

Willemse, L. (2014) The role of economic factors and *Guanxi* networks in the success of Chinese shops in Johannesburg, South Africa. *Urban Forum,* 25: 105-23.

Chapter Two

Doing Business with Xenophobia

Jonathan Crush and Sujata Ramachandran

> *"Are we so despised that because I sell a loaf of bread a little cheaper than my competitor I must be punished for it with my life?" (UNHCR News, 2007).*

INTRODUCTION

Common economic and social challenges confronting small-scale immigrant entrepreneurs from the Global South include limited market information, low levels of personal liquidity, poor access to credit and startup capital, high transaction costs, gender discrimination, over-regulation and intense competition (Barrett et al. 2003; Magatti and Quassoli, 2003; Halkias et al., 2011). The national and local policy environment within which immigrant businesses operate also plays a critical defining role in business failure and success. The environment includes legal restrictions and obligations, attitudes and policies towards migrant business activity, immigration and refugee legislation, and policing practices. As Levie and Smallbone (2009: 22-3) note, "the effects of the regulatory environment are transmitted through a broad range of state activities, including through the knock-on effect of immigration laws, which may not have had an intended influence."

While some attention has been given to the economic and policy environment in explaining variations in business performance among immigrant entrepreneurs (Ley, 2006; Teixera et al., 2007), much less has been paid to how the negative reactions of citizens to their activities and presence in the country of destination might impact on entrepreneurship. South Africa provides a particularly important case study of how citizen attitudes and behaviours materially affect the business climate for migrant entrepreneurs. In August 1997, for example, in the midst of "rainbow nation" euphoria following the country's first democratic elections, non-South African street traders were attacked and assaulted on the streets of Johannesburg. Many lost their merchandise and stands, some at gunpoint. The violence and intimidation were "accompanied by angry and vitriolic anti-immigrant rhetoric" (Peberdy and Rogerson, 2003: 80). This incident, largely overlooked by the state, emboldened a pattern of hostility towards migrant entrepreneurs that has reached epidemic proportions over the last decade.

Sometimes lost in the sobering statistics about the anti-immigrant violence that swept South Africa in May 2008 (over 70 people dead, 400 seriously injured, and 100,000 internally displaced) is the fact that many migrant-owned businesses were caught up in the mayhem (Hassim et al., 2008). Looting, burning and destruction of business property was widespread in the affected areas and many migrant entrepreneurs were among those hounded out of their communities. Such actions did not die out after May 2008. If anything, as this chapter demonstrates, they have become more insidious and pervasive, and are certainly not confined to the areas that erupted in 2008.

The remarkable growth of informal migrant entrepreneurship in South Africa since 1990, its innovative strategies, and the kinship, ethnic and business networks through which goods are acquired and resources accumulated, would have been much lauded had it not been for the striking detail that the actors in question are "foreigners" or "outsiders." As such, they are seen as undesirable and disadvantaging poor South African citizens with meagre avenues for income generation and survival. The growing presence of migrants in the informal sector has created noticeable tension in various quarters in South Africa, including government circles, ignoring the fact that in the free market economy of South Africa, immigrants and refugees, like citizens and commercial enterprises, ought to enjoy the freedom to establish, operate and expand their businesses (Maharaj, 2009).

Successive national attitudinal surveys by SAMP since 1996, as well as in-depth qualitative research and the personal testimony of many migrants, leave little doubt that South

Africans hold deep-rooted negative opinions about migrants and refugees in general and migrant entrepreneurs in particular (Crush, 2000, 2008; Crush et al., 2013). In the face of this body of evidence, recurrent denials by prominent political figures that xenophobia exists ring especially hollow (Crush and Ramachandran, 2014). Migrants and refugees interfacing with state institutions in various sectors report that these interactions are infused with attitudes and rhetoric that question their right to be in the country and regularly lead to the denial of services to which they are entitled by law and the constitution. Furthermore, when the majority of South Africans in national opinion surveys believe that refugees and migrants should not be entitled to legal and police protection, it is perhaps unsurprising that only the most egregious cases of police brutality garner public sympathy and attention – and even then only because they happen to be caught on video.

The first part of this chapter takes issue with the xenophobia "denialism" that permeates official and some academic discourse by presenting some of the results of SAMP's most recent survey of South African attitudes towards migrants and refugees (Crush and Ramachandran, 2014). Particular attention is focused on the linkages between attitudes and intended behaviours. In other words, how willing are South Africans to do something about the perceived "threat" of migrants and what measures are they actually willing to take? This analysis provides the background for understanding the problems and challenges migrant entrepreneurs face as they do business in the context of xenophobia. The second section of the chapter describes and analyses the nature of what we call "extreme xenophobia," that is, the prevalence of physical violence against migrant entrepreneurs in South Africa. This chapter focuses on the frequency and incidence of collective xenophobic violence, its impact on migrant entrepreneurship, and the evasions of the authorities.

A DANGEROUS CLIME

Being perceived as a "foreigner" in post-apartheid South Africa (particularly if one is from another African country) is inherently dangerous, so pervasive is the feeling among ordinary South Africans that you do not belong and should "go home" (Jinnah, 2010; Abdi, 2011; Ikuomola and Zaaiman, 2014). Trying to run a business in the South African informal economy is an especially hazardous undertaking as there is a widespread perception that migrant entrepreneurial activities inevitably disadvantage South Africans. This perception has been acted on in four main ways. First, the state (both central and municipal) has adopted a "protectionist" position, which leads to various regulatory and policing responses that seek to disadvantage, if not entirely eliminate, migrant entrepreneurship (Visser, 2010; Wafer, 2011). Second, the police on the streets run their own protection (or non-harassment) rackets to benefit financially from those able to pay. Third, South African competitors, particularly in the spaza sector, have increasingly adopted a strategy of what Charman and Piper (2012) call "violent entrepreneurship"; that is, the use of violence to intimidate and drive migrant entrepreneurs out of an area. Fourth, a minority of citizens have turned hostile attitudes into violent actions by forcibly shutting down migrant-owned businesses and attacking their owners and employees. Underlying all of these responses is a strong xenophobic undertow that is both manifest and measurable.

The World Values Survey (an independent global attitudinal survey) has consistently shown that South Africans are the least disposed globally to migrants coming from other countries to engage in economic activity. The most recent survey found that 30 per cent of South Africans want a total prohibition on foreign migrants who intend to work in South Africa (easily the highest figure of any country surveyed) (Table 2.1). Nearly half (48 per cent) want there to be strict limits on entry. Thus, 78 per cent are basically opposed to the idea of economic immigration to the country; no other country in the South has more than 50 per cent. South Africa (at 16 per cent) also has the lowest proportion of people in favour of skills-based immigration to fill gaps in the local job market and the lowest number (6 per cent) who favour an open-door policy towards economic migration.

SAMP's periodic surveys of South African attitudes towards the impacts of migration reveal more of the underlying economic hostility towards migrants (Table 2.2). Although there have been changes over time (with negative perceptions peaking in 2006), there has been a general growth in negativity about the social and economic impacts of migration since the 1990s. Between 1999 and 2010, for example, the proportion of South Africans who agreed that migrants use up resources increased from 59 per cent to 63 per cent. Those agreeing that they were responsible for crime increased from 45 per cent to 55 per cent and those that they bring disease from 24 per cent to 39 per cent. In terms of economic impacts, those agreeing that they deprive South Africans of jobs has remained steady at around 60 per cent. The proportion who felt that migrants bring skills needed by South Africa plummeted from 58 per cent in 1999 to 34 per cent in 2010. Only a quarter agree that migrants actually create jobs for South Africans.

Because migrants in South Africa come from all over the world it is important to know if particular opprobrium is reserved for those from certain areas. In the latest SAMP survey, migrants from other Southern African countries had the highest favourability ratings (25 per cent "completely favourable"), followed by migrants from Europe and North America (21 per cent) and the rest of Africa (17 per cent) (Table 2.3). Differences therefore exist but they are not particularly large and all migrants, wherever they are from, rate much lower than South Africans' evaluations of themselves (65 per cent favourable for Black South Africans and 56 per cent favourable for White South Africans). Since a significant number of migrants (and migrant entrepreneurs) are refugees, it is of interest that only 21 per cent of South Africans have a completely favourable impression of refugees. Unsurprisingly, irregular migrants are viewed with the most distaste (12 per cent favourable and 49 per cent completely unfavourable).

Table 2.1: South African Attitudes to Economic Migrants in Comparative Perspective

Country	Prohibit immigration (%)	Place strict limits on entry (%)	Let people in as long as jobs are available (%)	Let in anyone who wants to enter (%)
South				
South Africa	30	48	16	6
India	23	23	25	30
Ghana	18	39	36	7
Zambia	11	30	44	15
Brazil	11	33	47	9
China	8	21	51	20
Indonesia	6	15	72	8
Thailand	5	16	65	14
Malaysia	2	8	72	18
North				
Italy	8	49	37	6
United States	7	37	49	8
Germany	7	43	45	5
Australia	3	54	41	2
Canada	2	39	51	8
Source: World Values Survey				

Table 2.2: South African Perceptions of Impacts of Migration*

	1999 (%)	2006 (%)	2010 (%)
Social impacts			
Use up resources (e.g. water, electricity, housing)	59	67	63
Commit crime	45	67	55
Bring disease	24	49	39
Economic impacts			
Take jobs	56	62	60
Bring needed skills	58	25	34
Create jobs for South Africans	—	22	27

* Percentage who agree/strongly agree

Table 2.3: South African Impressions of Migrants and Citizens

	Completely favourable (%)		Completely unfavourable (%)	
	2006	2010	2006	2010
South African groups				
Blacks	70	65	5	5
Whites	55	56	7	4
Coloureds	45	49	12	7
Indians/Asians	38	42	20	12
Migrant groups				
Southern Africans	20	25	27	21
Europeans/North Americans	21	21	24	18
Rest of Africa	15	17	33	26
Refugees/Asylum seekers	19	21	32	27
Irregular migrants	6	12	65	49

South Africans do make clear distinctions between African migrants of different nationalities (Table 2.4). Within the SADC region, migrants from Botswana, Lesotho and Swaziland are viewed more positively than those from Zimbabwe and Mozambique. However, migrants from non-neighbouring countries rate even less positively: Nigerians (59 per cent unfavourable), Congolese (51 per cent unfavourable) and Somalis (50 per cent unfavourable). Since many informal migrant entrepreneurs are drawn from the ranks of Zimbabwe-ans, Mozambicans, Somalis and Congolese, it is not hard to imagine why they are singled out for harsh treatment. SAMP also found that levels of xenophobia are highest among self-employed South Africans in the informal economy. Levels are lower among both the unemployed and employees in the informal economy.

Table 2.4: South African Impressions of Migrants by Country of Origin

	Unfavourable (%)		Favourable (%)	
	2006	2010	2006	2010
Neighbouring countries				
Zimbabwe	52	44	12	15
Mozambique	47	40	14	15
Botswana	28	24	32	31
Swaziland	28	23	36	33
Lesotho	27	23	38	32
Other African countries				
Nigeria	66	59	7	7
Angola	54	48	9	9
DRC	54	51	8	9
Somalia	53	50	10	9
Ghana	50	45	11	11

Simply because the majority of a national population hold negative perceptions of a minority group such as migrants and refugees, it does not automatically follow that violent acts against that group will be pervasive or, indeed, occur at all. However, a significant minority of South Africans polled in attitudinal surveys have consistently expressed a will-ingness to take the law into their own hands. In 2010, for example, SAMP asked South Africans how likely they would be to take part in collective action against the presence of migrants (Table 2.5). As many as 23 per cent said it was likely that they would act to prevent migrants moving into their community, 20 per cent would prevent migrant children enroll-ing in the same schools as their own children, and 15 per cent would prevent migrants from becoming co-workers. Important for the argument of this chapter, 25 per cent said they would be likely to prevent a migrant from operating a business in their area.

By dividing the respondents into those that lived in hotspots affected by the May 2008 xenophobic violence and those that did not, it is possible to ascertain if areas with experience of widespread violence are more prone to violence in the future (Crush et al., 2013). While hotspot residents are more likely to prevent migrants from operating a business and moving into their community, they are less likely to oppose them becoming co-workers or enrolling their children in the same schools. However, the differences are not large and one in four residents of areas not directly affected by May 2008 also said they were likely to take action to prevent a migrant from operating a business in their community.

Table 2.5: Likelihood of South Africans Taking Preventative Action Against Migrants

How Likely Are You to Take Action to Prevent Migrants Doing the Following (% Likely/Very Likely):	All urban areas	Residents of 2008 hotspots	Residents of 2008 other areas
Operating a business in your area	25	27	24
Moving into your neighbourhood	23	27	21
Enrolling their children in school	20	18	21
Becoming a co-worker	15	14	21

Finally, the SAMP survey asked South Africans how likely they would be to take certain actions against people they suspected were irregular migrants in their community. Since South Africans believe that the vast majority of foreign migrants are in the country illegally, this is not very different to asking what they would do about migrants in general. Around a third said they would report them to the police, to employers or to community leaders (Table 2.6). Fewer (15 per cent) said they would combine with others to eject them from the community and 11 per cent said they were prepared to use violence against the migrants. The predilection to use violence was actually slightly stronger in areas not affected by the attacks of May 2008. What this means is that around one in every ten South Africans is predisposed to turn hostile attitudes into violent actions. This may seem a relatively low proportion in light of the prevalence of negative attitudes but multiplied it does suggest that 3.8 million (out of an adult population of around 35 million) South Africans would be prepared to use violent means to rid their neighbourhoods of foreign migrants.

Table 2.6: Likelihood of Taking Punitive Action Against Irregular Migrants

How Likely Are You to Take Action Against Irregular Migrants in Your Area (% Likely/Very Likely):	All urban areas	Residents of 2008 hotspots	Residents of 2008 other areas
Report them to police	36	34	36
Report them to employer	27	26	28
Report them to community association	27	24	29
Combine to force them to leave	15	15	15
Use violence against them	11	9	11

METHODOLOGY

There has been no systematic longitudinal analysis of the nature, distribution and intensity of violent incidents targeting migrants and refugees. Official statistics are not maintained and the tendency of government representatives and senior politicians to classify violent attacks on migrants and migrant businesses as "opportunistic crime" has only deepened the uncertainty about the occurrence of xenophobic violence and its underlying causes (Crush and Ramachandran, 2014). This chapter draws on the evidence from an extensive archive of news articles collected by SAMP since 1994 and detailed timeline reconstructions already in the public domain (Crush and Ramachandran, 2014). The overall aim of the research was to create a chronological account of attacks on migrant businesses, to categorize the types and frequency of attacks and to map the locations.

Several qualifications are in order. First, research on hate crimes in other contexts confirms that a sizeable proportion of such episodes go unreported and unrecorded (Martin, 1996; Wells and Polders, 2006; Gerstenfeld, 2013). The inventory on which this chapter is based does not claim to be exhaustive since many incidents undoubtedly go unreported by the press or human rights groups. Second, the lack of confidence in law enforcement agencies, poor prosecution of offenders, weak deterrent measures for xenophobic violence, as well as the continued presence of offenders in localized settings, are all likely to discourage migrants from reporting to the authorities (Gastrow, 2013). Third, the information in the database tends to be descriptive in nature, describing but not explaining why attacks take place or why they take the form that they do.

Although there is plenty of evidence of violent attacks on individual migrant entrepreneurs, this chapter focuses on acts of collective or group violence. Collective violence has been defined as the "instrumental use of violence by persons who define themselves as members of a group against another group in order to achieve political, social or economic objectives" (Zwi et al., 2002: 215). Aggressive social interaction organized on a group basis is the key feature here, whether this group or collective identity is assumed and transitory or has a permanent and stable character. This form of episodic social interaction involves perpetrators who distinguish themselves from the targeted victims either subliminally or directly. Moreover, this contact directly inflicts physical damage on the targeted persons and/or their possessions with some level of coordination and synchronization among the perpetrators, even in incidents that appear spontaneous with low levels of organization (Tilly, 2003). There are obviously different types of collective violence, varying in scope, duration and degree of organization. The damage caused by such violence also varies in scale and gravity with some acts having far-reaching and deadly consequences, such as those that swept South Africa in May 2008 (Crush and Ramachandran, 2010; Landau, 2012).

Collective violence has also been defined as a type of social control in which grievances and perceived wrongs are handled through unilateral aggression (de la Roche, 1996). The collectivization of violence generally occurs where there is strong partisanship and additional individuals support one side against the other. Solidarity is skewed in favour of the perpetrators and distanced from the targets of violence (de la Roche, 2001). A high frequency of collective violence is an indicator of profound social and cultural distance between the groups involved (the perpetrators and their intended targets). Other localized factors such as low institutional confidence, weak policing, and areas with long histories of violent crime, buttress a social environment where the likelihood and opportunities for collective violence remain robust (Monson et al., 2012). Institutional barriers to protection and justice for the victims activate and perpetuate the violence.

The incidents discussed in this chapter involve the intentional and spontaneous participation of groups in acts of collective violence against migrant businesses. The SAMP database contains information on over 250 separate incidents of collective violence since 1994. Migrant entrepreneurs and their businesses were also severely affected during the large-scale violence that occurred in May 2008. However, the events of that month are excluded from this assessment since they have been examined in depth elsewhere and are often treated as an exceptionally large singular event, even though there were at least 100 (and perhaps as many as 150) localized incidents of collective violence (Everatt, 2010; Hassim et al, 2008; Landau, 2012; SAHRC, 2010). The chapter is based on the identification and analysis of the largest or most significant episodes since 1994. Three distinct criteria, singly or in combination, were used for inclusion: first, the scale of damage had to be extensive, affecting several businesses; second, there had to have been displacement of and injuries to business owners; and third, the violence had to have been perpetrated by groups rather than individuals.

CHRONOLOGY OF COLLECTIVE VIOLENCE

From 1994 to August 2014 (excluding May 2008), there were at least 250 documented episodes of group-based violence against migrants and refugee businesses around the country. An analysis of the frequency of collective violence reveals a marked pattern of escalation (Table 2.7). Pre-2005 incidents constitute less than 5 per cent of recorded episodes. A definite upswing is seen from 2006 onwards, with the sharpest growth occurring after 2008. Excluding events in May 2008, nearly 90 per cent of recorded episodes of group violence against migrant businesses occurred since the beginning of 2008. The five years with the largest number of incidents were from 2010 to 2014. The highest annual number (20 per cent of the total) was recorded in 2010 during an upsurge in xenophobic attacks after the World Cup was held in South Africa. While these episodes differed in terms of the number of affected migrants and the severity of the damage, it is evident that small-scale, informal migrant businesses occupy a highly precarious position in South African settlements, having become especially vulnerable to situations of collective violence.

Table 2.7: Frequency of Collective Violence

Year	No. of incidents	Percentage
Pre-2005	9	4
2005	4	2
2006	9	4
2007	9	4
2008*	19	8
2009	17	7
2010	46	20
2011	22	10
2012	25	11
2013	36	16
2014 (to end-August)	32	14
Total	228	100
* Excluding May 2008 attacks		

GEOGRAPHIES OF COLLECTIVE VIOLENCE

Collective violence targeting migrant entrepreneurs is no longer confined to a few isolated locations. Since 2005, the majority of South African provinces have been touched by collective violence against migrant businesses. However, the Western Cape and Gauteng have experienced the highest levels of violence. The overall number of affected provinces and localities has increased considerably since 2005; indeed, the majority of provinces have witnessed repeated incidents since 2009. In 2005-6, incidents occurred in six distinct locations within three provinces (Figure 2.1). In 2009-10, they occurred in at least 14 separate locations extending over six of the nine provinces in South Africa (Figures 2.2 to 2.4). The year 2010 stands out with at least 37 separate locations in six provinces. The number of affected areas may have fallen somewhat to 22 in 2012 and 27 in 2013, but the number of affected provinces still stood at 6 and 7 respectively (Figures 2.5 to 2.7).

Figure 2.1: Collective Violence Locations, South Africa 2005–2006

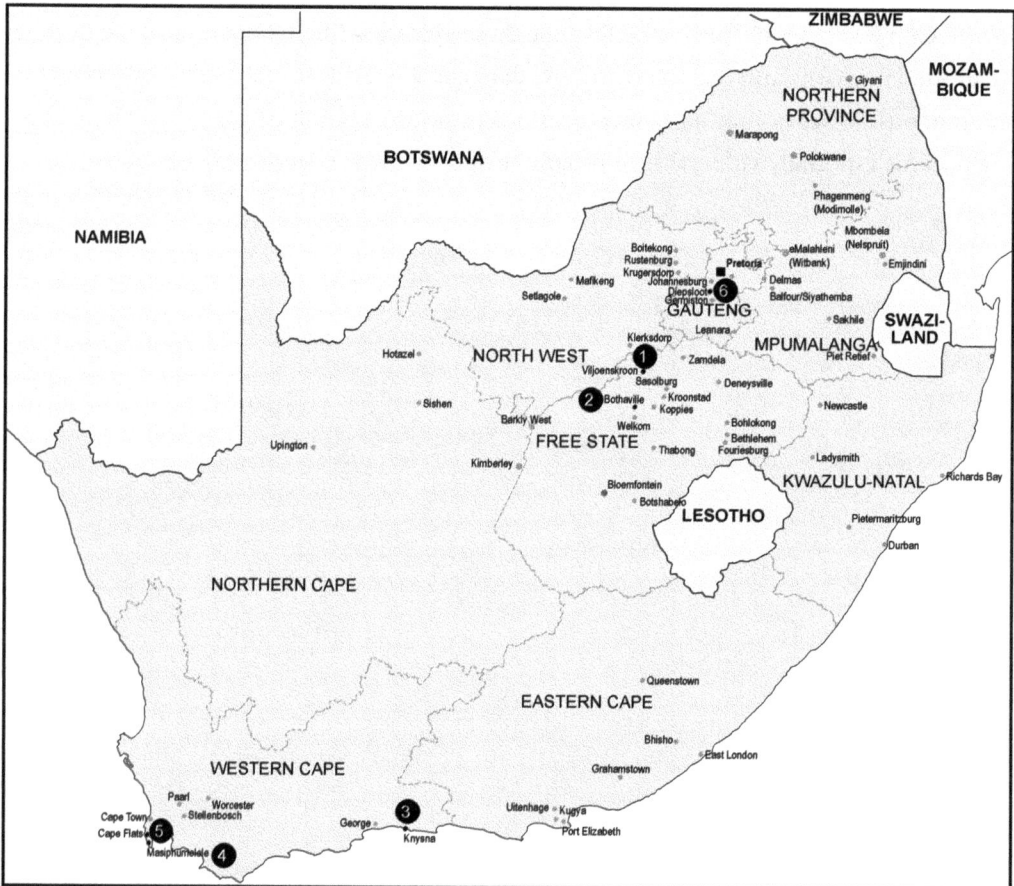

Figure 2.2: Collective Violence Locations, South Africa 2009–2010

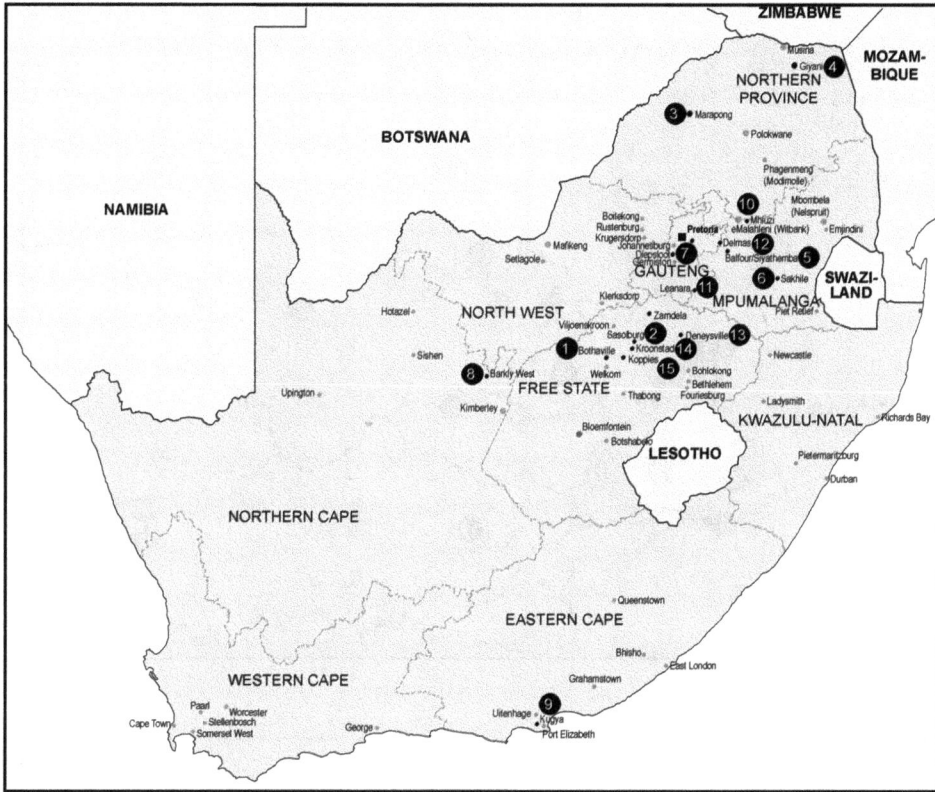

Figure 2.3: Collective Violence Locations, Gauteng 2009–2010

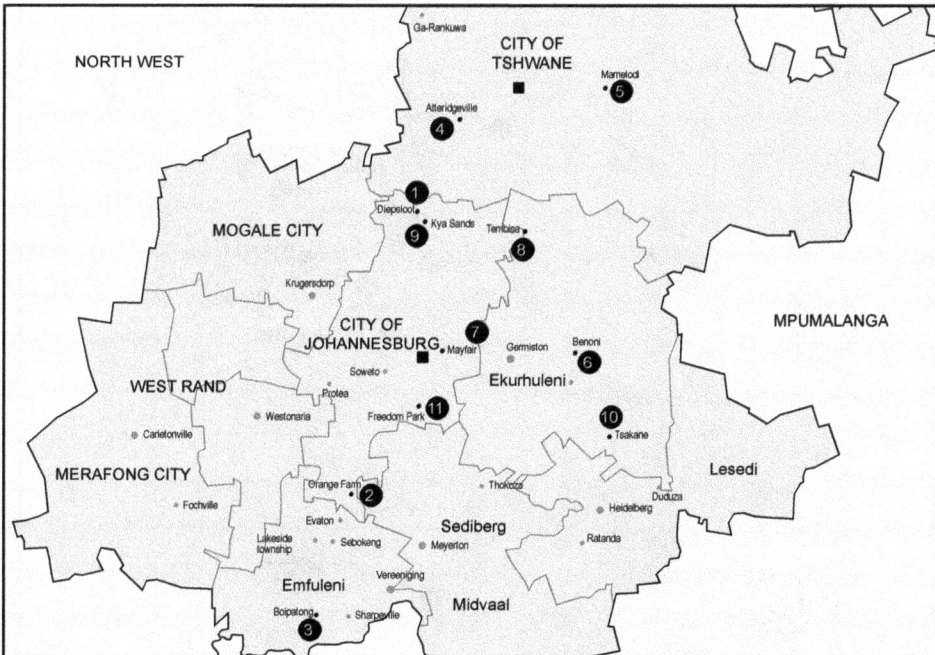

Figure 2.4: Collective Violence Locations, Western Cape 2009–2010

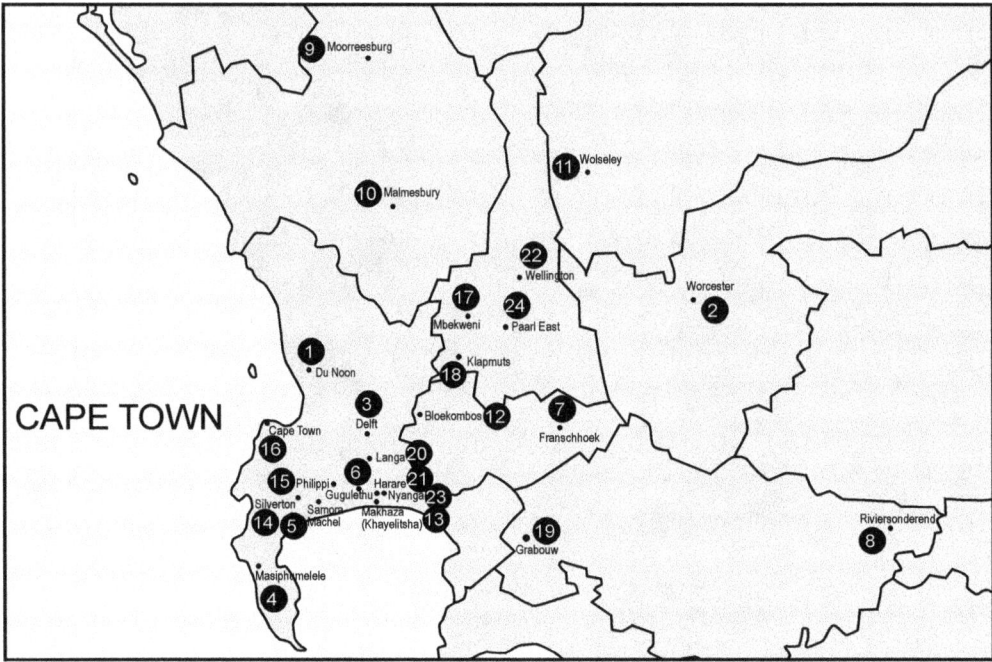

Figure 2.5: Collective Violence Locations, South Africa 2012–2013

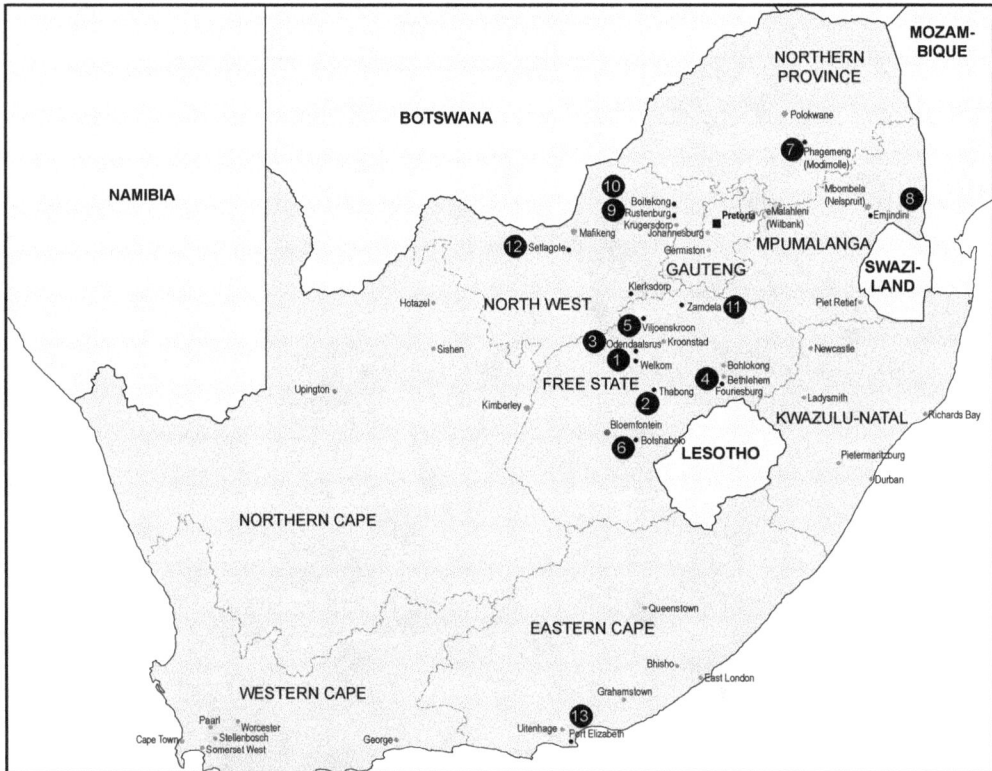

Figure 2.6: Collective Violence Locations, Gauteng 2012–2013

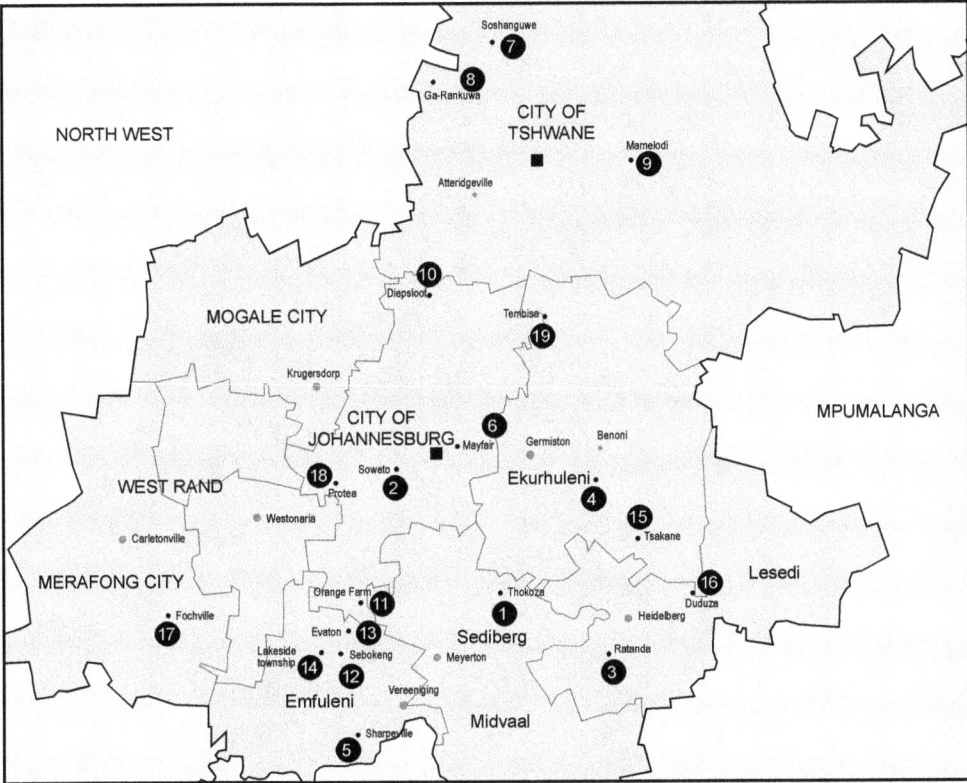

Figure 2.7: Collective Violence Locations, Western Cape 2012–2013

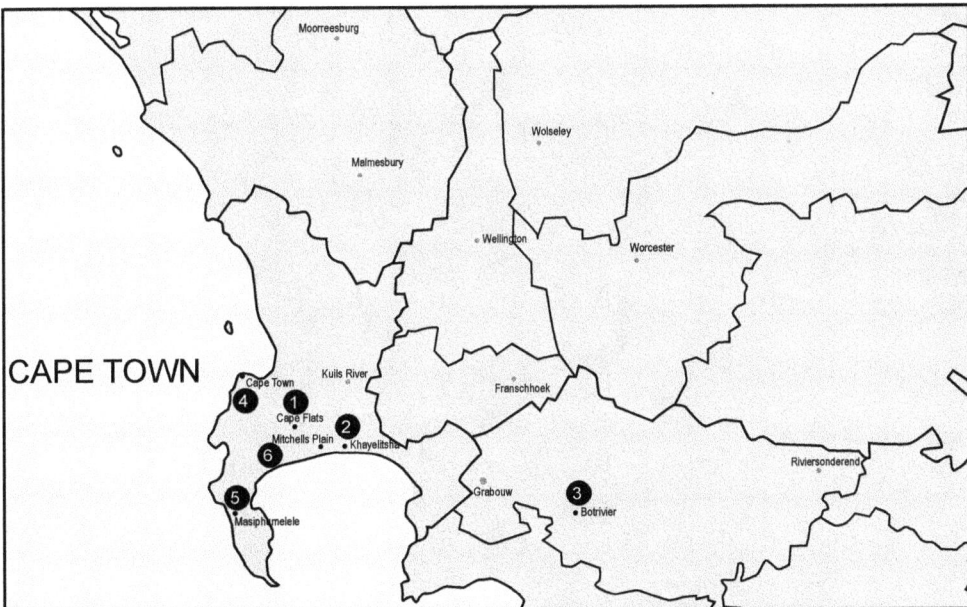

Key to Figures 2.1–2.7:

Figure 2.1: South Africa 2005–2006

1. Viljoenskroon
2. Bothaville
3. Knysna
4. Masiphumelele
5. Cape Flats
6. Diepsloot

Figure 2.2: South Africa 2009–2010

1. Bothaville
2. Sasolburg
3. Marapong
4. Giyani
5. Balfour/Siyathemba
6. Sakhile
7. Diepsloot
8. Barkly West
9. Kugya
10. Mhluzi
11. Leandra
12. Delmas
13. Deneysville
14. Kroonstad
15. Koppies

Figure 2.3: Gauteng 2009–2010

1. Diepsloot
2. Orange Farm
3. Boipatong
4. Atteridgeville
5. Mamelodi
6. Benoni
7. Mayfair
8. Tembisa
9. Kya Sands
10. Tsakane

11. Freedom Park

Figure 2.4: Western Cape 2009–2010

1. Du Noon
2. Worcester
3. Delft
4. Masiphumelele
5. Samora Machel
6. Gugulethu
7. Franschhoek
8. Riviersonderend
9. Moorreesburg
10. Malmesbury
11. Wolseley
12. Bloekombos
13. Makhaza (Khayelitsha)
14. Silverton
15. Philippi
16. Cape Town
17. Mbekweni
18. Klapmuts
19. Grabouw
20. Langa
21. Harare
22. Wellington
23. Nyanga
24. Paarl East

Figure 2.5: South Africa 2012–2013

1. Welkom
2. Thabong
3. Odendaalsrus
4. Fouriesburg
5. Viljoenskroon
6. Botshabelo
7. Phagemeng (Modimolle)

8. Emjindini
9. Rustenburg
10. Boitekong
11. Zamdela
12. Setlagole
13. Port Elizabeth

Figure 2.6: Gauteng 2012–2013

1. Thokoza
2. Soweto
3. Ratanda
4. Ekurhuleni
5. Sharpeville
6. Mayfair
7. Soshanguwe
8. Ga-Rankuwa
9. Mamelodi
10. Diepsloot
11. Orange Farm
12. Sebokeng
13. Evaton
14. Lakeside township
15. Tsakane
16. Duduza
17. Fochville
18. Protea
19. Tembisa

Figure 2.7: Western Cape 2012–2013

1. Cape Flats
2. Khayelitsha
3. Botrivier
4. Cape Town
5. Masiphumelele
6. Mitchells Plain

Several of the affected locations have witnessed repeated rounds of collective violence. Diepsloot, for example, was affected in 2006, and again in 2009, 2010 and 2013 (Harber, 2011). Other areas have experienced several incidents with short intervals between them. In the town of Delmas in Mpumalanga, for example, migrant businesses were assailed in February 2013 and again in April that year. In Mamelodi, migrant businesses were attacked in June 2014 and again in September. Since 2009, at least 32 distinct locations have witnessed two or more episodes of group violence (Table 2.8). Of these, collective violence has been repeated on three or more occasions in 12 areas: Delmas, Diepsloot, Duduza, Gugulethu, Khayelitsha, KwaNobuhle, Langa, Mamelodi, Motherwell, Orange Farm, Ramaphosa and Soweto. Some of these locations, such as Ramaphosa township, also witnessed extensive violence and destruction during May 2008 (SAHRC, 2010; Steinberg, 2008).

Table 2.8: Collective Violence Locations, 2009–2014

Locations	Province
Booysens Park, KwaDesi, KwaNobuhle, Kugya, Motherwell, Port Elizabeth	Eastern Cape
Bothaville, Botshabelo, Deneysville, Fouriesburg, Koppies, Kroonstad, Maokeng, Odendaalsrus, Sasolburg, Thabong, Viljoenskroon, Welkom, Zamdela	Free State
Atteridgeville, Benoni, Boipatong, Diepsloot, Duduza, Ekurhuleni, Evaton, Fochville, Freedom Park, Ga-Rankuwa, Imbeliseni, Johannesburg, Kya Sands, Lakeside, Mamelodi, Mayfair, Orange Farm, Protea, Ramaphosa, Ratanda, Sebokeng, Sharpeville, Soshanguve, Soweto, Tembisa, Thokoza, Tsakane	Gauteng
Giyani, Marapong, Phagemeng, Lebowakgomo, Lephalale	Limpopo
Botshabelo, Delmas, Emjindini, Leandra, Mhluzi, Sakhile, Siyathemba	Mpumalanga
Barkly West	Northern Cape
Boitekong, Boitumelong, Rustenburg, Setlagole	North-West
Bishop Lavis, Bloekombos, Botrivier, Cape Town, Delft, Du Noon, Franschhoek, Freedom Park, Grabouw, Gugulethu, Harare, Khayelitsha, Klapmuts, Langa, Malmesbury, Mbekweni, Mitchell's Plain, Moorreesburg, Nyanga, Paarl East, Philippi, Riviersonderend, Samora Machel, Silverton, Valhalla Park, Wellington, Wolseley, Worcester	Western Cape

TYPOLOGIES OF COLLECTIVE VIOLENCE

The nationwide attacks on migrants and refugees in May 2008 represent the nadir of xenophobic hostility in South Africa. There is an obvious temptation to characterize other, prior and subsequent, episodes of collective violence as "minor" incidents. Such a conclusion would be profoundly misplaced. The cumulative impact of months, indeed years, of low-level verbal and physical warfare against migrant entrepreneurs has taken a major toll on the lives and livelihoods of some of South Africa's most enterprising residents. Belligerent, discriminatory and abusive types of action have occurred. They include written or verbal threats and insults directed at migrant entrepreneurs; public intimidation of migrant entrepreneurs through protests or marches or other similar collective actions; involuntary migrant shop closures; direct physical violence against migrant store owners or their employees; looting of store contents; damage to the physical structure of shops, especially through arson; damage or destruction of other property belonging to migrants, including homes and cars; temporary or permanent forced displacement of migrant entrepreneurs and their families; and extortion for protection by local leaders, police and residents. Looting of store goods and damage to stores were easily the most common types of action recorded.

A number of incidents are worth recalling to illustrate the nature and intensity of collective violence. Between mid-2009 and late 2010, for example, more than 20 migrants were killed and another 40 received serious injuries in various attacks (CoRMSA, 2011). Of these, at least four people were killed during a series of violent confrontations over the presence of migrant traders in the Freedom Park township of Gauteng (Mashego, 2011). In mid-2011, 52 shops were plundered and three burnt down in Motherwell and three shops looted and one burnt down in KwaDesi (Maliza, 2011). In 2012, more than 700 shops were looted and/or destroyed and over 500 migrants were displaced because of public violence in Botshabelo in the Free State province (CoRMSA, 2012). That same year, two Bangladeshi traders (described as Pakistani citizens in some accounts) suffered third-degree burns and later died after a group of assailants threw a petrol-bomb on their container store in Thokoza and blocked the store's entrance preventing their escape (Smillie, 2012). In Valhalla Park in Cape Town, three shops were petrol-bombed during large-scale looting of Somali-owned businesses (Maregele, 2012).

During a particularly volatile period in Port Elizabeth in mid-2013, there was extensive vandalism, arson and plundering of an estimated 150 spaza shops operated by migrants and refugees (Sapa, 2013a; 2013b). One Somali refugee, Abdi Nasir Mahmoud Good, was publicly stoned to death while attempting to salvage his belongings from his ransacked store. Video footage was later released on YouTube showing the perpetrators, some of whom were children in school uniforms. Also in 2013, more than 200 migrant shopkeepers operating small-scale businesses in the town of Delmas, east of Johannesburg, were forced to close their stores after a spate of attacks. In a bout of violence over six days in June 2014, two refugees were killed when nearly 100 migrant businesses were looted or torched in Mamelodi East outside Pretoria. The violence was repeated in the Phomolong area of Pretoria two months later when three people were killed and several others wounded during a rampage that lasted for three weeks (Makhubu, 2014). Finally, before the army was called in to contain the unrest, a Somali trader was killed and three stores were torched when migrant traders were attacked during post-election violence in Alexandra township in mid-2014 (Poplak, 2014). As these examples of collective violence demonstrate, the scale of the attacks is sometimes sizeable and can spill over into neighbouring settlements. Looting and vandalism of migrant-owned shops have been especially common features of collective violence over the past several years. These actions, though criminal, may appear less grave when compared to severe injuries and loss of life, but they cannot be treated as inconsequential as they impose unwarranted hardships on migrant entrepreneurs through partial or complete loss of stock and destruction of their shops and investments.

The vulnerability of migrant shopkeepers has exposed them to other invidious forms of exploitation. Some 80 migrant traders operating from Extensions 8 to 12 in Diepsloot settlement north of Johannesburg, for example, were coerced into providing payment as "protection money" to local residents to avoid damages to and pillaging of their stores during service delivery protests (CoRMSA, 2010). A Johannesburg High Court order, in response to an urgent petition on xenophobic violence in Duduza and surrounding townships of the Ekurhuleni municipality, acknowledged the culpability of a ward councillor in instigating acts of violence against Somali, Bangladeshi and Ethiopian migrant traders (Serrao, 2013). Migrants claimed that he stoked xenophobia and then solicited bribes in exchange for their safety.

Collective violence against migrant businesses not only shatters the livelihoods of the targeted migrant groups, it impacts on South African citizens and businesses. Wholesalers, retailers and suppliers are inevitably affected when migrant business activities are disrupted or destroyed. Also, a significant proportion of migrant businesses rent space from South African property owners, who lose rental income when their tenants are expelled or their premises are vandalized (Gastrow and Amit, 2013). In addition, extensive damage to store structures degrades the existing and often meagre assets of local property owners. Other losers include poor local consumers who are forced to buy more expensive goods from larger stores or face the inconvenience of travelling longer distances to purchase necessities.

PRECIPITANTS OF COLLECTIVE VIOLENCE

It is never easy to tease out and identify intentions, motivations and underlying causes in turbulent situations, especially when the primary source is reportage and monitoring. Scholars researching collective violence have often articulated this dilemma (Short and Wolfgang, 2009; Tilly, 2003; Varshney et al., 2008). Some things are, however, evident. Some of the violence perpetrated against migrant businesses is obviously motivated only or primarily by criminal behaviour, especially robberies and looting, but to attribute all attacks to criminal motivation (as the state seeks to do) is reductionist and misleading. In general, the weak structural and social position of "foreigners" in localized areas as "outsiders", combined with limited access to protection and justice, certainly makes them more vulnerable to criminal attack. In other words, the attackers may not themselves be always motivated by xenophobia but it is xenophobia that makes their targets easy prey.

While the precipitants (or triggers) for any particular incident of collective violence vary, there is a clear general pattern both in terms of the choice of targets and the selective directing of violence toward migrants and migrant businesses. Local business competitors have certainly animated some of the collective violence against migrant entrepreneurs (Gastrow and Amit, 2012). A distinctive feature is the recent emergence and incendiary stance of loosely-formed groups, purportedly representing many or all South African small-business owners. These groups range from localized structures like the Zanokhanyo Retailers' Association operating in townships, settlements and urban areas such as Khayelitsha, Cape Town, to larger regional forums like the innocuously-named Greater Gauteng Business Forum. Since 2008, these groups have engaged in numerous public hate campaigns against migrant businesses, liberally using belligerent tactics ranging from forced store closures, coerced price increases, limits on the number of migrant businesses in an area, and public threats through letters or by radio. A few months after the May 2008 violence, for example, many Somali shopkeepers in Khayelitsha received threatening hand-delivered letters from the Zanokhanyo Retailers' Association ordering them to cease operating their stores (IRIN, 2008). In late 2010, the association again used intimidatory tactics to shut down Somali-owned shops in Khayelitsha, claiming that the terms of an agreement reached with Somali shopkeepers limiting the number of migrant businesses in the area were being violated (Damba, 2010). The Middelburg Small Business Community Forum claimed credit for mobilizing local authorities after the Steve Tshwete Municipality shut down 50 Somali shops and refused to issue them with trading licences (Misago and Wilhelm-Solomon,

2011). Accusing them of unfair competition and rising crime, the local forum stoked group violence against migrant-run shops in Lephalale in Limpopo in 2013 in the course of which five shops, two houses and three vehicles were razed (Crush and Ramachandran, 2014).

By early 2011, the Greater Gauteng Business Forum had become a very visible presence through its intimidation of migrant traders in the province of Gauteng. There are reports of the forum's direct involvement in campaigns to expel migrant businesses from locations such as Kathlehong, Soweto, Eldorado Park, Ramaphosa, Mamelodi and Diepsloot. The forum chairperson claimed that campaigns against "foreign traders" were "strictly business" and have "nothing to do with xenophobia or politics" (City Press, 2011), but the overt reasoning to justify these group actions draws from a familiar reservoir of xenophobic beliefs and a wilful misunderstanding of the rights of migrants and refugees in South Africa. Distorted ideas about migrants' presence and their impacts on South Africa are used to justify collective mobilization and violence against migrant businesses. For example, the Greater Gauteng Business Forum is reported to have stated that "these people are molesting our economy" (Mukhuthu, 2011). Forum members and other local business groups have expressed similar discriminatory sentiments: "We feel that foreigners who entered the country illegally or don't have a business licence to run spaza shops should leave because they are destroying our small local businesses and exploiting our people" (City Press, 2011). In 2013, the forum reiterated its central argument by maintaining that all migrant entrepreneurs must "go back home" because they are "here to destroy local business and people" asserting, as well, that "if nothing is done about it, there will be war" (Masombuka and Narsee, 2013).

The targeting of migrant businesses, particularly spaza shops, has been a common by-product of anti-government service-delivery protests in various parts of the country. In 2014, for example, one-third of the violent incidents involving looting and vandalism of migrant-owned shops took place during local anti-government or anti-municipality protests. Dissatisfaction over the pace of road construction and employment of locals for infrastructure projects in Sebokeng, for example, led to efforts to forcibly oust migrant businesses (Patel, 2013a, 2013b). Agitating for a better water supply, Hebron residents in North West province looted at least six shops in February 2014 after police cracked down on protesters. The connections between local dissatisfaction and resentment over service issues and attacks on migrant-owned shops need greater explanation. One hypothesis advanced by Abdul Hasan of the Somali Association of South Africa is that "they are targeting foreigners because we are the weaker link in the community, so they hit us to get government attention" (Kumwenda, 2010).

On several occasions, other kinds of protests have spiralled into xenophobic attacks on migrant businesses. More than 100 shops of Pakistani and Bangladeshi migrants were attacked over several days in early 2012 in Welkom, Odendaalsrus and Thabong, for example, when local youths went on a rampage after discussions over enhanced quotas for hiring South Africans on local mines stalled (SABC, 2012). In 2013, an estimated 200 businesses were damaged and plundered in Zamdela and neighbouring Deneysville and Koppies in Sasolburg during violent agitation rejecting the amalgamation of municipalities (Motumi, 2013; Nkonki, 2013). In 2014, allegations of dumped ballot boxes, election rigging and discontent over the outcome of the national elections led to unrest in Alexandra. This took a swift xenophobic turn when migrant shopkeepers were targeted (Poplak, 2014). Also in 2014, an unresolved labour dispute between the South African Municipal Workers' Union and the Metsimaholo Municipality of Free State prompted the violent public raiding of migrant businesses in Zamdela and neighbouring settlements of France and Armelia outside Sasolburg (Ndaba, 2014).

Participants in collective violence may not always use xenophobic language while attacking migrant stores, but an underlying xenophobic rationale is often there. Migrant entrepreneurs invariably characterize the general attitudes of the local community towards them in this way. Seven shops owned by Pakistani migrants were wrecked and ransacked in Boipatong during the course of an anti-government protest in February 2010, for example. The migrants themselves described the attacks as "hateful" and some participants defended their actions by arguing that "foreigners don't support our protests, and they are living a better life than us here in our country" (DMPSP, 2010). Zamdela township residents said that migrant businesses were targeted in early 2013 during a violent protest against the merger of Metsimaholo municipality in Sasolburg with the Ngwathe municipality near Parys because they did not "assist" the local community (Sidimba, 2013). In Duduza, local residents justified their collective, aggressive attacks on 200 migrant-owned shops in late 2013 as follows: "They come here and steal our jobs and now they are killing our children. We cannot accept this" (Hosken, 2013).

In other instances, there were direct triggers linked to the presence of migrants. For example, a Somali shopkeeper was killed and all Somali traders had to evacuate Booysens Park in 2013 when local residents associated them with criminal gangs and attacked them (McDonald, 2013). Amandla Wethu Workers' Union members assailed many Bangladeshi, Chinese, and Pakistani-owned businesses in Mthatha in the Eastern Cape after their president claimed that South African employees were being poorly remunerated (SABC, 2014). Some of the largest episodes of group violence have involved retaliatory vigilantism in response to the acts of one or two migrants. Instead of confining their response to the perpetrators, the vigilantes strike out at many or all persons of the same nationality or ethnicity as the migrant offenders, or even at all "foreigners" in the area. After a migrant shop owner in Cullinan, east of Pretoria, allegedly assaulted a child for stealing from his store, for example, local residents looted many shops owned by migrants and refugees and burned three of their vehicles (City Press, 2014; Sapa, 2014). Some 400 residents of Riviersonderend struck out at all Somali-owned shops in the area after a South African resident last seen in the company of Somalis was found dead. After a migrant shopkeeper reportedly shot a local youth for stealing from his store in Jeffreys Bay in early 2008, all Somali traders were attacked and forcibly ousted from the town (Mail & Guardian, 2008). In 2013, in Duduza on the East Rand, after an altercation over a mobile phone airtime voucher between a Somali shop owner and a local youth, who was shot, some 200 stores belonging to Somali, Ethiopian, Eritrean and Bangladeshi migrants were stripped of their contents and several structures were incinerated (Sosibo, 2013). In Lebokwagamo near Polokwane in April 2011, residents attacked all migrants from Ethiopia living in the area, looting and damaging their homes and businesses after one of their compatriots was accused of raping a girl (Matlala, 2011).

While xenophobic views and actions are not espoused or approved of by all local residents of affected settlements, their prevalence suggests that they do enjoy sufficient support and that there are few deterrents. Support from local community leaders also conveys a sense of legitimation and impunity, reducing the inhibition of potential offenders and, at the same time, enhancing the "opportunistic" aspects of the violence. Even official tolerance and passivity convey ambiguous messages that are only likely to perpetuate and shore up repeated cycles of violence. In several cases, affected traders hit by such attacks have shifted to another settlement only to end up facing attacks there too. In a general sense, this rhythmic configuration of collective, public violence is only likely to preserve and reinforce the social distance between South Africans and "foreigners." Mutual distrust and suspicion between groups is an inevitable outcome of a polarized context where xenophobic sentiments and practices are commonplace.

OFFICIAL EVASIONS

In a stance that has now become almost customary, South African politicians and senior officials at national, provincial and municipal levels are quick to label collective violence against migrants and refugees as "opportunistic crimes", committed by "criminal elements" or "hardened criminals", while simultaneously repudiating the role of anti-migrant prejudice (Polzer and Takabvirwa, 2010; Crush and Ramachandran, 2014; Freemantle and Misago, 2014). At national level, individual ministers and the Cabinet as a whole have repeatedly warned against viewing attacks on migrants and refugees as evidence of xenophobia. President Zuma recently informed South African MPs that xenophobia was not "such a huge problem in South Africa" (SABC News, 2013). Justice Minister Jeff Radebe made a similar observation in Parliament when some 80 stores and businesses owned by migrants were looted in Diepsloot: "The criminal activities that are perpetuated by some South Africans are not a reflection of xenophobic attacks against foreigners" (Patel, 2013b). A South African Police Services (SAPS) spokesperson insisted that "when we see children looting shops and people robbing people of their goods, it is to us a blatant sign of crime that is being excused as xenophobia" (Bauer, 2013).

The South African government recently took the unusual step of challenging *Al Jazeera's* online coverage of the stoning to death of a Somali refugee and other violence against migrants and refugees in Port Elizabeth (Patel and Essa, 2013). Government spokesperson Phumla Williams insisted that the article "painted an incorrect picture of…South Africa" and was "far from reality" and continued that "South Africa allows and welcomes foreign nationals" and has "strived to build a society based on the values of unity and togetherness" (Williams, 2013). With this came the standard denial of the presence of xenophobia in South Africa: "The looting, displacement and killing of foreign nationals in South Africa *should not be viewed as xenophobic attacks, but opportunistic criminal acts* [emphasis ours] that have the potential to undermine the unity and cohesiveness of our communities" (Hirsi, 2013).

Similarly, at provincial level, the Gauteng government was quick to condemn the "brutal and senseless attack" on two Bangladeshi traders in Thokoza in 2012 and urged South Africans *"to refrain from branding this attack as having been motivated by xenophobia* [emphasis ours]" (Office of the Gauteng Premier, 2012). After more than 100 complaints of looting and vandalism of migrant shops were registered in 2013 in various parts of Gauteng, government spokesperson Williams underscored the government's concern over the *"so-called xenophobic attacks* on foreign nationals [emphasis ours]" (Sapa, 2013a). When large-scale looting and attacks on migrant-owned shops occurred in 2013 in Port Elizabeth, provincial police characterized "the motive for the attacks on foreign-owned spaza shops" as *"not xenophobic in nature, but a criminal element that has seized an opportunity* [emphasis ours]" (Sapa, 2013c). This by-now-familiar argument was wheeled out again in early 2014 when violence occurred in Mamelodi East and police personnel attributed it to "criminal elements", denying that xenophobia was a factor.

The attribution of collective violence against migrant entrepreneurs to criminals and not in any way as evidence of xenophobia rings extremely hollow when the details of many of these attacks are examined. What makes the official position especially ironic is when officials themselves articulate sentiments that reproduce the xenophobic myths that they claim do not exist. A senior official in the Department of Home Affairs, for example, is reported to have informed South African MPs that "if you go to Alexandra, you go to Sunnyside, you go everywhere, spaza shops, hair salons, everything has been taken over by foreign nationals…they displace South Africans by making them not competitive" (van der Westhuizen, 2011). At an official meeting, then National Police Commissioner Bheki Cele characterized immigrants and refugees as "people who jump borders," were flooding into the country and destroying the livelihoods of South African informal traders. He continued: "The spazas… are better stocked than Shoprite. Our people have been economically displaced. All these spaza shops [in the townships] are not run by locals…One day our people will revolt, and we've appealed to the Department of Trade and Industry to do something about it" (Mtyala, 2011). Former deputy trade and industry minister Elizabeth Thabethe made similarly provocative statements about the supposed negative effects of Somali entrepreneurs in late 2013 at a national conference on SMMEs: "You still find many spazas with African names, but when you go in to buy you find your Mohammeds and most of them are not even registered" (Sowetan, 2013).

More recently, ANC Secretary-General Gwede Mantashe declared that the South African government was concerned about South African small businesses that were closing, having been "swallowed by foreign migrants" who "did not pay tax and comply with certain laws" (Ginindza, 2014). He informed an election campaign rally at Eldorado Park South in Johannesburg that, "if you go to Soweto, corner shops have been taken over by foreigners. We must do something about it." Responding to a wave of public criticism of his Licensing of Businesses Bill, DTI Minister Rob Davies claimed it was simply an effort to curb illegal imports:

All kinds of outlets [are] springing up that may well be involved in illegal imports and things of that sort…If you are found guilty of a number of offences, such as selling counterfeit goods…[and] you've been involved in illegal imports, found guilty of contravening the Foodstuffs, Cosmetics, and Disinfectants Act, been selling sub-standard products, employing illegal foreigners, or found guilty of conducting illegal business from the licensed premises, you've been doing drug trade or illegal liquor selling or anything of the sort…your licence is automatically revoked. So we say, easy in, easy out. You do any of those things, we don't want you (Radebe, 2013).

The Minister did not mention that existing legislation is more than able to deal with illegal imports, the employment of irregular migrants and illicit drug and liquor selling. He did not respond to criticisms that he viewed the informal economy as a hive of criminality and that the bill was actually a frontal attack on informal business and migrant entrepreneurship. For example, it would require all migrants to have business permits that cost far more than what all but a tiny minority of informal entrepreneurs can afford.

The opinions of politicians and officials about migrant entrepreneurs often seem indistinguishable from the intolerant views of ordinary citizens and this, in turn, reinforces negative beliefs and ideas in the populace at large. Failure to curb the situation by consistently restraining offenders and imposing stringent penalties on collective violence only expands the elements of "opportunism" attached to such acts, encouraging others to participate, and reinforcing the unprotected position of migrants and refugees as "outsiders" in affected areas. Thus, photographs in the South African media in July 2012 showed the Bishop Lavis (Cape Town) police "standing and doing nothing" while spaza shops were torched and looted in Valhalla Park (Maregele, 2012). Western Cape Minister for Community Safety Dan Plato later announced in a public statement that the Independent Police Investigative Directorate would examine the case and "take necessary action where any negligence or wrongdoing is identified" (Government of Western Cape, 2012). However, it is not clear if the case was actually investigated or disciplinary proceedings carried out against the SAPS personnel (Maregele, 2012).

Police passivity has been reported by migrants and the media in many episodes of violence targeting foreign-owned businesses. As far back as 2005, for example, some 150 Pakistani entrepreneurs operating spaza shops in Pietermaritzburg organized a protest march against the local police demanding accountability after a large mob looted goods worth

ZAR150,000 from one of them (Crush, 2008). Refugee shopkeepers from the Democratic Republic of the Congo, Ethiopia and Somalia who were forced out of Zwelethemba township near Worcester in the Western Cape in 2008 filed claims in the Equality Court in 2009 seeking redress for the unfair discrimination, xenophobia, and inadequate protection provided by police officials during this violent episode (de Jager, 2011). Despite the extensive looting and vandalism of Somali shops in Motherwell, Port Elizabeth, in 2013, local police said they were unable to offer protection (CoRMSA, 2011). Immigrants whose shops and homes were assailed in Wallacedene during a housing dispute in mid-2013 maintained that police personnel refused to provide assistance, insisting instead that they leave South Africa (Washinyira, 2013). Weak, hostile or indifferent police responses provide stronger incentives for repetition by reinforcing biases among existing offenders and signalling to potential offenders that migrant businesses are easy targets.

The victimization of migrant businesses through demands for protection money have also been reported. A report on policing in Khayelitsha, an area prone to regular violence against migrants and refugees, observed that local police personnel often demanded bribes from migrant traders and stole items from their stores (Khayelitsha Commission, 2014). Civil society groups accused the local police of checking immigration documents of affected traders instead of shielding them during the public violence that erupted in Mamelodi East and West in June 2014 (Amnesty International, 2014). Dissatisfied with the quality and consistency of police protection, spaza owners have adopted two main strategies. First, to protect their own businesses from attack, they have entered into local agreements with the police and South African entrepreneurs that they will support their efforts to prevent any new migrant businesses opening in an area. Second, they have begun to arm themselves with weapons to defend their stores and their lives. Armed clashes between attackers and store owners have become increasingly common in recent years.

Weak or lack of effective punishment for the perpetrators of violence sends permissive signals and tacit sanction. People have been arrested in various parts of South Africa over the past few years for public violence, looting, arson, malicious damage to property, possession of stolen goods and for their participation in collective violence targeting migrant businesses. But a great many have been released after verbal warnings and very few offenders have been indicted or faced prison sentences. For example, in 2011, the Germiston Magistrate's Court released without any penalty 71 Kathlehong residents arrested for distributing intimidating letters threatening "drastic action" against migrant-owned businesses (SABC,

2011). Again, 11 people were arrested for the death of Somali refugee, Nasir Good, but none of the offenders was formally charged or faced criminal proceedings. To date, there is evidence of the prosecution and conviction of offenders in only two serious incidents. The first case involved the burglary of three migrant-owned businesses in Buhlebesizwe No. 2 village near Kwaggafontein in 2011 for which five citizens were sentenced to individual terms of 15 years by a Mpumalanga judge (Nyaka, 2013). In the second case, one of the three accused in the murder of an Ethiopian trader, Thomas Ebamo, in 2012 was sentenced to 25 years' imprisonment in what was characterized by the presiding judge as a "savage act of xenophobia" (Oellerman, 2013). A seller of pots and carpets from his car, Ebamo had been robbed and dragged to his death after being tied to a vehicle's rear by his neck. However, these convictions and judgments are very much the exception.

CONCLUSION

Some migrant entrepreneurs may enjoy material advantages over ordinary South Africans in settlements where they operate their informal businesses, trading stalls or spaza shops. However, their status as "foreigners" and "outsiders" in South African society makes them markedly vulnerable to constant victimization, harassment and violence. More than that, these commonplace actions magnify the sense of constant insecurity experienced by migrants and refugees, compromising the ability of victims to fully integrate into South African society. The pervasive sense of fear and insecurity and the constant possibility of violence directed at their bodies and properties is a reality that they have to face on a daily basis in areas where they operate their businesses. As one Somali refugee put it, "we came to this country as refugees, because Somalia is being torn apart by war, but here another war is taking place, one that we don't understand, but we are the targets" (Citizen, 2007).

The terms of the debate on the rise of migrant entrepreneurship in South Africa have been limited and selective, reiterating (both implicitly and explicitly) the prejudiced, xenophobic idea that non-citizens are not entitled to police protection nor even running a small business, even if it is permitted by law and generated through their own initiative and inventiveness (Gastrow and Amit, 2013). Explaining collective violence through an undue emphasis on group rivalries for limited material resources allows the culpability to be shifted quickly onto the attacked group, migrants and refugees in this case, thus making the victims responsible for their own suffering. Collective violence against migrant businesses and migrants at large becomes an inexorable, uncontrolled feature of social reality in such a delimited stance, erasing and minimizing options for positive change or progressive interventions leading to the fuller acceptance of immigrants into South African society, economy and polity (Crush and Ramachandran, 2014).

Equally importantly, when assessments of "economic competition" are delimited on a group basis, particularly when the boundaries are drawn around nationality, citizenship and other forms of ethnicity, then they are rooted in discriminatory normative judgements about the different and unequal economic entitlements of citizens and foreigners in South Africa. The idea of economic competition itself is defined selectively and incompletely here, omitting the very real and stronger challenges to informal entrepreneurship posed by large retail grocery stores or supermarkets such as Shoprite, Pick n Pay and Usave (Crush and Frayne, 2011). It is difficult to imagine a scenario where the South African government would endorse or impose severe limits on the expansion of large commercial/retail stores in townships and poorer settlements because they truncate business opportunities for small-scale South African entrepreneurs. In terms of concrete, practical intervention, the focus turns in a reactionary manner to curtailing migrant entrepreneurship in place of the real, urgent need to support and enhance opportunities for all small entrepreneurs in marginal settlements through new incentives and programmes.

The official idea that collective violence against migrant-owned shops and businesses is best controlled through the imposition of tougher restrictions on migrant businesses rather than robust sanctions against perpetrators through hate-crime legislation and other measures is deeply ingrained. So, too, is the feeling that there is no need to ease suspicions about "foreigners" and their economic activities within the country. A recent ANC policy discussion document, for example, incongruously focused on "peace and stability" and recommended that "by-laws need to be strengthened" in a manner that meant "non-South Africans should not be allowed to run or buy spaza shops or larger businesses" (ANC, 2012). The document further suggested that asylum-seekers whose refugee applications had not been finalized by the Department of Home Affairs should be ineligible to operate and manage such shops, diverging from protections granted to this vulnerable group under national and international law. ANC Western Cape Secretary Songezo Mjongile endorsed these proposals by contending that the rise of migrant entrepreneurship was the underlying cause of friction and collective violence in townships and saying it was "unnatural that nearly all shops in townships are owned by foreigners. More locals need to participate and need to be supported…it creates tension" (Barnes, 2012).

Despite providing goods at cheaper prices to poor consumers, in affordable quantities and sometimes on credit, the success and resourcefulness of migrant entrepreneurs is regularly and falsely attributed to the use of illegitimate practices such as the sale of expired goods and failure to pay taxes. Police Commissioner Arno Lamoer admitted to Parliament's Police Portfolio Committee that migrant and refugee entrepreneurs constituted the victims in two-thirds of crimes such as robberies committed against small businesses in the Western Cape, but held them responsible for operating shops from homes or containers without trading permits, failing to bank their earnings, and sleeping in the store premises (Sapa, 2012).

Far from reducing xenophobia in South Africa, claims that collective violence against migrant businesses are simply acts of criminality legitimize and may even incite further violence. These acts are both criminal and opportunistic, but not in the sense suggested in public and political discourses in South Africa. These acts are criminal in that they can be considered as offences under the South African penal code and undermine the rule of law. Using this logic, one may argue that those who have engaged in such acts may be considered as "criminals." South African shop owners have certainly engaged long-term, hardened offenders to get rid of their "competition" through violence, and it may even be argued that "criminals" have committed some of these acts (Gastrow and Amit, 2013). But a strong case can be made that not all of those who have engaged in such violence have histories of criminal activity. Situations of mayhem and melee may allow some ordinary citizens to engage in such actions and the material benefits from participating in violent actions through looting cannot be detached from the analysis. Therefore, an element of opportunism is clearly present, which is why some observers have called it "opportunistic xenophobia" (Makhubu, 2014).

Selective notions about the barriers faced by South African small-scale entrepreneurs animate this debate, as do biased ideas about migrant traders, their activities, and reasons for their success. The deeply-embedded terrain of xenophobia further provides the fertile, volatile context in which a range of social, political and economic actors (including participants in violent attacks, South African traders, local councillors and, in some cases, police) have controlled the anxieties associated with the presence of migrants for their own narrow, self-serving interests. The escalating pattern of collective violence against migrant traders and their businesses signals the deeply-drawn divisions between insiders and outsiders, based on birth, citizenship and nationality. This highly repetitive cycle of violence targeting migrant traders underscores the precarious position they and other immigrants hold in South African society.

REFERENCES

Abdi, C. (2011) Moving beyond xenophobia: Structural violence, conflict and encounters with the 'other' Africans. *Development Southern Africa*, 28: 691-704.

Amnesty International (2014) Two refugees dead and many injured in attack. UA 148/14. 10 June.

ANC (2012) Peace and stability. ANC Policy Document 7 March.

Barnes, C. (2012) Cut number of foreign spaza shops – ANC. *Cape Argus*, 25 June.

Barrett, G., Jones, T. and McEvoy, D. (2003) United Kingdom: Severely constrained entrepreneurialism. In R. Kloosterman and J. Rath (eds.), *Immigrant Entrepreneurs: Venturing Abroad in the Age of Globalization*, (pp. 101-122). Oxford: Berg.

Bauer, N. (2013) Diepsloot: Crime, xenophobia – or both? *Mail & Guardian*, 28 May.

Charman, A. and Piper, L. (2012) Xenophobia, criminality and violent entrepreneurship: Violence against Somali shopkeepers in Delft South, Cape Town, South Africa. *South African Review of Sociology*, 43: 81-105.

City Press (2011) Campaign against foreign township traders spreads. 14 May.

City Press (2014) Foreigners escorted out of Cullinan. 19 February.

CoRMSA (Consortium on Refugees and Migrants in South Africa) (2012) CoRMSA condemns attacks on foreign nationals in Botshabelo. Johannesburg.

CoRMSA (2011) Protecting refugees, asylum-seekers and immigrants in South Africa during 2010. Johannesburg.

CoRMSA (2010) Database of violence against foreign nationals in 2009-2010. Johannesburg.

Citizen (2007) Rioters loot and burn Somali-owned shops. 14 February.

Crush, J. (2000) The dark side of democracy: Migration, xenophobia and human rights in South Africa. *International Migration*, 38(6): 103-134.

Crush, J. (2008) The perfect storm: The realities of xenophobia in contemporary South Africa. SAMP Migration Policy Series No. 50, Cape Town.

Crush, J. and Frayne, B. (2011) Supermarket expansion and the informal food economy in southern African cities: Implications for urban food security. *Journal of Southern African Studies*, 37: 781-807.

Crush, J. and Ramachandran, S. (2010) Xenophobia, international migration and development. *Journal of Human Development and Capabilities*, 11(2): 209-228.

Crush, J. and Ramachandran, S. (2014) Xenophobic violence in South Africa: Denialism, minimalism, realism. SAMP Migration Policy Series No. 66, Cape Town and Waterloo.

Crush, J., Ramachandran, S. and Pendleton, W. (2013) Soft targets: Xenophobia, public violence and changing attitudes to migrants in South Africa after May 2008. SAMP Migration Policy Series No. 64, Cape Town.

Damba, N. (2010) Somali shops closed down in Khayelitsha. *West Cape News*, 10 October.

de Jager, J. (2011) Addressing xenophobia in the equality courts of South Africa. *Refuge*, 28: 107-116.

de la Roche, R. (1996) Collective violence as social control. *Sociological Forum*, 11: 97-128.

de la Roche, R. (2001) Why is collective violence collective? *Sociological Theory*, 19: 126-144.

Displaced and Migrant Persons Support Program (DMPSP) (2010) Xenophobic attacks – Boipatong – Vaal. 29 February.

Everatt, D. (ed.) (2010) South African civil society and xenophobia: Synthesis. Strategy & Tactics and Atlantic Philanthropies, Johannesburg.

Freemantle, I. and Misago, J-P. (2014) The social construction of (non)crises and its effects: Government discourse on xenophobia, immigration and social cohesion in South Africa. In A. Lindley (ed.), *Crisis and Migration: Critical Perspectives* (pp. 136-157). New York: Routledge.

Gastrow, V. (2013) Business robbery, the foreign trader and the small shop: How business robberies affect Somali traders in the Western Cape. *South African Crime Quarterly*, 43: 5-15.

Gastrow, V. and Amit, R. (2012) Elusive justice: Somali traders' access to formal and informal justice mechanisms in the Western Cape. ACMS Report, University of the Witwatersrand, Johannesburg.

Gastrow, V. and Amit, R. (2013) Somalinomics: A case study on the economics of informal trade in the Western Cape. ACMS Report, University of the Witwatersrand, Johannesburg.

Gerstenfeld, P. (2013) *Hate Crimes: Causes, Controls, and Controversies.* London: Sage Publications.

Ginindza, B. (2014) ANC will add ministry for small business. *Business Report*, 9 April.

Government of Western Cape (2012) Looting of shops: IPID asked to investigate apparent lack of policing. 10 July.

Halkias, D., Thurman, P., Harkiolakis, N. and Caracatsanis, S. (eds.) (2011) *Female Immigrant Entrepreneurs: The Economic and Social Impact of a Global Phenomenon.* Farnham: Gower.

Harber, A. (2011) *Diepsloot.* Johannesburg: Jonathan Ball.

Hassim, S., Kupe, T. and Worby, E. (eds.) (2008) *Go Home or Die Here: Violence, Xenophobia and the Reinvention of Difference in South Africa.* Johannesburg: Wits University Press.

Hirsi, I. (2013) Somali man stoned to death in South Africa: Sister and community protest in St. Paul. *TC Daily Planet*, 6 September.

Hosken, G. (2013) Townships turn on foreign "killers." *Times Live*, 16 August.

Ikuomola, A. and Zaaiman, J. (2014) We have come to stay and we shall find all means to live and work in this country: Nigerian migrants and life challenges in South Africa. *Issues in Ethnology and Anthropology*, 9: 371-388.

IRIN (2008) Foreign competitors not welcome. 17 October.

Jinnah, Z. (2010) Making home in a hostile land: Understanding Somali identity, integration, livelihood and risks in Johannesburg. *Journal of Sociology and Social Anthropology*, 1: 91-99.

Khayelitsha Commission, (2014) Towards a safer Khayelitsha. Report of the Commission of Inquiry into Allegations of Police Inefficiency and a Breakdown in Relations between SAPS and the Community in Khayelitsha, Cape Town.

Kumwenda, O. (2010) South African police fire buckshot at township rioters. *Reuters*, 23 March.

Landau, L. (ed.) (2012) *Exorcising the Demons Within: Xenophobia, Violence and Statecraft in Contemporary South Africa*. Johannesburg: Wits University Press.

Levie, J. and Smallbone, D. (2009) Immigration, ethnicity and entrepreneurial behaviour. In J. Levie, D. Smallbone and M. Minnitti (eds.), *Perspectives on Entrepreneurship: Volume 1* (pp. 157-180). New York: Praeger.

Ley, D. (2006) Explaining variations in business performance among immigrant entrepreneurs in Canada. *Journal of Ethnic and Migration Studies*, 32: 743-764.

Magatti, M. and Quassoli, F. (2003) Italy: Between legal barriers and informal arrangements. In R. Kloosterman and J. Rath (eds.), *Immigrant Entrepreneurs: Venturing Abroad in the Age of Globalization* (pp. 147-172). Oxford: Berg.

Maharaj, B. (2009) Migrants and urban rights: Politics of xenophobia in South African cities. *L'Espace Politique* 8. DOI: 10.4000/espacepolitique.1402.

Mail & Guardian (2008) Somali shops looted in the Eastern Cape. 7 October.

Makhubu, N. (2014) Foreigners in fear after looting of shop. *Pretoria News*, 12 September.

Maliza, S. (2011) The HRC criticizes attacks on Somali shops. *Sunday Times*, 27 May.

Maregele, B. (2012) Plato to probe Bishop Lavis Police. *Cape Times*, 2 July.

Martin, S. (1996) Investigating hate crimes: Case characteristics and law enforcement responses. *Justice Quarterly*, 13: 455-480.

Mashego, A. (2011) Task team to tackle freedom park tension with foreigners. *New Age*, 25 January.

Masombuka, S. and Narsee, A. (2013) Send foreigners to camps. *Times Live*, 28 May.

Matlala, M. (2011) Ethiopian nationals attacked. *New Age*, 20 April.

McDonald, D. (2013) All Somali shops in Booysen Park looted. *News24*, 30 May.

Misago, J-P. and Wilhelm-Solomon, M. (2011) Evicted Somali traders cry foul. *Mail & Guardian*, 4 September.

Monson, T., Takabvirwa, K., Anderson, J., Polzer Ngwato, T. and Freemantle, I. (2012) Promoting social cohesion and countering violence against foreigners and other 'outsiders.' ACMS Report, University of the Witwatersrand, Johannesburg.

Motumi, M. (2013) Foreigners run scared in Sasolburg. *Post*, 24 January.

Mtyala, Q. (2011) Cele's xenophobic outburst. *Cape Times*, 7 October.

Mukhuthu, Z. (2011) Minister's remarks rile traders. *Sowetan*, 9 March.

Ndaba, B. (2014) Mobs loot foreign businesses in Zamdela. *Star*, 17 July.

Nkonki, T. (2013) Sasolburg unrest likened to xenophobic attacks. *Eyewitness News*, 24 January.

Nyaka, F. (2013) Five sentenced to robbery of foreign nationals. *New Age*, 19 February.

Oellerman, I. (2013) 25 years for 'savage act of xenophobia.' *Witness*, 20 March.

Office of the Gauteng Premier (2012) Gauteng Condemns the Attack on Bangladeshi Nationals in Thokoza. 30 January at https://www.facebook.com/GPPremierOffice/posts/262525377152972

Patel, K. (2013a) Sebokeng's cocktail of joblessness, drugs and xenophobia. *Daily Maverick*, 27 May.

Patel, K. (2013b) 'Xenophobic' violence spreads, threatens chaos. *Daily Maverick*, 31 May.

Patel, K. and Essa, A. (2013) African migrants battling rising persecution. *Al Jazeera*, 6 June.

Peberdy, S. and Rogerson, C. (2003) South Africa: Creating new spaces? In R. Kloosterman and J. Rath (eds.), *Immigrant Entrepreneurs: Venturing Abroad in the Age of Globalization* (pp. 79-100). Oxford: Berg.

Polzer, T. and Takabvirwa, K. (2010) Just crime? Violence, xenophobia and crime: Discourse and practice. *SA Crime Quarterly*, 33: 3-10.

Poplak, R. (2014) Hannibal Elector: From Alexandra to Zuma, via Malema: Violence, silence & nothing wrong with Nkandla. *Daily Maverick*, 11 May.

Radebe, K. (2013) Big brother's new business bill. *Moneyweb*, 20 March.

SABC (2011) Case against 71 Kathlehong residents dismissed. 30 April.

SABC (2012) Attacks mount on shops owned by foreigners. 5 February.

SABC (2013) Xenophobia must not get out of hand: Zuma. 20 June.

SABC (2014) Foreign nationals' shops vandalized, looted in Mthatha. 5 February.

SAHRC (2010) Investigation into issues of rule of law, justice and impunity arising out of the 2008 violence against non-nationals. South African Human Rights Commission, Johannesburg.

Sapa (2012) Foreigners streaming into Western Cape. 8 February.

Sapa (2013a) Foreigners' shops looted in PE. 16 September.

Sapa (2013b) Somali-owned PE shops re-open after attacks. 19 September.

Sapa (2013c) 111 arrested for PE protests. 18 September.

Sapa (2014) Foreigners escorted out of Cullinan. 19 February.

Serrao, A. (2013) Hostility against foreigners on the rise. *IOL News*, 31 October.

Short, J. and Wolfgang, M. (2009) Perspectives on collective violence. In J. Short and M. Wolfgang (eds.), *Collective Violence* (pp. 3-32). New Brunswick: Transaction Publishers.

Sidimba, L. (2013) Why foreign shops were targeted. *City Press*, 27 January.

Sosibo, K. (2013) Attacks on Duduza 'not random.' *Mail & Guardian*, 20 September.

Sowetan (2013) Foreign-owned businesses hampering rural growth – DTI. 10 October.

Smillie, S. (2012) Bangladeshi traders die after torching. *Star*, 1 February.

Steinberg, J. (2008) South Africa's xenophobic eruption. ISS Paper 169, Institute for Security Studies, Pretoria.

Teixeira, C., Lo, L. and Truelove, M. (2007) Immigrant entrepreneurship, institutional discrimination, and implications for public policy: A case study in Toronto. *Environment and Planning C: Government and Policy*, 25: 176-193.

Tilly, C. (2003) *The Politics of Collective Violence*. Cambridge: Cambridge University Press.

Van der Westhuizen, C. (2011) Torn between two discourses. *The Star*, 30 August.

Varshney, A., Tadjoeddin, M. and Panggabean, R. (2008) Creating datasets in information-poor environments: Patterns of collective violence in Indonesia, 1990-2003. *Journal of East Asian Studies*, 8(3): 361-394.

Visser, A. (2010) Race, poverty, and state intervention in the informal economy: Evidence from South Africa. PhD Thesis, New School University, New York.

Wafer, A. (2011) Informality, infrastructure and the state in post-apartheid Johannesburg. PhD Thesis, Open University.

Waldinger, R., Aldrich, H. and Ward, R. (eds.) (1990) *Ethnic Entrepreneurs: Immigrant Business in Industrial Societies*. Newbury Park: Sage.

Washinyira, T. (2013) Cape Town: Immigrants accuse cops of abuse as their businesses are destroyed. *Daily Maverick*, 27 June.

Wells, H. and Polders, L. (2006) Anti-gay hate crimes in South Africa: Prevalence, reporting practices, and experiences of the police. *Agenda*, 20: 20-28.

Williams, P. (2013) Response to *Al Jazeera*: Article on South Africa. *Al Jazeera*, 22 June.

Zwi, A., Garfield, R. and Loretti, A. (2002) Collective violence. In E. Krug, L. Dahlberg, J. Mercy, A. Zwi and R. Lozano (eds.), *World Report on Violence and Health* (pp. 215-229). Geneva: WHO.

Chapter Three

Making an Area Hot: Interrupting Trade in an Ethnic Enclave in Johannesburg's Inner City

Tanya Zack

INTRODUCTION

In October 2013, the City of Johannesburg (CoJ) forcibly removed all informal traders operating in public spaces in the inner city. As many as 6,000 traders were affected. "Operation Cleansweep" catapulted the City into a stand-off with traders and resulted in court proceedings, which granted temporary reprieve for traders and required that the City articulate a legal and developmental response to the street-trading issue. How would such a response differ from current City policy? And what might such a response be in the Ethiopian entrepreneurial enclave of Jeppe in the inner city of Johannesburg? Jeppe itself is an intense ethnic retail enclave where much of the on-street and in-building retail activity can be classified as informal trade and where much of the appropriation and reconfiguration of space does not fit within City by-laws. These questions are particularly pertinent as the City is formulating its response and developing plans for the future of informal trading in the inner city.

Scott and Storper (2014: 8) note that "(t)he essential nature of urban land is that it is simultaneously private and public, individual and collective, and that its shape and form express the intertwined dynamics of the individual actions of firms and households and collective action on the part of diverse institutions of control and governance." They acknowledge the conflicts and deterioration that can emanate from uncoordinated actions at this scale and add that "without institutions able to implement relevant planning and policy measures, these dysfunctionalities would unquestionably undermine the viability of the city, for market logic alone is congenitally incapable of regulating the urban commons in the interests of economic efficiency and social wellbeing" (Scott and Storper, 2014: 8). This implies that municipal policy framing and coordination are critical. It also draws attention to the intertwined dynamics that shape urban land and the material conditions that policy must respond to.

A reflection on Johannesburg's policy history and its shortcomings indicates that the task of designating trading space is not simply a technical site selection and allocation process. It is also about responding to intertwined economic, social and spatial logics. While they are at all times the result of macro and micro dynamics, these aspects of informal trade are contextual and warrant examination on the ground. The placement and management of informal trade in the inner city may require that the City craft both general prescriptions for this activity as an aspect of the agglomeration economy that requires broad level intervention and governance, as well as particular responses for site specific conditions.

This chapter begins with an account of the changing policy environment towards informal trade from the pre- to the post-apartheid period, showing how policy shifts and ambiguities have affected the context within which informal traders operate. It then turns to the case study area of Jeppe in inner-city Johannesburg, examining the conditions of on-street and in-building trade and the intertwined business relationships within this migrant ethnic retail enclave. The rupture wrought by Operation Cleansweep in Jeppe is discussed using information from interviews with affected street traders and shopkeepers. The chapter concludes that an appropriate developmental response to supporting informal trade would need to be responsive to localized social and economic conditions and relations in different parts of the inner city.

POLICIES TOWARDS INFORMAL TRADING: APARTHEID AND BEFORE

There is a long history of informal trade in Johannesburg and an equally long history of municipal policy both in opposition to and in support of these activities (Gotz and Wooldridge, 2000). Negative attitudes towards informal trade stretch as far back as the early 20th century and the low tolerance of the authorities for coffee-cart sellers catering to a growing African population (Rogerson and Beavon, 1984; Beavon and Rogerson, 1986). Restrictions, court action, prosecution and active harassment of traders by the Johannesburg City Council continued until the courts ruled in favour of traders during the 1950s.

Arrests of coffee-cart traders declined for a period, but the City responded with building by-laws and claims that these businesses were a public health threat (Beavon and Rogerson, 1986). In the 1960s, it amended its by-laws to regulate coffee-cart sellers, but refused to grant licences – effectively making most traders illegal (Gotz and Wooldridge, 2000). The City's heavy-handed raiding of coffee-carts finally led to their demise (Freedman, 1961). An estimated 2,000 traders had to find other means of livelihood and many turned to hawking alternative goods, including fruit and vegetables. The coffee-cart was replaced by illegal street trading while the restrictive actions of the City kept the numbers of hawkers at about 200 during the 1970s (Beavon and Rogerson, 1986).

The 1980s saw greater tolerance, and even support, of street trading by the central government (Rogerson, 1987). The focus on deregulation and economic reform generated policy and legislative change aimed at lifting restrictions on business activities. Small and informal businesses were included in these reforms, as evidenced by the 1986 White Paper on Urbanization and the 1986 Temporary Removal of Restrictions on Economic Activities Act. Perhaps most significantly, the 1993 Amended Business Act allowed for trading to occur except in areas expressly declared as prohibited or restricted trading areas by municipalities. The climate of reform gave rise to burgeoning informal retail activities in city centres (Rogerson, 2003). In Johannesburg fewer traders were prosecuted in the 1980s and the number of valid hawker licences increased to 7,000 in 1988 (Gotz and Wooldridge, 2000).

Since the 1980s, most street traders have been survivalists. Yet programmes to support street trade have inevitably focused on the "entrepreneurial potential" of this activity and its graduation out of the informal sector. The state's deregulation has therefore not been coupled with effective programmes to stimulate income enhancement or transition to more formalized retail outlets (Rogerson, 2003). Inadequate access to credit and business management skills, as well as competition from formal retail, has therefore hindered the prospects for formalization.

POST-APARTHEID POLICY

For the last three decades, increased informal trading activities on the streets of Johannesburg have added to the pressures on public services and been accompanied by a municipal discourse that readily associates street trade with congestion, littering, and even crime (Dinath and Zack, 2014). The context for the City's response to the surge of street trading has been a desire to stem the dramatic decline in formal investment in the inner city (Tomlinson et al., 1995). In the late 1980s and early 1990s, property owners and investors made calls for municipal investment in the inner city in an effort to attract private investment (CoJ, 1993). In 1992 the Central Johannesburg Partnership (CJP) was established to serve business interests in the inner city. Initially the CJP research was directed by North American approaches to tackling urban decay, which included a zero-tolerance approach towards "illegal informal trade" (Beall et al., 2002). The CJP also proposed the establishment of City Improvement Districts (CIDs), where the management of public space would be undertaken through partnerships between the private sector and the municipality. The notion of the management of public space as a key to renewal permeated CJP discourse and that of the City. In 1993, the City devised formal municipal solutions for street trading, premised on management and control. These focused on the creation of market spaces for street traders. Small numbers of traders were accommodated in formalized off-street market spaces.

Inner-city revitalization was taken to a new level with the City launching a bold vision, and the private sector rallying behind the call for an ideal future city centre that would earn descriptors such as "vibrant," "safe," "liveable," "accessible," "dynamic" and "focused on the 21st century" (Royston, 1997). After years of inertia the municipality was under pressure to respond to street trading (Gotz and Wooldridge, 2000). The City's 1999 Inner City Street Trading Management Strategy foregrounded management, by-law enforcement and infrastructure development. Informal trade was to be accommodated within a hierarchy of markets (CoJ, 2006). The managerialist and urban regeneration focus, emphasizing the location of traders in linear markets and the reduction of sidewalk trading, was coupled with a drive for development of the sector through training initiatives. Plans were rolled out for the development of several markets under the management of the newly established municipal entity, the Metropolitan Trading Company. These were accompanied by plans for the restriction of trade in many parts of the city (GJMC, 1999). The establishment of CIDs was also significant for street trading. Various models unfolded with some CIDs prohibiting street trading altogether and others offering high levels of cleaning, security and management to linear markets in their areas. The emphasis on trading inside designated off-street markets reduced the support for sidewalk trading (Charlton, 2014).

Further citywide long-term economic and spatial plans were developed in the early 2000s. The iGoli 2002, iGoli 2010 and Joburg 2030 plans all emphasized the vision of Johannesburg as a "world class city" and foregrounded the importance of building a robust economy (CoJ, 2002). These plans offered few strategies for dealing with the social and developmental imperatives of the inner city, but acknowledged the importance of the area. In 2000, the inner city was adopted as a mayoral priority area. An Inner City Position Paper (CoJ, 2001) called for a turnaround of the inner city and introduced the idea of area-based or precinct planning. The Johannesburg Development Agency (JDA), a municipal-owned entity established in 2001, focused on a precinct approach to revitalization of the inner city. The managerial approach towards street trading continued with the Inner City Management Strategy arguing for the elimination or, failing that, management of the negative consequences of informal street trading (Rice, 2006).

In the mid-2000s, official responses to street trading were more ambiguous, characterized by holistic and inclusive language in policy frameworks, strengthened partnerships for inner-city rejuvenation, maintaining the messages of managed trading spaces, and opening up large areas of trading on sidewalks in less regulated ways. At that time, integrated planning frameworks were prioritized by the national government and the CoJ responded with its first Growth and Development Strategy (GDS) (CoJ, 2006a) and a five-year Integrated Development Plan (CoJ, 2006b). The GDS 2006-2011 committed the City to a set of principles, led by "proactive absorption of the poor." Together with the additional principles of "balanced and shared growth" and "facilitated social mobility," this strengthened the formal introduction of pro-poor thinking in the City – something that had been introduced in the 2005 Human Development Strategy (HDS) (CoJ, 2005). The HDS emphasized that poverty, inequality and exclusion were concerns that could not wait for the benefits of economic growth to reach all the citizens of Johannesburg. The HDS and GDS made a case for acknowledging and stimulating emerging economic opportunities (Dinath and Zack, 2014).

This period of progressive policy responses across the city was, on the one hand, supported by a compassionate response to the enormous pressure for trading space in the inner city, and on the other, contradicted by a re-emphasis of the control and management position, led by the private sector. In 2005, the demands made by informal traders for additional trading space peaked and the City responded to this pressure by providing metal stands (colloquially known as "cages") for street vendors along many inner-city sidewalks. This was contrary to its own written policy against sidewalk trading as the location of the stands defied the City's by-laws. Coincident with the release of the GDS, the private sector issued a report that re-emphasized that there should be no trading on sidewalks in the inner city. The negative impacts of informal trade cited included cluttered sidewalks, havens for criminal activity, dirtying of public areas and hindrances to maintaining, cleaning and policing of public areas (CJP, 2006).

Ten years after the announcement of the Inner City Vision, a summit was held in May 2007. One of the objectives was to ensure that the strategy addressed the fact that the inner city was not geared to absorb the increasing number of poor people trying to move closer to opportunities only found in dense urban settings. A new agenda for the inner city was mapped out in the Inner City Regeneration Charter. With regard to street trading, the charter stated that a stricter enforcement regime would be implemented and would coincide with the roll-out of new trading spaces. The City would make every effort to avoid arbitrary actions against traders. The following year, the City instituted a training programme aimed at turning traders into small business owners (Dinath and Zack, 2014). However, sporadic evictions of traders continued and in 2009 new informal trading by-laws were approved (CoJ, 2012).

The developmentalist approaches that had been initiated in the previous decade were reinforced in post-2010 policies. This included the GDS 2040 (CoJ, 2011a), which was unambiguously developmentalist, focusing on the eradication of poverty. The Johannesburg Informal Trading Policy released in the same year made provision for smart cards, periodic markets, incubation, cooperative development and participatory structures for traders (CoJ, 2011b). The Inner City Transformation Roadmap (2014a) took forward the work of the 2007-2012 Inner City Regeneration Charter and directed work towards tackling problems of the inner city in a coordinated and holistic manner. It focused on area-based management and partnership approaches to inner-city revitalization. The roadmap extended the location of trade to "markets, linear markets and designated roads," implying that sidewalks were not excluded as an acceptable location for informal trading space (CoJ, 2014a).

OPERATION CLEANSWEEP

Against the backdrop of a long history of ambiguous practices and recent progressive policy utterances around street trading, Operation Cleansweep was launched in October 2013. The fact that the authorities took such violent action was something of a surprise. Operation Cleansweep was designed to remove both legal and illicit traders from sidewalks and regulated market spaces across the central business district (CBD). Uniformed men and women from the South African Police Services (SAPS), South African Revenue Service (SARS) and Johannesburg Metropolitan Police Department (JMPD) moved in and out of buildings, breaking open the locks of roller-shuttered doors and removing goods from shops. There was shouting, chasing, whipping and threats, and teargas was fired. The municipal metal stalls that street hawkers traded from were loaded onto JMPD flatbed trucks.

The forcible removal of traders from Johannesburg's streets was widely reported and the media highlighted the plight of those who were denied income-earning opportunities for many weeks. The impact was especially dramatic in Jeppe, where the sidewalks are among the most intensely traded footpaths in the inner city. Official explanations for the police operation included crime prevention, tackling criminality, resolving impediments to service delivery, reducing congestion and improving cleanliness. Claims were made that hawkers were contravening by-laws, and public announcements were made during the operation to indicate that the City and police were targeting irregular migrants, business theft suspects, and traders in counterfeit goods (Nicolson and Lekgowa, 2013). Some argued that street trading was responsible for "crowding, blocking pedestrian walkways, structures erected that cause obstruction (to) pedestrians" (Magubane, 2013). A city spokesperson labelled Operation Cleansweep a "strategic intervention vehicle" intended to "tackle service delivery challenges in the inner city." He said the operation would address illegal trading, illegal dumping and littering, land and building invasions and other by-law contraventions, illegal connection of infrastructure including theft of electricity, and the lack of a sense of civic pride and ownership (Nxumalo, 2013).

In the aftermath of Operation Cleansweep, talks ensued between the City and traders' associations. City officials talked of a plan – ostensibly a spatial plan – that would define where informal trading would be permitted so that the situation would not return to the supposedly chaotic conditions that preceded the operation. The City refused the street traders permission to return to trading during this time, but officials did embark on a process of verifying "legal" traders. The process was delayed and frustrations within the trader community grew. Street traders engaged in meetings, submitted memoranda and staged public protests. When these interactions did not elicit a positive response from the City, the traders turned to litigation. A case was filed at the High Court for an urgent interdict against Operation Cleansweep that traders be allowed to return to trading immediately. The High Court ruled that the matter was not urgent and set a date for the case to be heard early in 2014. Traders and their legal teams applied, and were granted, leave to appeal. The Constitutional Court set aside the High Court decision regarding the lack of urgency of the case and ruled that all legal displaced Johannesburg CBD street traders could return to their legal trading sites with immediate effect (Constitutional Court, 2014).

The City meanwhile established an operational team led by the Chief Operating Officer and commissioned the University of the Witwatersrand to undertake research into informal trading, transnationalism and xenophobia (Wits, 2014). The Department of Economic Development began to devise an alternative strategy for informal trading in the inner city. These actions were not necessarily coordinated, but in mid-2014 the department set up a consultative process aimed at producing a set of plans for street trading in the inner city. The Informal Trading: Inner City Promulgation and Designation of Trading Areas stakeholder consultation process intensified deliberations that were already underway within and between trader associations, academic institutions and private sector organizations. At stake was the designation of spaces for the restriction or prohibition of informal trade within the inner city.

The City, traders and private property organizations had been involved in separate deliberations over informal trading in the inner city and the consultative process brought to the fore the need for a more comprehensive and developmental plan. The Wits (2014) research highlighted a policy history towards informal trade that was inconsistent, often at odds with the citywide strategy, and uncoordinated with ground-level management and law enforcement actions. The documentation prepared for the City's consultation process on the designation of trading space in the inner city indicated that street trading was to be legitimized under certain conditions (CoJ, 2014b). Alongside a continued concern with management, regulation and spatial order it raised the need for a "greater focus on development" (CoJ, 2014b, p. 24). But suggestions for developmental interventions were minimal. Without providing detail, the City referred to the need to see informal business as an incubator for entrepreneurs, the development of value chain opportunities, better support services and skills development (CoJ, 2014b). What these and other developmental considerations might mean in practice is unclear. City of Johannesburg plans for informal trade have, in the main, not been based on grounded research. There are few accounts of actual practice or the needs of informal traders in the inner city streets and there is no reliable enumeration data (Bénit-Gbaffou, 2014).

CONDUCTING BUSINESS IN JEPPE

The north-eastern portion of the Johannesburg CBD is known by users and traders as Jeppe and is named after the main route – Jeppe Street – on which the precinct centres. High-rise buildings have been incrementally appropriated over two decades as an intense shopping hub hosting mostly Ethiopian migrant entrepreneurs. Micro retail operates on every sidewalk, in municipally-provided stands and on makeshift tables, in cupboard-sized shops facing the sidewalks, and in shops of varying sizes within buildings. The modernist buildings were designed in the mid-20th century to cater to medical practices. Their configuration has proved highly adaptable to retail use: up to six floors of intense shopping space with some retail units as small as two square metres. At street level, and within buildings, the boundaries of formal and informal trade are blurred (Zack, 2013).

The many hundreds of street traders and micro retailers in Jeppe comprise a booming agglomeration economy. Here merchants from other countries in Sub-Saharan Africa arrive on a daily basis to buy cheap clothing, household wares and accessories. While many shoppers are hawkers from surrounding black townships and smaller urban centres and rural areas in South Africa, much of the business of shops and hawker stands in Jeppe is cross-border trade (Zack, 2013). This trade is a manifestation of the low-end globalization described by Mathews and Yang Yang (2012), where the transnational flows of people and goods are oiled not by high finance but by small amounts of capital and through informal transactions. As more Ethiopians have joined the throng of traders, the area has taken on the characteristic of an ethnic enclave wherein social relations, individual behaviours and economic transactions are strongly dictated by social networks and structures (Aldridge and Waldinger, 1990). The reliance on ethnic linkages described in literature on ethnic entrepreneurial enclaves also features in Jeppe (Light and Karageorgis, 1994). The number of restaurants, traditional clothing stores, ethnic homeware outlets, and stores offering travel services, wedding planning and photographers has increased as this Ethiopian quarter matures.

A key to the success of micro enterprises in Jeppe and to the graduation from stands to more established shops is the symbiotic relationship between street traders and shopkeepers. Many shopkeepers, for example, supply street trader stalls. As one noted: "I buy plastic products for the home and I supply the traders in this whole area with plastic things I am wholesaling and retailing. Actually we are all also wholesalers" (Interview No. 13, 8 November 2013). Another aspect of this relationship is informal access to credit. Financial support is offered through credit, introductions to suppliers and access to informal banking and savings networks. The boundaries of these benefits spill beyond the Ethiopian community. For example, one shopkeeper whose life as a vendor began in rural South Africa selling household items door to door, graduated to a small shop space in Jeppe and then expanded to the four shops he owns in this area. He attributes his success to the credit he was able to access from Chinese migrant wholesalers:

> It's amazing that we come here. Chinese people come from their country. But we meet here. But they trust us. We help each other. I get credit up to R50,000. And if a new guy wants space, a Chinese guy will help him set up shop. He will give him stock to fill the shop and the guy will pay later (Interview No. 13, 8 November 2013).

And this shopkeeper was now extending credit to others: "There is a Congolese trader down the road. I helped her as hawker, I gave her credit, helped her stock. Now she has a little shop. She still buys from me." The agglomeration economy of Jeppe facilitates other financial tools, including group saving. Informal savings clubs and a general practice of thrift is part of the economic success of operating in this high-risk environment: "We are always saving, even people who only earn R50. The culture of saving is in everything, we waste nothing. We eat together, we share a plate and it costs each person very little" (Interview No. 13, 8 November 2013).

While storage is a necessary component of wholesale trade and many traders and shopkeepers rent storerooms in the upper floors of buildings in the area, those traders with less capital are likely to rely on the formal shops for stock. There is a considerable convenience attached to being able to offer a customer bulk supplies of an item and purchasing that stock in the moment of the sale. In this way the proximity of different scales of business in the area benefits both the larger and smaller vendor. Buying power extends beyond credit and savings:

We know how to make an area hot. We bring supplies of new stock quickly. And by working together we are strong. We negotiate the cheapest prices with Chinese suppliers and we supply each other (Interview No. 14, 5 November 2013).

This shopkeeper was referring to the intensity of trade in Jeppe and the ways in which Ethiopian vendors help others to establish business there.

The nature of goods sold and the business model in Jeppe are important elements in maintaining the vibrancy of the area. The lines between trading, retailing, wholesaling, intermediation and even couriering in Jeppe are blurred. In many instances, shopkeepers are also intermediaries, bringing goods from Chinese wholesalers to sell to other shopkeepers. And customers may be couriers for Ethiopian businesses in other areas: "There are customers here who are carrying things to Ethiopians in Musina. They take bags of things labelled for different traders" (Interview No. 13, 8 November 2013). The major form of trade in the area is in cheap clothing, often with counterfeit brand name labels imported from China.

Frequent police raids have had a dramatic impact on the counterfeit market and more established retailers have grown reluctant to carry the risk of counterfeit goods. The demand for these goods remains high, however, and smaller retailers are readier to bear the risk. As one street trader on Delvers Street noted: "I need to sell counterfeit because I can't compete with the prices of the big guys who sell unbranded clothes. They can buy so many bales and can drive the prices down so that we can't compete with them" (Interview No. 15, 12 November 2013).

Landlords and leaseholders charge extremely high rentals for shops in Jeppe. A monthly rent of ZAR2,000 per square metre is not unusual. This compares with the rental rates elsewhere in the inner city of under ZAR180 per square metre (Zack, 2013). In addition, the informal property market in this area operates according to the practice of "key money." This is a non-refundable advance payment made to secure the property. It is separate from the monthly rental and is paid to the landlord or leaseholder of a building or to the previous incumbent of a shop. It may even be paid to an incumbent or leaseholder of a municipal trader stall. A trader who operated from a stall on Delvers Street said he had "bought" a stand from a friend by paying key money amounting to ZAR55,000. The price was lower than the going rate for the extralegal "sale" of stalls in the area and he believed that he was getting a good deal because the friend was returning to Ethiopia: "I paid quickly because it's a good price for a stand in Delvers" (Interview No. 18, 7 November 2013).

OPERATION CLEANSWEEP AND MIGRANT ENTREPRENEURSHIP

The evaluation of the impact of Operation Cleansweep on an enclave dominated by migrant entrepreneurs draws on interviews with 18 Ethiopian traders and shopkeepers on two streets in Jeppe in the weeks following the campaign. Interviews focused on how Operation Cleansweep affected their business and about the relationship between shopkeepers and street traders. The responses highlight particular dynamics that might be important considerations in supporting a sustainable informal trading sector in the inner city.

The immediate negative impact of Operation Cleansweep is evident from the personal testimony of those most affected. A couple who had worked together from a stand on Jeppe Street, for example, reported that they had lost everything:

> *Because we have a family and whatever we earn we have to spend we have never been able to save. So the stand is our lifeline. We also support some family members back in Ethiopia. We work hard, but we managed. Now we have lost everything* (Interview No. 1, 13 November 2013).

Another trader reported that his wife was beaten by police who demanded to know where her store was. He said the police had also taken ZAR2,500 from her (Interview No. 2, 9 November 2013). A woman who had left a job at a butchery in a neighbouring town to become a street trader said she had been paying a rental of ZAR2,000 to the owner of the stand. The owner had required a year's rental upfront. She had paid the money and borrowed ZAR20,000 for stock. During the raid the metro police confiscated her goods as well as the stand: "I can't pay my flat rental this month. I made a big mistake to leave my job" (Interview No. 3, 7 November 2013).

Confiscation of goods by the police was a common complaint. A street trader who was very nervous about being interviewed said he had worked in the area for 10 years. His cage and stock were confiscated by the police who also followed him to his home where they cut open a mattress in search of money and vandalized his home. His wife and children had gone back to Ethiopia after the incident (Interview No. 4, 9 November 2013). One woman who had rented a stand from the municipality for a number of years described her experience as follows:

> *I have never sublet my stand and I don't sell counterfeit goods. But the police came one after the other. They were taking things. It seemed they were taking things for themselves. I tried to take my things but they sprayed pepper spray. I*

could not even get to my handbag and I also lost the R3,200 that was in there because it also disappeared (Interview No. 5, 5 November 2013).

The police not only raided the business operations of traders but their storage units as well. An informal trader who had worked on Delvers Street said she did not sell counterfeit goods, paid her rent to the municipality and thought she was safe, but "suddenly the metros (police) arrived and started loading everything from the cage…I have lost everything except a small amount of stock in my store and I have nowhere to sell that. I can't pay my rent for my flat this month" (Interview No. 6, 5 November 2013). Another trader whose stall was removed from Delvers Street said: "I had a storeroom in one of the buildings. It was broken by metro police two days after they took the cages. So I have really lost almost everything. I have a bit of stock in another storeroom" (Interview No. 7, 9 November 2013).

A trader whose confiscated stock was worth ZAR30,000 and who, like many others, had paid key money (of ZAR80,000) for the stand that had been removed, said he had moved out of his flat and was sharing a room with someone as he could not afford his rental (Interview No. 6, 5 November 2013). A shopkeeper on Delvers Street said (in reference to an informal transaction for a municipally-owned trader stand): "I bought a stand for R80,000 last winter. It has been removed in the raid and now my shop has very few customers because that stand attracts customers" (Interview No. 17, 5 November 2013). Another trader described what happened when he tried to resist, and then report, the police action:

> *What is going on? I don't sell counterfeit goods but they took all my stock. There was no warning. They just arrived and loaded my stuff. I have never run from the police because I am legal. My goods were legal…Now it's as if the police are looting. They are not protecting the law. I tried to protect my goods. But they beat me and forced me to leave. I followed them to the police station when they left. The Commander came and listened to my story. Then he ordered the police to arrest me. The next day they told me that I must pay R3,000 to be released. Everything is dark for me now* (Interview No. 8, 6 November 2013).

Many Ethiopian traders disappeared from the streets in the weeks after Operation Cleansweep. The social networks operating in this ethnic enclave enabled them to seek assistance from fellow Ethiopians in other areas. There they might be given an opportunity to sell goods at a transport node or door to door. Such an arrangement had to be short term, as they needed to be ready to take advantage of the revival of opportunity on the streets of Jeppe if and when that came.

Traders were not the only entrepreneurs affected by Operation Cleansweep. Many formal shopkeepers number traders among their customers and the disruption of their activities had a negative impact on them as well:

> *The street traders were my main customers. Now that they are gone my profit has fallen. Some of them owe me money but I don't think they will pay because they have lost everything... This November feels like a February because customers and profits are very low. These days I only have customers for singles and not for stock* (Interview No. 9, 13 November 2013).

> *My business has reduced. I am now relying on selling on weekends to people who stock from the countryside. The hawkers used to buy from me. Now that they have gone I open my shop and just sit here on weekdays* (Interview No. 10, 7 November 2013).

> *Street traders buy a lot from me. I can also sell my leftover stock after a season to the hawkers. Now I am stuck with it. But they also bring customers* (Interview No. 11, 9 November 2013).

The low-profit and high-turnover sales formula in this area is premised on the potential for selling in bulk:

> *Since the raids my business has been low. I sell cheap things, I make so little profit from these socks and hats and vests that I can only manage if I sell wholesale. But my customers are hawkers and they are not stocking now because they have lost money (Interview No. 16, 12 November 2013).*

Shopkeepers continued to offer credit to hawkers who were trying to avoid police harassment. One shopkeeper on Delvers Street indicated that the principle of giving credit, sometimes with a short turnaround payment time of a single day, persisted: "Now the hawkers are running around from metro, taking small amounts of goods. We have to give them stock and credit and they sell on a daily basis and pay us back" (Interview No. 12, 12 November 2013).

CONCLUSION

The deliberations on informal trading in the wake of Operation Cleansweep are challenging what has largely been a formalistic policy approach in Johannesburg. It is clear that future policy and practice will need to be more comprehensive and developmental. While the need for broad policy and guidelines for informal trade across the inner city cannot be discounted, detailed solutions and even differential prescriptions need to be developed at a precinct level, which take cognisance of the spatial and non-spatial influences on the viability of trade. Informal trade practices in Jeppe illuminate the complex mix of factors that support street trade in this area. To the extent that these factors are dependent on an ethnic economy and the trade conditions it has generated, they are particular to that space.

The credit practices in Jeppe are stimulating the rapid transition of traders to more formalized spaces and means of operating. This aligns with the City's concern to graduate traders and grow entrepreneurs. In Jeppe, any strategy aimed at stimulating entrepreneurship should learn from and build on development that is already happening informally. Opportunity is created and multiplied in this agglomeration economy under conditions of extreme density of traders and customers. This is a key factor in "making this area hot." Customers have wide choice and can comparison shop within a short distance. The marginal profits being extracted require that high sales volumes be sustained. Shops benefit from selling to street traders who, in turn, are able to keep lower levels of stock on site because they have ready access to stock. Suppliers, creditors and retailers are known to one another and credit is extended on the basis of trust and social networks.

Close relationships exist between formal and informal trade in Jeppe and the proximity of stalls and street-facing shops is seen as positive by both groups, which contradicts an official perception that street trading inhibits the custom of formal shops. Certainly, the beneficial relationship between trading stalls and shops may not be true for all parts of the inner city, but the policy response in Jeppe should be tailored to allow for such an interface. An approach that simply seeks to reduce the number of street traders may have the unintended effect of reducing benefits to more formalized shops.

The importance of tailoring policy responses to street trade to the actual and varying conditions across the inner city is demonstrated in an examination of the peculiar dynamics within the so-called Ethiopian quarter. In that space a developmental response to street trading would need to be sensitive to and support the local and ethnic economic practices that contribute to the viability of the area. A blanket response would be inappropriate since the inner city is not a homogenous economic space. Considerable variations across space and local-level spatial and economic realities need to be accounted for if the City is to support and strengthen the potential of informal trade. Such a localized response would be in line with the City's own precinct approach to revitalization in the inner city, which recognizes the value of area-based planning and management.

Sweeping critiques of informality in the inner city have inspired large-scale harassment and blanket law enforcement approaches. Yet the relationships between formal and informal trade, the requirements of traders, the interface with customers and the economic linkages that sustain this trade are not necessarily uniform but are shaped by very localized relationships. While the informal sale of stands and the payment of key money in Jeppe may not coincide with City policy, for example, these practices illuminate the high value of trading space in this area. This may require differentiated tariffs to encourage fair allocation of stands, but it also requires a deeper understanding of the mechanisms of the informal property market. Or again, the tendrils of the informal economy in Jeppe reach across sub-Saharan Africa and even globally. This means that the City needs to consider the informal economy in this area as a crucial component of cross-border trade and that the trade opportunities in this manifestation of low-end globalization should be better understood and supported.

Operation Cleansweep is an extreme example of a logic about street trading that is focused on control and on limiting the perceived ills of this activity. The application of blunt law enforcement tools has consequences way beyond the spatial clearing and ordering of space. Operation Cleansweep wrought significant personal and economic hardship in Jeppe. A more developmental view offers an alternative to an approach that is solely focused on responding to perceived chaos. It is directed at understanding and optimizing opportunity in the area and sector.

REFERENCES

Aldridge, H. and Waldinger, R. (1990) Ethnicity and entrepreneurship. *Annual Review of Sociology*, 16: 111–135.

Beall, J., Crankshaw, O. and Parnell, S. (2002) *Uniting a Divided City: Governance and Social Exclusion in Johannesburg.* London: Earthscan.

Beavon, K. and Rogerson, C. (1986) The council v the common people: The case of street trading in Johannesburg. *Geoforum*, 17: 201–216.

Bénit-Gbaffou, C. (2014) Management models: Lessons from the Retail Improvement District (RID) and Park Station Pilot Traders Management Committee, in Alternative Formalities, Transnationalism and Xenophobia in the Inner City of Johannesburg. School of Architecture and Planning, University of the Witwatersrand, Johannesburg.

Charlton, S. (2014) The case for managed trade in public space and the spatial dimensions of the informal economy, in Alternative Formalities, Transnationalism and Xenophobia in the Inner City of Johannesburg. School of Architecture and Planning, University of the Witwatersrand, Johannesburg

CJP (2006) Johannesburg inner city informal trading management. Unpublished report, Johannesburg.

CoJ (1993) Towards a development framework for the inner city. Unpublished paper, Johannesburg City Council, Johannesburg.

CoJ (2001) Inner City. Unpublished position paper, City of Johannesburg, Johannesburg.

CoJ (2002) *Joburg 2030*. Johannesburg: City of Johannesburg.

CoJ (2005) *Human Development Strategy: Jo'burg's Commitment to the Poor.* Johannesburg: City of Johannesburg.

CoJ (2006a) *Growth and Development Strategy 2006.* Johannesburg: City of Johannesburg.

CoJ (2006b) *Integrated Development Plan 2006–2011.* Johannesburg: City of Johannesburg.

CoJ (2011a) *Johannesburg Growth and Development Strategy 2040.* Johannesburg: City of Johannesburg.

CoJ (2011b) Informal trading policy for the City of Johannesburg. City of Johannesburg, Johannesburg.

CoJ (2012) City of Johannesburg Metropolitan Municipality Council Informal Trading By-Laws. Provincial Gazette No. 66 (14 March 2012), Local Authority Notice 328, Johannesburg.

CoJ (2014a) *A Place of Opportunity: The Inner City Transformation Roadmap (Final Draft).* Johannesburg: City of Johannesburg.

CoJ (2014b) Informal trading: Inner city presentation for stakeholder consultation. City of Johannesburg, Johannesburg.

Constitutional Court (2014) South African Informal Traders Forum and Others v City of Johannesburg and Others; South African National Traders Retail Association v City of Johannesburg and Others (CCT 173/13 ; CCT 174/14) [2014] ZACC 8; 2014 (6) BCLR 726 (CC); 2014 (4) SA 371 (CC) (4 April 2014)

Dinath, Y., and Zack, T. (2014) Explaining the impasse: Why informal economic activity has not been consistently supported by the City, in Alternative Formalities, Transnationalism and Xenophobia in the Inner City of Johannesburg. School of Architecture and Planning, University of the Witwatersrand, Johannesburg.

Freedman, M. (1961) The problem of prohibition and control of illegal street trading in urban areas of the Transvaal. *Public Health*, 61(12): 7–29

GJMC (1999) Declaration of restricted trading areas in the Johannesburg Inner City. Urgency Report 1 of Executive Committee, City of Johannesburg, Johannesburg.

Gotz, G. and Wooldridge, D. (2000) Local government innovation: A case study of the greater Johannesburg metropolitan council's inner-city office and three urban development projects. Local Government Learning Network, Johannesburg.

Light, I. and Karageorgis, S. (1994) The ethnic economy. In N. Smelser and R. Swedberg (eds.), *The Handbook of Economic Sociology* (pp. 647–669). Princeton, NJ: Princeton University Press.

Magubane, K. (2013) Cosatu throws its weight behind informal traders' march. *Business Day*, 25 October.

Mathews, G. and Yang Yang, N. (2012) How Africans pursue low-end globalization in Hong Kong and mainland China. *Journal of Current Chinese Affairs*, 41: 95–120.

Nicolson, G. and Lekgowa, T. (2013) Operation cleansweep: Johannesburg metro police arrests human rights lawyer. *Daily Maverick*, 6 December.

Nxumalo, M. (2013) Hawkers demand right to sell on street. *Mail & Guardian*, 24 October.

Rice, E. (2006) Informal traders' markets in Johannesburg: Creating an enabling environment for development of micro-enterprise? Honours Report in Marketing Management, University of Johannesburg, Johannesburg.

Rogerson, C. (1987) The state and the informal sector: A case of separate development. In G. Moss and I. Obery (eds.), *South African Review* 4 (pp. 412–422). Johannesburg: Ravan Press.

Rogerson, C. (2003) The absorptive capacity of the informal sector in South Africa. In D. Smith (ed.), *The Apartheid City and Beyond: Urbanisation and Social Change in South Africa* (pp. 161–172). New York and London: Routledge.

Rogerson, C. and Beavon, K. (1984) A tradition of repression: The street traders of Johannesburg. In R. Bromley (ed.), *Planning for Small Enterprises in Third World Cities* (pp. 233–245). Oxford: Pergamon Press.

Royston, L. (1997) *The Golden Heartbeat of Africa*. Johannesburg: GJMC.

Scott, A. and Storper, M. (2014) The nature of cities: The scope and limits of urban theory. *International Journal of Urban and Regional Research*, 39: 1-15.

Tomlinson, R., Hunter, R., Jonker, M., Rogerson, C. and Rogerson, J. (1995) *Johannesburg Inner City Strategic Development Framework: Economic Analysis*. Johannesburg: Greater Johannesburg Transitional Metropolitan Council City Planning Department.

Wits (2014) Alternative Formalities, Transnationalism and Xenophobia in the Inner City of Johannesburg. School of Architecture and Planning, University of the Witwatersrand, Johannesburg.

Zack, T. (2013) Seeking logic in the chaos precinct: 'Jeppe'. In E. Pieterse and A. Simone (eds.), *Rogue Urbanism: Emergent African Cities* (pp. 283–291). Johannesburg and Cape Town: Jacana and African Centre for Cities.

Chapter Four

A Transnational Space of Business: The Informal Economy of Ivory Park, Johannesburg

Andrew Charman and Leif Petersen

INTRODUCTION

South African townships and informal settlements receive economic migrants from beyond and within South Africa. The settlers have a variety of motivations for temporary or permanent relocation, though generally they share a desire for economic opportunities having left areas of economic marginality and/or political instability. Internal migration has been described, from the state's perspective, as a process of "hollowing out" the countryside while stimulating the growth of large cities (RSA, 2006:17). Though this analogy does not account for oscillating movements between urban and rural areas, the overall trend towards urbanization is indisputable (SSA, 2012). Population movements have most notably affected the major urban industrial centres and the province of Gauteng in particular, which received over 1 million net migrants over the inter-censal period 2001-2011.

The movement of people contributed towards the increase in population by 15 per cent between 2007 and 2011 (SSA, 2012: 15). Of the total Gauteng population of 11.9 million in 2011, 1.1 million persons were recorded as immigrants or persons born outside

South Africa (SSA, 2012: 25). As South African's economic heartland, Gauteng is also the primary destination for "transit migrants," some of whom travel to the region to conduct business, including the export trade into the region. Others seek to build social networks to help facilitate their movement outside Africa (Landau and Segatti, 2009). A significant proportion of international migrants have taken up residence in the various townships and informal settlements on the periphery of the Johannesburg and Ekurhuleni metropolitan municipalities. One such settlement is Ivory Park, which is situated on the northern boundary of the City of Johannesburg and provides the setting for this chapter's analysis of the social (and transnational) nature of informal markets.

Migration and the experience of transnationality in South African differs from the situation in the Global North where poor economic migrants find accommodation within cities as a result of the demand for low-skilled cheap labour in industries and the service sector. As a result, migrants tend to be spatially separated from the non-migrant working classes (Rouse, 2004). In the South African context, the scope for transnational spaces dominated by migrants is more constrained and must therefore be negotiated. Migrants and South Africans live in the same areas and compete in a labour market that is over-subscribed with low-skilled work seekers. Just over one quarter of the Gauteng labour force is unemployed (SSA, 2013: xiv). Competition for formal sector employment is fierce, as is rivalry for housing and allied resources including land. While migrants generally have a precarious legal status, a considerable number have successfully obtained employment and run businesses (micro enterprises) as a result of their greater skills, industrious work ethic, political subservience, prior entrepreneurial experience and more sophisticated social networks (CDE, 2008; Liedeman, 2013).

The broad scope of migrant entrepreneurial activity has been identified in several studies and includes the selling of curios, ethnic clothes and foods; car repair; hairdressing; operating restaurants, nightclubs, cafes, music shops and import-export businesses; and traditional healing (Rogerson, 1996, Peberdy and Rogerson, 2002). The dynamic nature of migrant entrepreneurship has been widely observed in different contexts. Kloosterman and Rath (2001), for example, report that migrants are able to mould opportunities that did not previously exist through their innovative behaviour. In South Africa, Mudi-Okorodudu (2011: 4) argues that "immigrants are creative and resourceful actors who actively engage their challenging context to achieve economic freedom." Liedeman (2013) highlights the significance of social networks in affording migrant spaza shopkeepers an advantage in labour, investment and reinvestment, and in procurement of goods to create a competitive advantage. Migrant micro entrepreneurs have also been credited with creating employment opportunities for South Africans within their businesses (Kalitanyi and Visser, 2010). However, other studies have suggested that new employment opportunities tend to be restricted to kin or other migrants (Charman et al., 2012; Liedeman, 2013).

The relative success of the migrant population in attaining work or setting up viable small businesses has amplified tensions around ethnicity and nationality within townships and informal settlements. These tensions have resulted in conflicts and violence in different spatial and temporal contexts. The depth and breadth of hostility towards migrants, as identified through attitudinal surveys, provides evidence, in the views of some researchers, of the racist and xenophobic attitudes of South Africans with "xenophobia scores" greatest among poor and uneducated persons (Crush, 2008; IOM, 2009:15; CDE, 2008). There is a substantial literature documenting and seeking to examine the dynamics of xenophobic politics in South Africa, with one strand of literature focusing on the frustration among jobless Black South Africans and their political allies (Hadland, 2008; Steinberg, 2008; IOM, 2009; ACMS, 2011). This literature has brought the grassroots political mobilization of anti-migrant actions into clearer focus. The higher order linkage between township activism and national economic policies remains opaque, however, as does the role of the state in contributing towards anti-migrant politics. Importantly, the literature shows that violence is geographically bounded, occurring in some localities but not others (Bekker et al., 2008). This provides a counter-narrative to reductionist arguments about pervasive xenophobic sentiment within township politics and shows that in some communities South Africans are both accommodating of migrants and defensive of their entitlement to live, work and conduct businesses.

Limited attention has been paid to date to the transformation of space accompanying negotiations between established residents and new settlers in townships and informal settlements. Some have noted that spatial controls and restrictions on migrants restrict opportunities and frame oppositional politics (Landau and Misago, 2009). But the significance of changes in everyday life, witnessed daily in market places, streets, open spaces and residential homes that accommodate and integrate transnational space, has been understated. This chapter explores the role, operations and social placement of informal micro enterprises and the relationship between migrants, immigrants and South Africans in the particular context of one township, Ivory Park, in Gauteng.

The major concern is with the contribution of transnational market spaces to the township informal economy. Migrants have been particularly resourceful in utilizing these spaces; the street being of particular importance because many entrants into the informal economy engage in street trade and street activities, either as self-employed micro entrepreneurs or informal workers (Ligthelm, 2008). From a policy perspective, enhancing the township business environment means recognizing the role of the street as a multi-functional urban space that accommodates a range of activities and uses, and promotes mixed-use development and intensification of activities.

The research on which the chapter is based was undertaken in Ivory Park in 2012-2013. The chapter is divided into three sections. The first introduces the study site and provides details on the research approach and methods. It also offers a generalized description of the scope and scale of the enterprises identified. The second section lays out the argument that insiders and outsiders derive mutual benefits from the proliferation of informality and describes some of the negotiations that have resulted in transformed spaces that accommodate transnationalism. The final section examines the achievements of immigrant entrepreneurship in four spatial contexts. The chapter concludes with a reflection on the limits of transformation, returning the discussion to consider the power dynamics and ethnic tensions that weaken the negotiated achievement of transnationality in Ivory Park.

IVORY PARK: A POST-APARTHEID TOWNSHIP

Ivory Park is a post-apartheid township settlement that came into existence in the early 1990s, accommodating the homeless and migrants to the city. The township was formally established in 1997 when the City demarcated 14,627 residential stands and began constructing houses, laying out road infrastructure, and building schools and other community facilities. It was designed as a dormitory settlement, built to accommodate people but lacking any provision for business or trade. Organic processes of change have greatly altered the original settlement plan, including the building of additional accommodation units and the growth in local business activity.

Internal and international migrants have played a key part in this reconfiguration, creating a demand for informal housing and stimulating the growth of the informal economy through their labour, entrepreneurship and inventiveness. Over the past 20 years, the proliferation of informal micro enterprises within Ivory Park and the spatial transformation towards a settlement characterized by entrepreneurship and business have begun to challenge the various meanings of the township as a place of residence. The township's population has expanded rapidly to over 206,000 residents (SSA, 2012), including many economic migrants from throughout South Africa, as well as from countries such as Mozambique and Zimbabwe.

The research was undertaken in a portion of Ivory Park, Extensions 2 and 5, equal to about one quarter of the township in geographic size. The data below refers to this portion of the township. Data is not yet available on place of birth of residents but the first language breakdown shows how heterogeneous the area has become. A quarter of the residents are Zulu first language speakers (primarily internal migrants from KwaZulu-Natal) but no other ethnicity constituted more than one quarter of the population (Figure 4.1). All of South Africa's official languages are represented in the area, while five per cent classified their first language in the "other" category, most of whom are likely to be non-South African. The Census may have undercounted the immigrant cohort, with some possibly recorded under "English" and some with a first language that is spoken in South Africa and neighbouring countries, such as isiNdebele (Zimbabwe), Xitsonga (Mozambique), Sesotho (Lesotho), Setswana (Botswana) and siSwati (Swaziland).

Figure 4.1: Languages Spoken by Ivory Park Residents

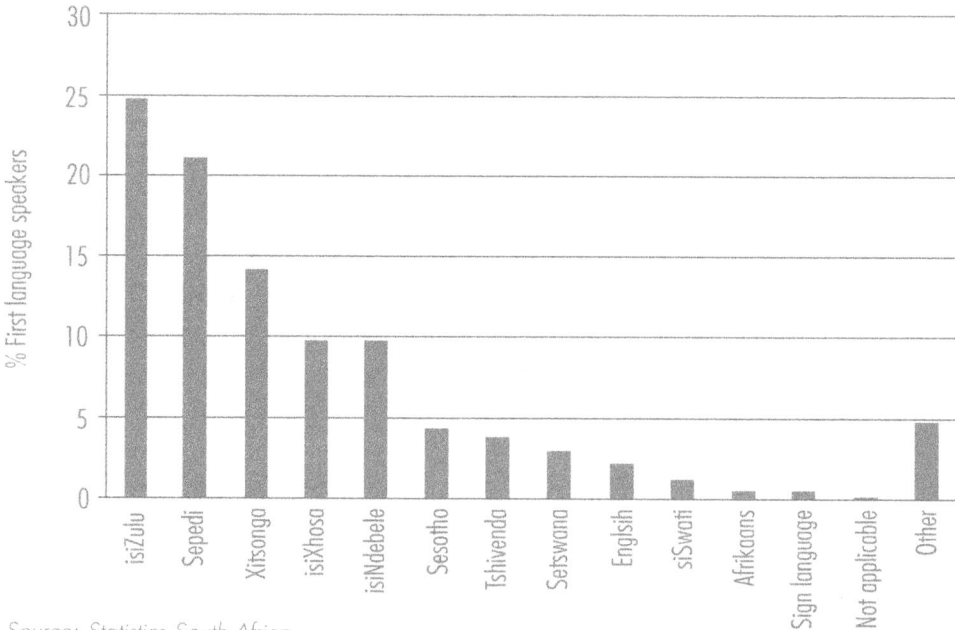

Source: Statistics South Africa

The demographic composition of Ivory Park provides further evidence of its migrant character (Table 4.1). For example, the average household size is only 2.4 in contrast to the national average of 3.4 and regional average of 3.0 (SSA, 2012: 60). The area also has a comparative scarcity of children and youth and an unbalanced gender breakdown (with males predominant at 54 per cent). About half of the resident population of working age were employed in 2011 (Table 4.2). Those not employed can be divided between the unemployed, not economically active (a category used by Statistics South Africa to describe those persons not available for work, including students) and a relatively small number of "discouraged" work seekers not looking for employment.

Table 4.1: Demographic Profile of Ivory Park

Population	Households	Household size	Male	Female	% Male	% Female
45,454	19,158	2.4	24,771	20,684	54.4	45.6

Source: Statistics South Africa

Table 4.2: Employment Status of Ivory Park Adult Residents

Name	Employed	Unemployed	Discouraged work seeker	Other not economically active	Not applicable
Ext 2	12,672	5,814	1,143	5,550	8,088
Ext 5	4,767	2,157	306	1,965	2,988
Total	17,439	16,935			11,076

Source: Statistics South Africa

METHODOLOGY

The research reported in this chapter was undertaken in 2012-2013 in several phases as a collaborative investigation between the Sustainable Livelihoods Foundation, a non-profit research organization, and UrbanWorks, a firm of architects. In the first phase of the study, the researchers recorded and mapped the distribution of all micro-enterprise activities within a defined geographic area, measuring 1.6km^2 with a known population of 45,453 residents in 2011 (SSA, 2012). A sub-area of Ivory Park was selected for the purpose of the research to enable the researchers to complete the survey in six weeks. The selected area was chosen as it was bounded by major roads and included a main taxi rank in the centre of the site. The researchers investigated the area on bicycle and foot, traversing every street and pathway in an effort to document and map all economy activity. Business activities were identified through observation, engagement with residents and chain sampling (Charman et al., 2014).

The research identified 2,361 micro-enterprise activities. The most common informal businesses sell liquor, fresh food (vegetable and meat products) and grocery items, which are mainly obtained from formal sector businesses and manufacturers. In terms of business categories, the five most frequently identified activities were liquor sales (697), street trade in commodities (314), grocery retail shops (191), fast-food sellers (145), street traders in fruit and vegetables (143) and hair-care businesses (143). The micro enterprises are located in both residential and non-residential sites. The businesses in residential areas comprise liquor retailers, spaza shops, and service businesses such as child care and hair salons. Those in non-residential localities include street traders, services operating from buildings close to the high street, and businesses operating on open ground, such as car washers, micro manufacturing and traders.

The second phase of the research sought to understand the social ordering and architecture of the street as a market place. The objective was to understand the spatial definition of contrasting business activities, including their market location, design of infrastructure, marketing strategies and relationships over the use of space. The research focused on the street context and examined these dynamics in four distinct and varied localities: the high street taxi rank, the high street intersection, the neighbourhood street, and a mid-point along the high street (Charman et al., 2014). As part of the research process, a price survey of 134 street trading businesses was conducted. The survey adhered to a census approach, interviewing all of the identified businesses that were willing to participate in the research. The survey obtained data on the age, gender and demography of the seller, the goods they sold, and the average profit from daily, weekly or monthly sales.

In the third phase, the researchers worked with eight street photographers (identified through the business census) through a participatory "photovoice" process. Photovoice is an action research tool whereby the participants take photographs of a social subject and then, through their photographs, situate the subject within an intellectual framework that addresses their concerns or articulates a particular message. In line with the participatory methodology, the researchers conducted workshops with the participants in which the topic of "street life" provided a framework for discussing their experiences and views of the street as a social and economic space within the township. Of the eight photographers, five were South Africans (of diverse ethnicity), two were Zimbabweans and one was Mozambican. Their brief was to capture daily photographs of street life over one month, post their photographs on a Facebook page and engage in the social debate that the project would stimulate (https://www.facebook.com/photovoiceivorypark).

INSIDER-OUTSIDER DYNAMICS

Ivory Park has a significant transnational character forged through the continual reshaping of relationships between insiders (the first settlers) and outsiders (who include more recent arrivals, as well as the marginalized, both old and new). One of the core social sites in which this change has been shaped is within informal markets and the informal economy more broadly. In a range of geographical contexts, from the street environment to controlled spaces such as the taxi rank and housing market, informal markets have provided a forum for social engagements on the "rights" to live or work in the settlement. This has involved multiple negotiations over the rules, obligations and expectations between those holding de facto rights and those seeking usufruct rights. These negotiations are framed by local, generally unwritten, formal and informal power relationships, which are commonly fraught with tension. An important component in the negotiated outcome is the role of the community through its everyday representation as a moral authority and arbitrator for the common good.

The entry of migrants into Ivory Park fostered a demand for accommodation, business structures and entrepreneurial opportunities, each of which necessitated negotiations and deals with the residents. Insiders are principally those families who acquired the original land grants, either through state transfers or market transactions. The first businesses in Ivory Park were invariably started by these residents with micro-enterprise characteristics based on the home-based business model that had developed in the township environment, epitomized by spaza shops and shebeens (Ligthelm, 2005). In the early days, some of these micro enterprises were highly profitable, but over time those that survived under the ownership of insiders provided a supplementary income stream at most.

One of the original land holders, a Rasta musician known as DJ Sweetest, recalled how some of the original settlers had once lived in an informal settlement in Alexandra and moved voluntarily to Ivory Park under threat of forceful eviction. He had emerged as a community leader in this process. These settlers were a heterogeneous mix: diverse in culture, language, outlook and economic status. When the township was formally developed, most of these families were able to acquire landholdings and Reconstruction and Development Programme (RDP) houses. The relatively large plot size (more generous than subsequent allocations as the RDP was rolled out) enabled the beneficiaries to rent out portions of their holdings or to construct "backyard" structures for residential or business lease. DJ Sweetest, for example, rents out two business container structures, three backyard shacks and, on the remaining portion of open ground, runs a "Gym at Your Own Risk" gymnasium. The gym is a meeting place for men of diverse nationalities who either exercise to build muscle and body shape or simply hang out.

Within the insider community of Ivory Park, it is seen as quite acceptable to generate income by renting accommodation or business structures to outsiders. By contrast, within the neighbouring settlements of Rabie Ridge and Tembisa, class and culture sensibilities militate against these strategies with backyard structures either absent or restricted to extended family members. In Ivory Park, the rental of property underpins the informal economy and there are few limitations to rental entrepreneurship. Home owners extend their business interests to the realm of the street where the sidewalk is expropriated and offered for rent; electricity and water are accessed, marked up and resold; storage space on private landholdings is leased; and containers are leased and accommodation units are built wherever space permits.

Informal markets in non-residential localities, such as streets and open ground, have historically been more accessible than residential trading spaces to newcomers. Sites on the street offer the lowest entry barriers for emerging businesses with access primarily determined through negotiation over the use of space, either through appropriation or a commercial arrangement. Migrant start-ups thus generally begin as street operators, either complementing existing businesses or providing an original service or product offering. Though easier to enter, these markets are nevertheless subject to implicit and explicit local rules, including clear understandings of use rights and restrictions on competitive activities. Local market traders reported how no trader could occupy another person's site or stand, or sell the same goods as others at a discount. Street trading business rules are based on a common understanding that all street traders are poor and should therefore allow fair opportunities for each trader to derive a modest living. In the solidarity of the street, traders accept the need to make room for new entrants to sell basic necessities such as fruit and vegetables, so long as the local market rules are adhered to.

The orientation of the street markets towards the poor and entry level businesses has resulted in a proliferation of greengrocers, fast food stalls, and retailers of sweets and mobile phone airtime, with some specialist traders selling clothing accessories, cosmetics, appliances and electrical goods, homeware and hardware, and car spares. With the street environment providing an important social space for meeting and interaction, service businesses such as hair salons have moved away from residential locations and are now commonly found on the major streets that bisect the township. This has resulted in a process of spatial transformation that has begun to blur the boundary between residential and non-residential business spheres.

The relationship between insiders and outsiders in Ivory Park is thus based on mutual benefit. Insiders gain financially through rents (typically earning ZAR1,000 per month for a single room unit), but can also access the flourishing business activities of entrepreneurial migrants, which lessens their dependence on the distant formal economy. In many cases, migrant informal micro enterprises provide local employment and afford considerable advantages to residents, providing access to goods and services that are convenient, appropriate to people's needs (and influenced by cultural preferences) and often cheap. Thus, in two distinct ways, first as residents renting accommodation, and second as micro entrepreneurs, migrants contribute economically to community wellbeing. In this manner the informal economy provides a mechanism for building social cohesion through negotiation and the determination of terms of an agreement.

With insiders and outsiders both recognizing that they have mutual economic interests, other forms of social relationships have begun to strengthen ties and erode differences. Apart from shared interests such as safety and security, insiders and outsiders share worship and belief systems; participate jointly in leisure activities, particularly within the confines of public drinking and street theatre venues, gambling sites and eateries; and share common concerns with the welfare and educational development of children. Group identities also often coalesce among football fans, for example. These shared interests enhance and reinforce a sense of community within Ivory Park that cuts across ethnicity and nationalism and permits difference without conflict.

SURVIVALISTS AND ENTREPRENEURS

Although non-residential open markets are spaces of entrepreneurship and, increasingly, innovation, most businesses appear to be survivalist in character. The most profitable businesses include those selling take-away foods, where daily profits can easily reach ZAR450 for well-situated businesses, followed by those selling clothing and apparel where daily profits can exceed ZAR1,000, but more typically provide a daily income of about ZAR250. Yet for those micro entrepreneurs selling snacks (chips and sweets), cigarettes and fruit and vegetables, which constitute market entry level products and comprise the most numerous trader category, the median profit is ZAR150 per day. Given that many work long hours, from sunrise to sunset, the hourly return is slightly below minimum wages for retail trade workers. These vendors are best described as economic survivalists. In enterprise terms, their operations are unsophisticated and highly vulnerable to market-related idiosyncratic shocks, such as inclement weather, police harassment, theft and stock spoilage.

Across the spectrum of informal economy activity, migrant entrepreneurs generally run the more profitable businesses. This is not to suggest that South Africans are unable to operate equally profitable concerns, nor that all migrants are entrepreneurially successful. Many of their start-ups are very poor. But they do appear to hold the entrepreneurial advantage, especially when South African businesses are relatively uncompetitive in terms of business location or enterprise size. The cohort of 34 fruit and vegetable vendors (all the street traders within this enterprise category, which excludes multiple-product sellers) provides insights into comparative entrepreneurial differences particularly because one migrant groups is more successful than South Africans (the Mozambicans) and one is not (the Zimbabweans). The South African and Zimbabwean fruit and vegetable sellers made an average daily profit of ZAR68 and ZAR64 respectively, while the Mozambicans, by contrast, made an average daily profit of ZAR193 (Table 4.3).

Why should the Mozambican traders be so much more successful? The answer lies in a combination of factors including more innovative business approaches, collective procurement of stock, high levels of industriousness and physical advantages. Some of the most profitable vendors were men and their business strategy was based on hawking a shopping trolley through the side streets, a task that require considerable strength and physical stamina.

Table 4.3: Ivory Park Fruit and Vegetable Vendor Profits

	South Africans ZAR	Mozambicans ZAR	Zimbabweans ZAR	Median ZAR
Average daily profit	68	193	64	150
Average weekly profit	340	517	187	406
Source: SLF FIME dataset				

Many factors combine to create micro-entrepreneurial success in the informal economy, including business positioning, ethnic networking and marketing innovations (Ligthelm, 2005, 2008; Liedeman, 2013; Charman et al., 2012). However, it would be misleading to narrow entrepreneurial success down to any one feature. Individual entrepreneurial attributes, such as work ethic or business self-confidence, are undoubtedly important, but these are not exclusive to migrants and cannot be correlated with business success in the absence of an in-depth psychological study. One important characteristic that appears to distinguish some migrant businesses from South African enterprises is the role of ethnic networks where migrant businesses operate within stronger networks.

Migrant businesses in Ivory Park almost exclusively employ members of the same ethnic group, usually family members, friends, friends of friends or, at the very least, members of the same clan. In many instances, the employees work under a form of apprenticeship or partnership and are not, strictly speaking, wage employees. South African grocery businesses similarly utilize family labour, though in general employ less labour than migrant businesses (51 per cent of South African shops have no employees). There was almost no evidence of South Africans working in migrant-run stores in Ivory Park (Table 4.4). The data strongly indicates that employment opportunities are restricted to ethnic networks for both South African and migrant businesses.

Migrant entrepreneurs notably benefit from transnational networks, which enable them to obtain products from their home country at a favourable price. The goods are often brought into South Africa through informal transport networks that appear highly efficient and very cost effective. Through these means, for example, vendors are able to obtain fresh fish and vegetable products from Mozambique; and groundnuts, mopane worms, dried leaf vegetables and homeware crafts (such as brooms) from Zimbabwe.

Table 4.4: Employment in Grocery Shops, Ivory Park

National Origin of Business Owner/Employee Numbers								
Employee Numbers	Lesotho	Mozambique	South Africa	Zimbabwe	Ethiopia	Somalia	Bangladesh	Pakistan
0	0	15	37	5	11	3	4	0
1	1	24	19	9	29	3	14	1
2	0	1	5	1	10	3	4	0
3	0	0	1	0	1	1	0	0
4	0	0	1	0	1	0	0	0
5	0	0	1	0	0	0	0	0
7	0	1	0	0	0	0	0	0
8	0	0	1	0	0	0	0	0
% with no employees	0	36	51	33	20	30	18	0
Shops employing non-nationals								
Employee origin	Lesotho	Mozambique	South Africa	Zimbabwe	Ethiopia	Somalia	Bangladesh	Pakistan
South Africa	0	1	0	0	0	0	0	0
Zimbabwe	0	0	1	0	0	0	0	0
Malawi	0	0	0	0	1	0	0	0
Mozambique	0	0	2	0	0	0	0	0

Note: Apart from the above five cases, all other shop employees were of the same national origin as the owner/s

Source: SLF FIME DataSet

SPATIAL INFLUENCES ON ENTREPRENEURSHIP: TAXI RANKS

This section of the chapter explores the spatial influences on entrepreneurial activities through four vignettes, focusing on high street retailers at the Ivory Park taxi rank, residential spaza shops, mobile (vegetable) hawkers and micro manufacturers operating from open ground. The clustering of informal enterprise at transport nodes such as the taxi rank provides evidence of favourable conditions for street-based enterprise as these are spaces with high concentrations of foot and commuter traffic. The numerical dominance of a diverse set of migrants trading in this space is evident from Figure 4.2, although South African-owned micro enterprises can also be found. Many of the resident street traders (primarily

South Africans) in the rank could be described as economic survivalists; they are owner operated, established in temporary ramshackle structures, and procure stock daily for sales. Conversely, many of the migrants run more substantial businesses, operating from brick and mortar structures. A considerable number are employee operated, and the owners (or partners) have invested in similar stores or outlets in other localities.

Migrant businesses include food outlets, butcheries, hair salons, traditional healers, specialist shops selling car spares and street traders selling fruit, cigarettes and sweets. Possibly as a response to the absence of the corporate retail sector (such as supermarkets and shopping malls), and to meet local consumer demand, migrant entrepreneurs have set up shops trading in products more familiar in formal malls and high street shopping environments: electronics, cosmetics, clothing and clothing accessories.

Figure 4.2: Business Ownership in the Ivory Park Taxi Rank Precinct

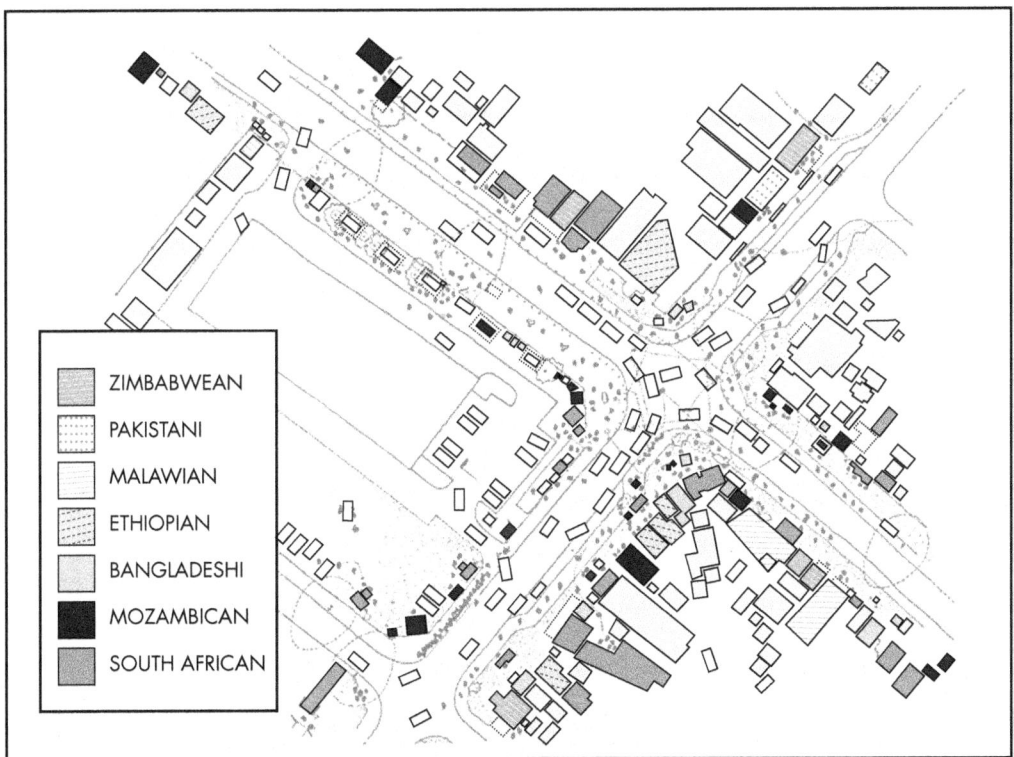

Note: The black dots indicate pedestrians, highlighting areas of density. The rectangular shapes (with no fill) indicate vehicles

The varied ownership structure and ethnic networks enjoyed by migrant retailers afford various supply chain advantages. In addition to the competitive advantages of size and scale, migrant retailers are able to acquire goods at reduced cost either directly from the manufacturer or from informal markets in the producing countries. They then resell the goods at a lower price than comparable goods sold in stores in the formal economy. The great majority of manufactured and electronic goods sold in the Ivory Park retail stores are imported, mostly from China. Different ethnic groups concentrate in particular sectors. For example, Pakistani retailers sell electrical goods and cosmetics – in one case operating their business from an old shipping container within the taxi rank. Nigerians operate gold exchange/pawn broking businesses, which open doors on an appointment basis only. Ethiopians sell clothing and apparel, while Ghanaians specialize in second-hand clothes.

The size of the price discount available to customers is usually sufficiently attractive to compensate for the variable but generally inferior quality of the goods, and the limited after-sales service, such as the absence of goods return policies. Some retailers also sell substitute brands and goods that have circumvented taxation systems in both the producing and destination country, thus offering the consumer a combination of price discount, shopping convenience and brand value. Ivory Park's high street retailers use a variety of techniques to enhance their business. Shops trade for extended hours with some operating seven days a week. Music is used to accentuate the business profile, blasting through speakers placed on the pavement to reduce the noise of commuter traffic. Several shops compete musically through contrasting ethnic genres. Specials are commonly advertised through fliers handed out to passing commuters.

HOME-BASED SPAZA SHOPS

The residential positioning of spaza shops is central to their business logic. Most serve a small geographical niche market, usually the residents that live within a 50-100 metre radius of the store. Spaza shops are spatially distributed in a relatively uniform pattern throughout Ivory Park. Each shop has a geographical comparative advantage based on its residential proximity. Historically, these South African businesses were secure in this advantage, largely because price competition was deemed an unacceptable business strategy (Charman et al., 2012). In recent years, migrant entrepreneurs have entered this market through buying up the trading rights to existing shops, or purchasing or renting properties in a strategically advantageous location. Migrant retailers have since come to dominate the residential grocery market.

Ethiopians, Bangladeshis and Somalis operate some of the more established and most sophisticated enterprises in terms of product range, service offering and prices. The pattern of enterprise distribution suggests that this spatial outcome has been enhanced by the networking strategies of the entrepreneurs. The case of the Ethiopian spaza shops is suggestive of this social influence. Fifty four of the 218 grocery shops in the research site are owned by Ethiopians. Each store has been positioned with enough distance from other Ethiopian stores that it can operate in its own distinctive spatial area, with few locational competitors. The collective impact of this competitive strategy has been severely felt by small-scale spazas, particular those run by South Africans, Mozambicans and Zimbabweans. Some of these shops have responded to this competition through retailing liquor, and sometimes take-away foods, to neighbours whose customer loyalty they count on.

STREET HAWKERS

The street has long been the core space for the informal sale of fruit and vegetables, fresh meat and items such as clothing and household goods. However, migrant entrepreneurs are redefining market parameters through the mobile hawking of goods throughout the residential areas. Their basic strategy is to bring the market to people's front door. By taking their products into residential areas, hawkers thus save people the journey to the street market. Fruit and vegetable vendors have been particularly innovative. Most are young Mozambican men who sell fruit and vegetables door to door using commandeered shopping trolleys. Products are packaged into popular mixes of affordable size (generally as ingredients for one meal) and tied in bags. The range of vegetables sold is diverse and includes garlic and chillies whose influence on local diets has been popularized through the experience of Mozambican cuisine. Mobile hawkers also sell meat, offal, brooms and brushes, and clothes. Product hawkers use different sounds to announce their presence in the street. The meat sellers use a shrill whistle and vegetable sellers have a particular cry, "*amavegieeeeee*" (i.e. vegetables). Clothes sellers are more discrete, knocking on doors and seeking to engage the residents in conversation.

The hawkers operate from midday onwards until all their stock is sold, pushing trolleys over many kilometres in hilly terrain to sell their goods. As one young Zimbabwean man commented, "People think that this work is for fools, but they don't realise how much I can make. One day I make R1,400." The hawkers are especially active in the late afternoon, selling produce for immediate consumption. They typically also work in small syndicates, linked through ethnic networks to a wholesaler operator who delivers on-site. An important component of hawker entrepreneurship, particularly for those selling clothes, accessories or household goods, is the provision of credit. Hawkers record the purchaser's name and accept payment at an agreed later date. Although there is some risk in credit provision, the sellers claim that more than 80 per cent of recipients repay their monthly instalments and settle the total debt.

The willingness of insiders to honour business deals with outsiders is a sign of the acceptance of migrant traders because the informal credit system rests on the integrity of the community and mutual respect between trader and purchaser. Despite their informality, these transactions are underpinned by the pressure of community sanction and local neighbourhood relationships in which respectability exerts a strong arbitrative influence over business. Both vendors and purchasers understand that in instances of default, the sellers have the right to turn non-repayment into a matter of public knowledge, which could bring dishonour on the household.

OPEN-AIR MICRO MANUFACTURERS

South Africa's informal economy is usually seen as an economy of trade with little micro manufacturing (Wills, 2009). Yet, in Ivory Park, many products are locally manufactured, including speaker boxes, furniture, mattresses and bed stands, burglar bars, window frames and security gates, shoes and sandals, bricks, car seat covers and clothing. Migrants are at the forefront of innovation and productivity in this sector. Their prominence owes much to a combination of skills, collective (and cooperative) workmanship, recognition of market opportunities for unique products and cheap prices, and the availability of open spaces within which to conduct business.

Most micro manufacturing takes place on small patches of public open ground. Furniture manufacturers and bed-makers (commonly Zimbabweans and Mozambicans) work in teams of compatriots. The team approach enables the entrepreneurs to share tools and equipment, purchase collectively and in bulk, upscale production volumes, and transfer skills from experienced to newer members. In one case, 20-30 Mozambicans engage in the simultaneous manufacture of bedding units. This business activity is particularly innovative in that it utilizes scrap material including shipping pallets for bed bases and reclaimed bed springs that are reupholstered. A complete bed unit sells for ZAR600, a low price targeting the poor and new settlers. The market emphasis largely appears to be on price rather than quality.

Shoe micro manufacturers in Ivory Park have created a market niche within a sector otherwise dominated by imports and second-hand shoes. These are manufactured more as cultural adornments than generic products. Mozambican cobblers, for example, produce sandals made from leather, including a range with animal skin features and designs. Such products are unique and superior to the imported plastic and synthetic sandals found at the taxi rank retail outlets.

CONCLUSIONS

Much has been written in the South African context about the escalation in township conflict between insiders and outsiders, often characterized as South Africans versus migrants and refugee outsiders (Charman and Piper, 2012; Mudi-Okorodudu, 2011; Maharaj, 2009; ACMS, 2011). Far less has been written on the ways in which the insider-outsider tensions have been resolved. Little is known, for example, about the impact that agreements between South African property owners and foreign renters have had on relationships, let alone the possibility that these negotiations have helped to build social inclusion. This chapter has sought to address this gap, focusing on the Ivory Park informal economy and the various spaces in which such interactions take place. The chapter has shown how an emergent transnationality within the Ivory Park informal economy has transformed spaces, notably those in which business is conducted. These transnational connections comprise labour, investment capital and access to factory products and farmgate sales. A new identity has thus been forged with foreign migrants constituting part of an emergent community with a particular Ivory Park identity and multi-cultural composition.

Despite the noticeable shift towards transnationality through the deepening of informality, there are boundaries at which the gap between insiders and outsiders, and in some instances the divide between South Africans and non-South Africans, is sustained. These social boundaries exist in various contexts in which power is mobilized or circumscribed. Within the informal economy this dynamic of power defines the framework and sets the terms within which transnational social relations take place. In the case of the local public transport sector, for example, the boundary is illuminated by the role of the Ivory Park taxi association whose authority determines who may operate taxis, who may drive cars and who may conduct business (or political activities) within the rank precinct. The taxi association local leadership is largely conservative and isiZulu nationalist in political outlook, but appears to place business before politics in its decisions about inclusion and exclusion. In the aftermath of a brutal attack and murder of a Mozambican taxi driver in July 2013 by police on the East Rand, for example, the Ivory Park taxi association instructed all drivers to dress in a suit and tie to express their respectability and distance themselves from politicization of the incident (Whittles, 2013).

In the context of the street economy, social boundaries are more fluid and determined by multiple actors, including the home owners of contiguous properties who usually impose ownership claims on adjacent street trader businesses, individual neighbourhood petty thugs, and street committees and neighbourhood watch bodies. Such organized bodies use their "authority" as representatives of the community to coerce businesses to comply with their demands and, according to one leader, were instrumental in gaining access for migrant vendors to stands along the street. These organizations, and individuals, demand compliance from outsiders through their role in protecting businesses from crime and their actions to apprehend criminals. The compliance of vendors reinforces the power of these authorities, but also provides migrants with recourse against uncooperative homeowners with whom they must often negotiate to use street space or obtain electricity or water.

Most of the migrant business are economically survivalist and operate in a similar manner to their South African counterparts. But wealth remains unequally distributed. Larger businesses potentially exert different and greater influence on local markets, reshaping market rules to dominate and monopolize. The transition away from South African ownership in the spaza shop sector was legitimate and probably bound to happen because of the inherent weaknesses in the business model. In neo-liberal terms, the market has performed a clearing function, replacing inefficient and uncompetitive enterprises with new, improved business activities. Migrant spaza shops are successful because of their competitiveness. But embracing price discounting has meant breaking a local informal economy rule with respect to its use as a retail strategy. Other "rules" have also been broken. Shops open earlier and trade later into the night, heightening the security risk for customers and shopkeepers alike. The unspoken understanding of what products the grocery shop should stock and what products they ought to avoid has come to an end. Such changes have led to the emergence of mini-markets, or large shops akin to small supermarkets. While the economic benefits through cheaper goods have been felt by consumers, who undoubtedly support migrant-run grocery shops, the loss of local entrepreneurship and employment has been expressed as a concern by former South African shopkeepers.

As social spaces, spaza shops were an important part of the fabric of the community, providing a repository for memories and a hub for social connection between shopkeepers (often retired South Africans) and customers. Shopkeepers were once repositories of local information, much of which was transferred through casual conversation or subtle greetings both through respect towards the elderly and because the shopkeepers knew their customers. In addition, the shopkeepers would provide surveillance over the neighbourhood through their observation of movements and interrogation of customers on events that had unfolded. Most migrant shop owners are unable to replicate these roles because their business model relies on employees, with few owners being based in the community. The new business model features frequent turnover in shop ownership, while shop employees can change on a regular basis. The relationship between shopkeeper and customer has thus become strictly commercial.

In view of the government's economic objective to promote small business, Ivory Park's emerging transnationalism and its manifestation in micro enterprises demonstrates the significant enhancements that migrants add to the economy. Residents have benefited from greater access to products and services. Traders have secured livelihoods. Workers have gained employment, though most employment opportunities appear to be restricted ethnically. Neither migrant nor South African businesses provide employment to people from other nations. The diversity of products and services lessens the dependence of residents on retailers situated outside of the township. The activities of street vendors, in particular, in identifying and occupying new market sites, introducing a diverse range of products, business activities and opportunities, and bringing scarce manufacturing skills into the township economy have indeed enhanced the Ivory Park economy.

ACKNOWLEDGEMENTS

The financial assistance of the Sustainable Livelihoods Foundation's Formalizing Informal Micro-Enterprises Project is acknowledged. Findings, opinions and conclusions are those of the authors and are not to be attributed to this project, its affiliated institutions or its sponsors. We thank Teresa Legg for the map.

REFERENCES

ACMS (2011) Mobilisation against foreign traders in South Africa. Migration Issue Brief 5, African Centre for Migration & Society, University of the Witwatersrand, Johannesburg.

Bekker, S., Eigelaar-Meets, I, Eva, G. and C. Poole. (2008) Xenophobia and violence in South Africa: A desktop study of the trends and a scan of explanations offered. Stellenbosch University, Stellenbosch.

Besem, V. (2005) Entrepreneurship and identity among a group of Ghanaian women in Durban (South Africa). PhD Thesis, University of Zululand, KwaZulu-Natal.

CDE (2008) Immigrants in Johannesburg: Estimating numbers and assessing impacts. Centre for Development and Enterprise, Johannesburg.

Charman, A., Petersen, L. and Govender. T. (2014) Street trade in Ivory Park, Gauteng Province, South Africa. In Mörtenböck, P. and H. Mooshammer (eds.) *Informal Market Worlds Atlas: The Architecture of Economic Pressure*. Rotterdam: NAI Publishers.

Charman, A., Petersen, L. and Piper, L. (2012) From local survivalism to foreign entrepreneurship: The transformation of the spaza sector in Delft, Cape Town. *Transformation: Critical Perspectives on Southern Africa*, 78: 47–73.

Charman, A. and Piper, L. (2012) Xenophobia, criminality and violent entrepreneurship: violence against Somali shopkeepers in Delft South, Cape Town, South Africa. *South African Review of Sociology*, 43: 81-105.

Crush, J. (2008) The perfect storm: The realities of xenophobia in contemporary South Africa. SAMP Migration Policy Series No. 50, Cape Town.

Hadland, A. (ed.) (2008) *Violence and Xenophobia in South Africa: Developing Consensus, Moving to Action*. Pretoria: HSRC.

IOM (2009) Towards tolerance, law and dignity: Addressing violence against foreign nationals in South Africa. International Organisation for Migration Regional Office for Southern Africa, Pretoria.

Kalitanyi, V. and Visser, K. (2010) African immigrants in South Africa: Job takers or job creators? *South African Journal of Economic and Management Sciences*, 13: 376-390.

Kloosterman, R. and Rath, J. (2001) Immigrant entrepreneurs in advanced economies: Mixed embeddedness further explored. *Journal of Migration and Ethnic Studies*, 27: 189-202.

Landau, L. and Misago, J-P. (2009) Who to blame and what's to gain? Reflections on space, state and violence in Kenya and South Africa. *Africa Spectrum*, 44: 99-110.

Landau, L. and Segatti, A. (2009) Human development. Impacts of migration: South Africa case study. UNDP Human Development Research Paper 2009/5, New York.

Liedeman, R. (2013) Understanding the internal dynamics and organisation of spaza shop operators: A case study of how social networks enable entrepreneurialism amongst Somali but not South African traders in Delft South. MA Thesis, University of the Western Cape.

Ligthelm, A. (2005) Informal retailing through home-based micro-enterprises: The role of spaza shops. *Development Southern Africa*, 22: 199-214.

Ligthelm, A. (2008) A targeted approach to informal business development: The entrepreneurial route. *Development Southern Africa*, 25: 367-382.

Maharaj, B. (2009) Migrants and urban rights: Politics of xenophobia in South African cities. *L'Espace Politique*, 8. DOI: 10.4000/espacepolitique.1402.

Mudi-Okorodudu, C. (2011) Immigrant street traders in South Africa: The economics, the struggle and tensions. Paper presented at Rethinking Development in an Age of Scarcity and Uncertainty Conference, New York.

Peberdy, S. and Rogerson, C. (2002) Transnationalism and non-South African entrepreneurs in South Africa's small, medium and micro-enterprise economy. In J. Crush and D. McDonald (eds.), *Transnationalism and New African Immigration to South Africa* (pp. 20-40). Cape Town: SAMP.

Rogerson, C. (1996) Urban poverty and the informal economy in South Africa's economic heartland. *Environment and Urbanization*, 8: 167–179.

Rouse, R. (2004) Mexican migration and the social space of postmodernism. In P. Jackson, P. Crang and C. Dwyer (eds.), *Transnational Spaces* (pp. 24-39). London: Routledge.

RSA (Republic of South Africa) (2006) *National Spatial Development Perspective 2006*. The Presidency, Pretoria.

SSA (2012) Census 2011. Statistical release. Statistics South Africa, Pretoria.

SSA (2013) Quarterly Labour Force Survey, Quarter 2. Statistics South Africa, Pretoria.

Steinberg, J. (2008) South African's xenophobic eruption. ISS Paper 169, Pretoria.

UN Habitat (2004) *State of the World's Cities*. London: Earthscan.

Whittles, G. (2013) Macia's attack was 'xenophobic.' *Eyewitness News*, 4 March.

Wills, G. (2009) South Africa's informal economy: A statistical profile. WIEGO Working Paper (Urban Policies) No 6, Cambridge MA.

Chapter Five

Resilience and Innovation: Migrant Spaza Shop Entrepreneurs in Soweto, Johannesburg

Trynos Gumbo

INTRODUCTION

Twenty years into democracy, the South African government faces a mammoth task of fighting persistent poverty and inequality and rising unemployment, particularly in urban centres. Participation in the urban informal economy, which is widely characterized as a survival strategy, has been growing in importance since South Africa's attainment of democratic rule in 1994 (Rogerson, 1999; Skinner, 2000). The trend has been most conspicuous in South Africa's four largest metropolitan cities, all of which have witnessed a major upsurge in informal activities that have brought extensive transformation and restructuring of urban economies in the country (Rogerson, 2002; Geyer, 2009; Van Eeden, 2011). Of particular interest and relevance is the rise in the participation of foreign nationals in South Africa's informal economy (Horn, 2011).

In the last two decades, South Africa has become a major destination country for both economic and forced migrants. Most live in urban areas where they compete with locals and each other for jobs and other services. Because many migrants fail to secure formal employment on arrival they join the burgeoning informal economy, particularly street and spaza shop retail trading. South Africa has also earned a reputation for the opportunities it offers to migrants who wish to start and operate small-scale informal businesses. Through their resilience and entrepreneurial prowess, migrants have started to dominate spaza shop retail trading in the country's most populous townships (Liedeman et al., 2013). Migrant spaza shop owners have recorded major entrepreneurial success, in some cases heightening tensions with disgruntled local spaza shop owners and criminal elements who subject them to xenophobic attacks, rob them, loot their stock and vandalize or even burn their businesses (Charman et al., 2012; Liedeman, 2013). To understand the strategies and resilience factors in micro entrepreneurship by migrants in South African cities, a survey was conducted on migrant spaza shop entrepreneurs in Soweto, the largest, most populous and sprawling low-income suburb of the City of Johannesburg.

Against the backdrop of unfriendly and unsupportive business environments and resentment from local spaza shop owners (Charman and Piper, 2012; Crush et al., 2013), the research aimed to disentangle the successful and resilient strategies adopted and implemented by migrant spaza shop owners. This chapter shows how migrant entrepreneurs, particularly Africans from Ethiopia and Somalia as well as Asians from Bangladesh and Pakistan, maximize the business opportunities that present themselves within densely populated areas with a large customer base. Conspicuous differences were observed in the way local South Africans and foreign nationals conduct their spaza shop businesses. However, there was little variation in the way foreign nationals conduct business; hence, neither place of origin nor racial differences between African and Asian migrants had any effect on their resilience and innovativeness. The only difference was the advantages enjoyed by Ethiopians and Somalians due to the strong unity that emanates from their shared religious experience which encourages mutual support and cooperation.

The chapter also highlights the challenges faced by migrant spaza shop entrepreneurs in starting and growing their businesses, particularly the lack of support from institutions such as local municipalities and resistance by local spaza shop owners who disapprove of the competition. The chapter ends by offering policy recommendations and emphasizing the lessons that could be learnt by South African shop owners to improve their own business operations and livelihoods. These include the sharing of experiences and business skills, perseverance strategies, and community engagements facilitated by community organizations made up of both locals and foreign nationals as well as local council officials.

METHODOLOGY

This chapter focuses on the operations of migrant spaza shop owners and operators in the township of Soweto. The information that is presented was gathered and analyzed using mixed-method approaches. A survey was implemented to gather detailed information about the resilience factors behind the successful operations of migrant spaza shop owners and the innovative business strategies that they employ to outclass local owners. In total, 120 migrant spaza shop entrepreneurs were studied between January and April 2014. Participants in the study were purposively chosen from six out of the 30 wards in the township.

The questionnaire had both open-ended and closed questions so as to allow the collection of both statistical and qualitative data on the operations of migrant spaza shop owners. Various information on the operational characteristics of spaza shops was collected including income, rentals for using space, asset values and the number of customers served in a day. Qualitatively, data on the places of origin of migrant spaza shop owners and operators as well as the strategies they use to run their businesses was collected. To get a glimpse of how South Africans conduct their businesses, interviews were conducted. Thirty qualitative interviews were also conducted with South African spaza shop owners. In general, the interviews yielded information on the strategies that are used to stock, market and price products, locational strategies and customer handling as well as savings habits.

CHARACTERISTICS OF MIGRANT SPAZA SHOPS

Attracted by the potentially lucrative market of a high-density population, albeit with relatively low incomes, migrants are increasingly visible in the spaza shop sector in Soweto. All of the migrant spaza shop entrepreneurs interviewed for this study were from the African and Asian continents (Figure 1). Forty-five per cent were from Africa, mainly Ethiopians (39 per cent of the total interviewed) and Somalis (16 per cent). The other 55 per cent was made up of Asians mainly from Bangladesh (26 per cent) and Pakistan (19 per cent) (Figure 5.1).

The study revealed that most migrant spaza shop owners live on the plots where their businesses are located. The African migrants mostly used their shops as places of residence to cut the costs of running their businesses. Although the Asians also lived where they worked, they seldom used the same structures and some lived far from their spaza shops. Living within the business premises not only cuts costs but also increases security as the operators monitor activities within and around their shops, given the high rate of crime in South African townships.

Figure 5.1: Country of Origin of Migrant Spaza Entrepreneurs

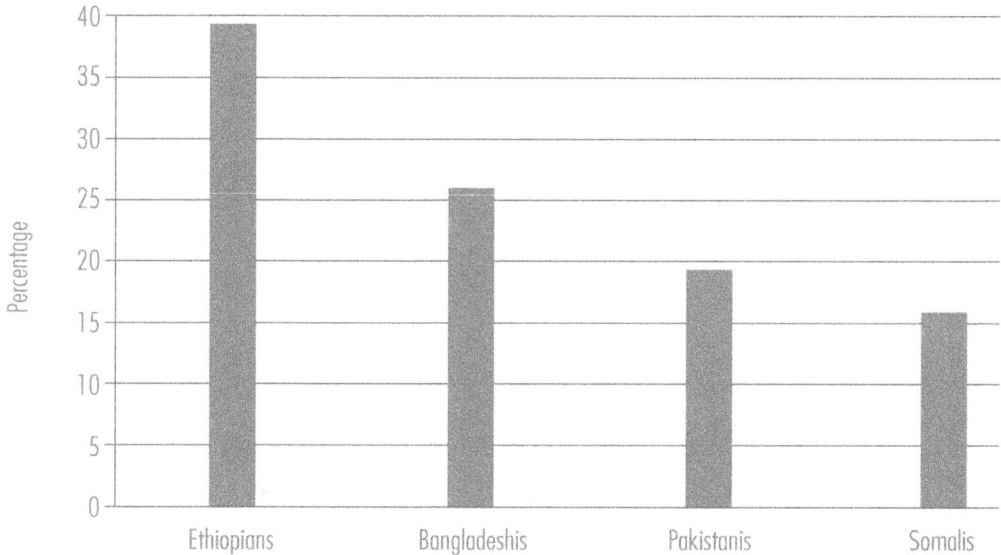

The study also revealed that most of the migrant spaza shop retailers had lived in South Africa for less than 10 years (Figure 5.2). Only 23 per cent had lived in the country for more than 10 years and 9 per cent for more than 15 years. Forty-four per cent were recent arrivals, having been in South Africa for less than five years. Almost all had arrived in South Africa after the first democratic elections in 1994.

The recent penetration of the Soweto market by migrants is illustrated by the length of time that they have been running their spaza shops (Figure 5.3). Nearly three-quarters of those surveyed had been in operation for less than five years, with 22 per cent in operation for less than a year. Only 3 per cent had been in Soweto for more than 10 years. Interestingly, while 44 per cent of the migrants had been in the country for less than five years, 71 per cent had been in the business for the same time period. This suggests that a quarter of the migrants had pursued other income-generating activities after arriving in South Africa, before opening a spaza shop in Soweto.

Figure 5.2: Length of Residence of Migrant Spaza Shop Owners in South Africa

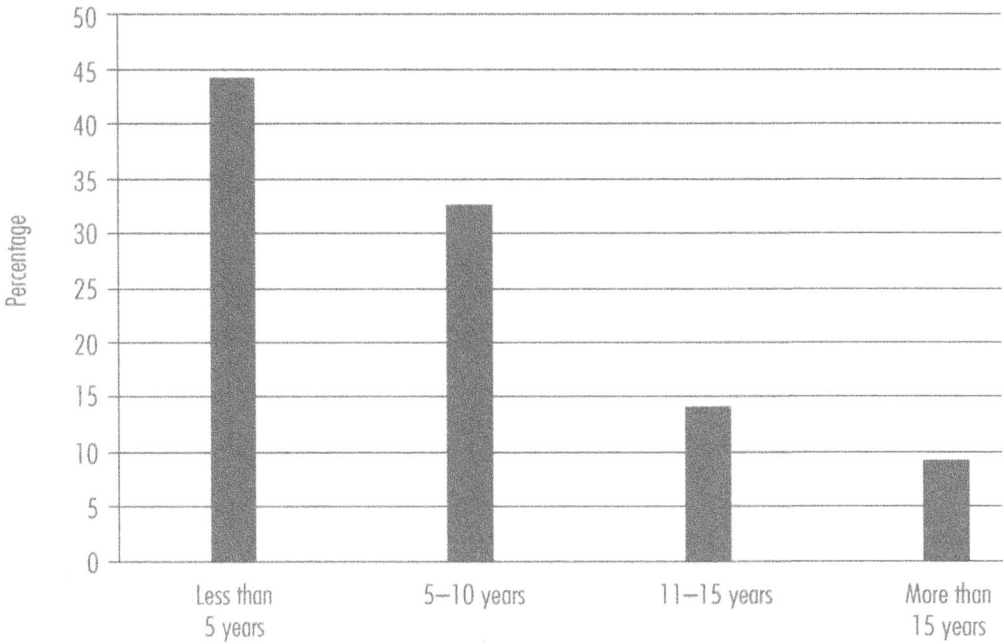

Figure 5.3: Duration of Operation of Migrant Spaza Shops in Soweto

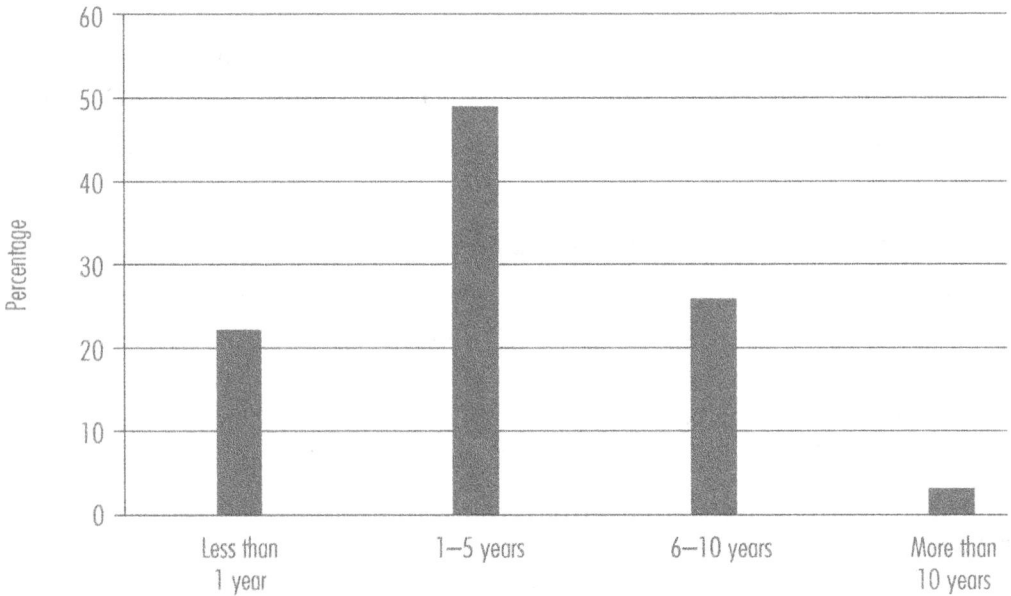

Most of the migrant spaza shop owners were male. The Africans, in particular, said they came alone to South Africa to generate income and remit to their country of origin. The few that had migrated to South Africa with their families preferred to employ other male foreign nationals than have their wives help them in the businesses. Some provided mentorship to male relatives so that they could start their own businesses while others simply wanted to take advantage of the availability of cheap labour in the form of jobless foreign nationals.Asian men rarely had their wives working with them in their spaza shops either. They preferred to run their businesses alone or employ other foreign nationals or, occasionally, locals. The migrant spaza shop owners were generally reluctant to employ South Africans as shopkeepers or assistants. In contrast, women and children tend to run the spaza shop businesses owned by South Africans, mostly as shop assistants. While some local women own spaza shops, no migrant women do.

SUCCESS OF MIGRANT ENTREPRENEURS

The migrant spaza entrepreneurs in Soweto have enjoyed considerable success, out-performing many local businesses. Most have invested significantly in their businesses, an indication that these are not simply survivalist enterprises. A total of 38 per cent had over ZAR40,000 in assets and 9 per cent had assets of over ZAR50,000 (Figure 5.4). Only 2 per cent had business assets of less than ZAR20,000 (Figure 5.4). A second indication of success is that they enjoy a large customer base. The majority (89 per cent) serve more than 50 customers per day, with nearly 50 per cent serving over 100 per day (Figure 5.5). The size of the customer base is attributable to the provision of readily available and conveniently located (both in terms of time and distance) basic goods at affordable prices. Many spaza shops have regular customers who shop there for daily necessities such as bread and milk.

The resilience of migrant spaza shop entrepreneurs is attributable to their strict savings behaviours. Many entrepreneurs endure personal hardship and suffering, maintaining simple lifestyles to save money and channel their profits towards the growth of their businesses. Those who are successful save money to buy delivery vehicles and other essential equipment and machinery such as refrigerators to use in their business operations. They invest in their businesses and also remit part of their profits to their countries of origin. Most operate their spaza shop businesses without bank accounts because they lack the documentation required by banking institutions. The majority have asylum-seeker papers, which are accepted by the Post Office but not by commercial banks. They are therefore forced to carry significant amounts of cash in running their spaza shop businesses despite the risk of losing the money through looting and robbery.

Figure 5.4: Migrant Spaza Shop Asset Values in Soweto

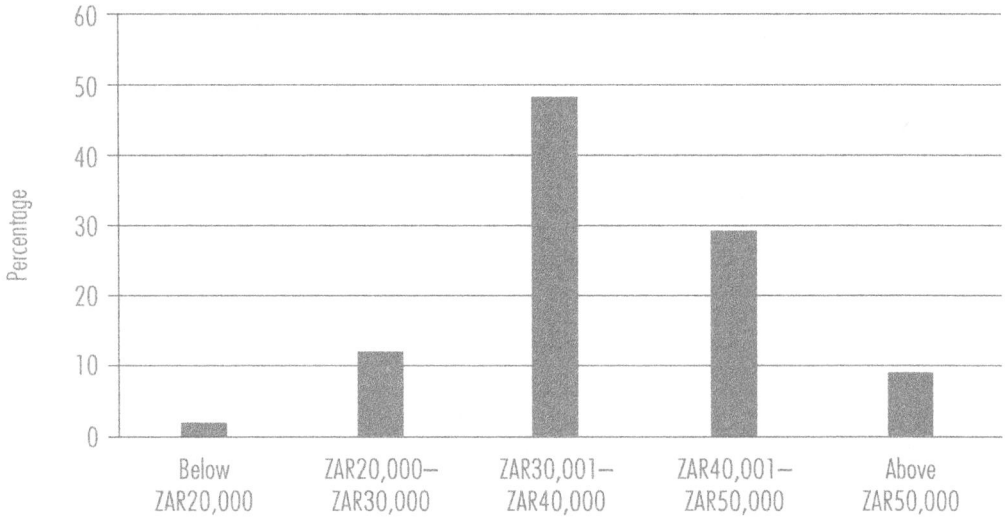

Figure 5.5: Customers Served by Migrant Spaza Shops in Soweto

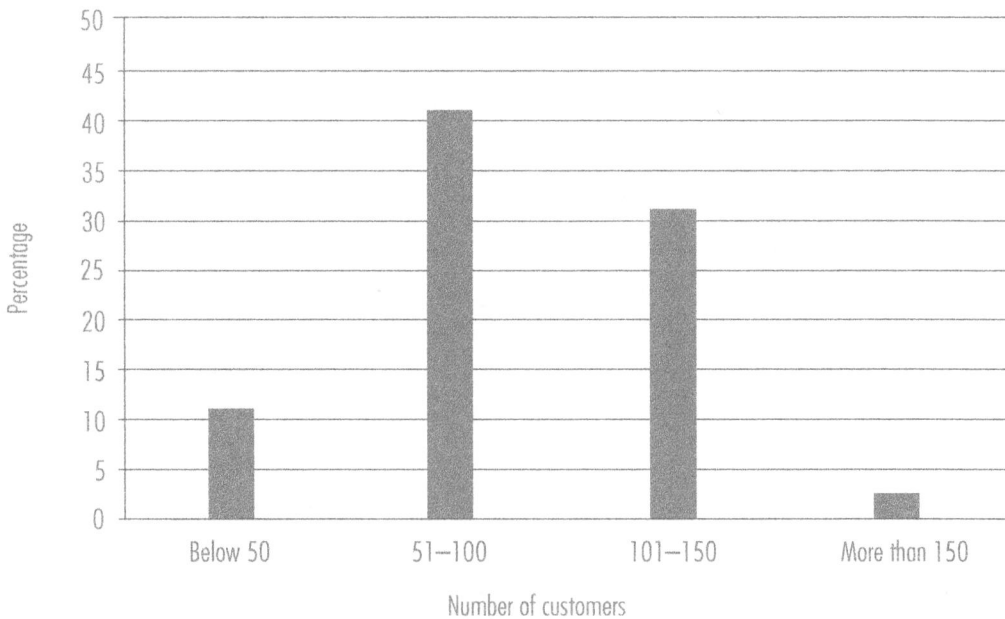

The migrant entrepreneurs contribute financially to the community through rental income paid to owners of the spaces they use for their businesses (Figure 5.6). Most of the landlords are South Africans. The vast majority (96 per cent) pay more than ZAR1,500 per month in rentals. Nearly a quarter (22 per cent) pay between ZAR2,500 and ZAR3,000 per month and 8 per cent pay more than ZAR3,000 per month. As renters, migrant spaza entrepreneurs do not pay fees or levies to the municipality which leads to negative perceptions of their operations on the part of officials. They are generally not part of the local authority's community plans, projects and programmes, and hence they mainly operate with the blessing of their landlords and customers.

Figure 5.6: Migrant Spaza Shop Rentals in Soweto

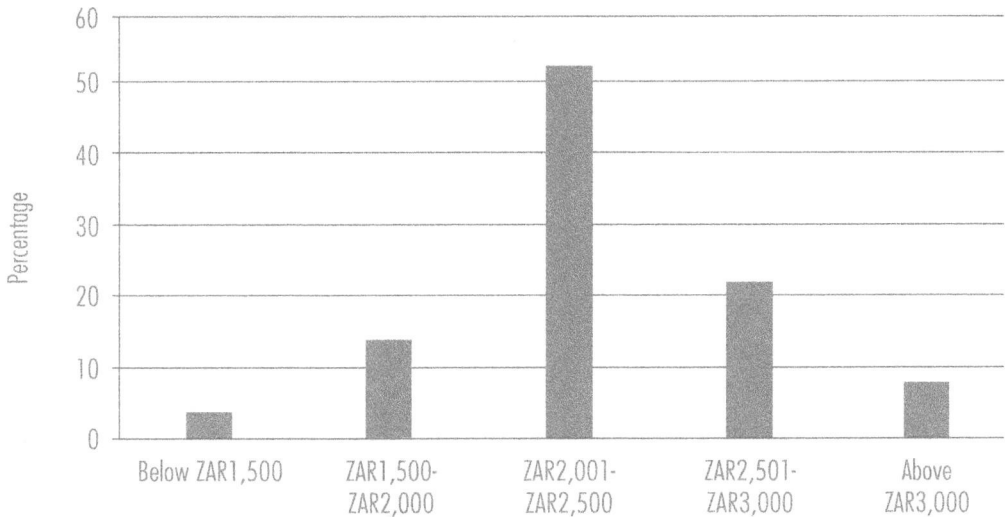

BUSINESS STRATEGIES

Migrant entrepreneurs employ a number of business strategies that give them a competitive advantage over local businesses within the same sector and market. These include the strategic location of their spaza shops, buying a variety of stock in large quantities, strict saving behaviours, lowering their prices, aggressive marketing and generating loyalty by providing credit (Table 5.1). Spaza shops owned by migrants tend to be located at strategic points such as street corners to improve accessibility and enhance visibility. The strategy is used to capture as many customers as possible and boost sales. The general tendency is to build structures to be used as shops attached to the houses they have leased and protruding towards the streets. This practice contravenes the building regulations of the City of Johannesburg and does pose dangers as the buildings reduce visibility for motorists, particularly at corners.

Table 5.1: Resilience Factors and Business Strategies of Migrant Spaza Entrepreneurs

Resilience factors and innovative business strategies	Details of findings
Mentorships and on the job training	• High reliance on mentorship by associates
Strong financial and group ties	• Social, religious, migration and business ties • Informal financial support mechanisms within groups such as hire purchase
Strategic location of spaza shops	• Street corners to maintain visibility
Frequent and flexible stocking	• Buying stock to meet demand as reflected by the market
Strict saving habits	• Maintain simple lifestyles to save for the business
Small profit, quick returns	• Aim not to maximise profits at once e.g. for a loaf of bread a 20c profit is made
Long operating hours	• Operating hours are usually from 6am-9pm
Aggressive marketing	• Advertising using bright paintings, product names and local shop names
Swift adaptation	• Language, customer preferences and expectations
Generating customer loyalty	• Offering credit and striving to meet expectations

Migrant spaza shop entrepreneurs gain their business skills through informal training and mentorship. Most gained their business skills through informal means, either in their country of origin before they came to South Africa or after their arrival in Johannesburg. On arrival, new migrants are accommodated by friends and relatives who own spaza shops where they are mentored and equipped with the basics of running a business. There is a symbiotic relationship whereby newcomers learn entrepreneurial skills and earn some income during their internship, which is later used to start their own business, while the spaza shop owners benefit from the cheap labour. Mentorship can take a year or more before they have the financial security and a suitable space to start their own business within the township. There is therefore strong reliance on on-the-job training; few migrant entrepreneurs gain their business skills through formal education. Closely related to mentorship practices is the financial support extended to "graduates" to enable them to start their own spaza shops. The support is rendered through family, religious and migration ties. Financial support takes a variety of forms including soft loans that attract very low or no interest and interest or hire purchase arrangements where a business is established for an associate who takes ownership once the start-up money has been repaid in full.

Many purchase their non-perishable stock in bulk from formal wholesalers such as Devland Cash & Carry, Makro and Jumbo. However, they are flexible when it comes to stocking perishable items such as bread and small items such as cigarettes and sweets that can be ordered on a daily basis. For example, bread is delivered to the spaza shops every morning by suppliers and the quantities stocked depend on the day of the week. Likewise, soft drink stocks are increased in summer and reduced in winter. Migrant spaza entrepreneurs stock a variety of products to cater for customers of different income levels; for example, Coca-Cola, a relatively expensive brand, alongside the cheaper and therefore more popular Refresh. Generally, the migrants spend between ZAR200 and ZAR600 a day on perishable stock and other small items that are always in demand and more than ZAR1,000 for non-perishable goods.

Migrant spaza shop owners go out of their way to forge strong relationships with community members, customers and suppliers, thereby generating trust among their key business stakeholders. They also sell goods on credit to promote loyalty and repeat custom, especially where the customer is short of money. Their selling strategies promote small profits but quick returns. This creates stiff competition among themselves and with local spaza owners but provides goods to Soweto residents at very affordable prices. Hence a crucial strategy employed by migrant entrepreneurs to attract and keep customers is to price their goods lower than locally-owned spaza shops. Cumulatively, they still make good returns supported by flexible and responsive stocking. Their stock moves fast and they are able to generate reasonable revenue over time. Local spaza owners claim that they sell higher quality and healthier products than migrants. However, most low-income community members cannot afford these goods and prefer to buy cheaper products from migrant spaza shops. Furthermore, the local style of ordering goods is different from that of migrant entrepreneurs as locals tend to order on set days and not on the basis of demand for a particular product. The only exception is bread, which is delivered every day by suppliers.

Migrant entrepreneurs tend to keep their spaza shops open for very long hours. They open around 6am to capture customers buying food for breakfast and close around 9pm to accommodate neighbours and others seeking daily necessities, such as bread, milk and mobile phone airtime. They also engage in a variety of aggressive marketing strategies. For example, their shops are brightly painted with graphics of basic commodities. This attracts a wide base of customers from within the neighbourhood and passers-by from other communities who are drawn to the strategically placed shops by the bright colours. Products commonly associated with children, such as the popular yoghurt drink Mayo, are pictured on the structures to attract young people sent by their parents on errands. Furthermore, the shops have African and local names, which promotes a sense of identification with the community they serve.

The migrants also make an effort to learn the basics of local South African languages to improve communication with customers and suppliers. A basic grasp of the dominant local languages in Soweto, such as isiZulu and Setswana, helps to facilitate transactions when supplies are ordered. Similarly, it makes it easier for migrant shopkeepers to communicate with their customers, particularly children, who are frequently sent by their parents to make purchases and cannot express themselves properly in English.

Despite their popularity with Soweto consumers, migrant spaza owners are extremely security conscious due to the high rate of crime and the threat of xenophobic attacks orchestrated by resentful business owners. Against the backdrop of criminality and resentment and disapproval of their business activities by local spaza owners, migrants have devised ways of securing their goods, including having very small windows that they use as counters and reinforcement with burglar bars. The goods are clearly displayed within the shop so that customers can easily see through the bars and request the product for purchase or point and direct the shopkeeper to the item. Some owners use their business premises as places of residence not only to secure their goods during the night but to reduce the costs of accommodation and running a business. The practice can, however, compromise hygiene if they sell food products such as bread, milk and mealie-meal. In a few instances, their residential rooms are separated only by a door from the shop.

Although the migrant entrepreneurs face harassment and sometimes experience looting and robbery, the factors that pushed them to leave their countries of origin are considered by most to be far worse than their current circumstances. Spaza shop entrepreneurs from Ethiopia, Bangladesh, Pakistan and Somalia all identified political instability and economic hardship as their main reasons for leaving their countries for South Africa. Exposure to suffering in their countries of origin has made them resilient in the face of the hardships they experience as they operate their shops in South Africa.

CONCLUSION

Despite the hostile operating environment that confronts many migrant entrepreneurs in South Africa, they display considerable resilience and have recorded notable success within the urban informal economy in many of South Africa's cities. In particular, they have identified and exploited a gap in the low-income market through participation in spaza shop businesses. Migrant spaza entrepreneurs in Soweto outcompete and are resented by the majority of local spaza entrepreneurs. Several mitigating strategies could be developed to reduce tensions between the two. First, it would be in everyone's interest to formulate local economic and community development policies and strategies that facilitate the participation and financial contribution of migrant entrepreneurs in a broader range of community activities. Second, one way to resolve disagreements would be through the development of community organizations composed of local council officials, local large formal retailers as well as local and migrant spaza entrepreneurs. Third, business partnerships between locals and migrant spaza shop entrepreneurs (for example, with regard to ordering products from wholesalers), would go a long way towards improving business relationships within the township. Fourth, migrant spaza shop entrepreneurs need to be encouraged to employ responsible and hardworking local youths and impart business acumen and skills to them. Fifth, policies on the establishment of spaza shops at local level, particularly the extension of houses for the purposes of creating business premises, need to be developed, implemented and enforced. This is necessary to ensure that the residential environment is not distorted by spaza businesses and their operation does not disrupt the functioning of local services such as transportation, sewerage and electricity. Finally, the space occupied by spaza shop businesses should ideally be separated from residential areas in order to promote more hygienic conditions. However, the symbiosis between migrant spaza entrepreneurs and South African landlords would make this difficult to enforce.

REFERENCES

Charman, A. and Piper, L. (2012) Xenophobia, criminality and violent entrepreneurship: Violence against Somali shopkeepers in Delft South, Cape Town, South Africa. *South African Review of Sociology*, 43: 81-105.

Charman, A., Petersen, L. and Piper, L. (2012) From local survivalism to foreign entrepreneurship: The transformation of the spaza sector in Delft, Cape Town. *Transformation: Critical Perspectives on Southern Africa*, 78: 47-73.

Crush, J., Ramachandran, S. and Pendleton, W. (2013) Soft targets: Xenophobia, public violence and changing attitudes to migrants in South African after May 2008. SAMP Migration Policy Series No. 64, Cape Town.

Geyer, H. (2009) Notes on spatial-structural change in urban South Africa: The 1990s. *Journal of Urban and Regional Analysis*, 1: 27-39.

Horn, A. (2011) Who's out there? A profile of informal traders in four South African city central business districts. *Town and Regional Planning Journal*, 59: 1-6.

Liedeman, R., Charman, A., Piper, L. and Petersen, L. (2013) Why are foreign-run spaza shops more successful? The rapidly changing spaza sector in South Africa. Econ3x3, Sustainable Livelihoods Foundation, Cape Town.

Liedeman, R. (2013) Understanding the internal dynamics and organisation of spaza shop operators: A case study of how social networks enable entrepreneurialism among Somali but not South African traders in Delft South, Cape Town. MA Thesis, University of the Western Cape.

Rogerson, C. (1999) Local economic development and urban poverty alleviation: The experience of post-apartheid South Africa. *Habitat International*, 23: 511-534.

Rogerson, C. (2002) Urban economic restructuring: The changing SMME economy of inner-city Johannesburg. In R. Donaldson and L. Marais (eds.), *Transforming Rural and Urban Spaces in South Africa During the 1990s Reform, Restitution, Restructuring* (pp. 333-360). Pretoria: African Century.

Skinner, C. (2000) Getting institutions right: Local government and street traders in four South African cities. *Urban Forum*, 11: 49-69.

Van Eeden, A. (2011) The geography of informal arts and crafts in South Africa's four main CBDs. *Town and Regional Planning Journal*, 59: 34-40.

Chapter Six

The Role of Economic Factors and *Guanxi* Networks in the Success of Chinese Shops in Johannesburg

Lodene Willemse

INTRODUCTION

Over the last few years, China has played an increasingly important role in the global economy, resulting in a significant increase in Chinese migration to cities and towns worldwide (Kohnert, 2010). Push factors include political and economic reforms in China, especially the "opening up" of the country in 1978 when emigration legislation was deregulated, making it easier for people to travel outside China (Huynh et al., 2010; Kohnert, 2010). Uneven economic expansion in China resulted in high unemployment, a lack of professional opportunity and increased population pressure, which fuelled Chinese emigration (Ma, 2008; Sales et al., 2009). Pull factors include improved diplomatic relations between China and other countries, increased economic opportunity and the process of chain migration. China's establishment of diplomatic relationships and bilateral trade agreements with other nations, together with new clauses in migration laws, all lowered the borders between China and her trading partners, easing the movement of her people (Gadzala, 2009; Huynh et al., 2010; Park, 2010). Chinese migrants are also attracted by established agglomeration economies, which consist of existing clusters of Chinese investors, industrial bases and business and physical infrastructure that can provide greater economic opportunity and the chance to make a better living (Yeoh and Kong, 1994; Wilhelm, 2006; Rogerson, 2009; Kohnert, 2010).

Many Chinese engage in "chain migration" to other countries. The pioneers entice the younger generation to follow in their footsteps and continue family businesses or start their own (Yip, 1995; Phan and Luk, 2008; Dobler, 2009). The experiences of Chinese migrants vary according to economic, social, cultural and political conditions in China and the country of settlement, but are not uniformly positive. Although difficult economic conditions forced many to migrate to other countries, economic challenges and the burden of sending money home mean that hardships persist. Migration is also associated with separation from family members, which has a negative impact on social lives, and foreign residence may hinder their ability to engage in local politics and maintain connections with China (Mohan and Kale, 2007; Sales et al., 2009).

The primary economic activities of the Chinese in foreign countries include import/export, wholesale distribution and retail businesses. Two types of Chinese entrepreneurship can be distinguished: the "intermediary" who services the general population and the "enclave entrepreneur" who services his or her own ethnic community as well as the general public (Selvarajah and Masli, 2011). Most Chinese import their products from China, which reduces the number of intermediaries, costs and selling price. Wholesale distribution centres often develop into regional shopping hubs that provide goods to local and international retailers and consumers. Other economic activities include the manufacturing of textiles, clothing, furniture and agro-processing products; engineering and construction projects and services to the local Chinese communities including schools; newspapers; stores selling Chinese medicines; traditional Chinese medical practitioners including acupuncturists, doctors and herbalists; and massage parlours, hair salons and laundries (Wilhelm, 2006; Mohan and Kale 2007; Park, 2009a).

The most important economic activity is the establishment of Chinese shops and restaurants in areas commonly known as Chinatown close to the central business districts (CBDs) of cities (Harris, 1999; Phan and Luk, 2008; Gadzala, 2009; Sales et al., 2009; Dittgen, 2010). Typically, Chinese shops (also called "shop houses") in Singapore and North America are multi-level buildings where the ground floors are usually Chinese shops, the second floors are used as storage facilities for stock or as meeting places for local Chinese associations to maintain cultural traditions, while the third floors are the living quarters (Lai, 1990; Yeoh and Kong, 1994; Yip, 1995). A recent phenomenon among younger migrants is the development of "condominium malls" that are detached from the living quarters (and especially popular in Australia, Canada and Indonesia). Each unit in a condominium mall is purchased and owned by individual investors who form a corporation to own the building collectively, and charge levies to ensure maintenance and renovations in communal areas such as corridors, parking lots and loading zones (Wang, 1999; Ip, 2005; Jacobsen, 2006; Phan and Luk, 2008).

While Chinese migrants are often perceived as a homogeneous group, there are many fissures within the diaspora. Chinese migrants may share a common cultural heritage, but there are many regional distinctions among them that manifest in their origins, settlement patterns, language, class, gender, age and differences in legal status (Ip, 2005; Dobler, 2009; Kohnert, 2010; Park, 2010; Harrison et al., 2012). However, most Chinese migrants are driven by the desire to achieve a good quality of life not only for themselves and their families but also for their ethnic group. The Chinese already in a place therefore try to provide migrants with job opportunities, to support newly-arrived entrepreneurs in starting their businesses, and to become role models (Selvarajah and Masli, 2011).

Existing studies of the Chinese in South Africa focus mainly on the migration process and the factors relating to their migration, describing the Chinese diaspora and providing a broad overview of their general business activities (Wilhelm, 2006; Laribee, 2008; Park, 2009a, 2009b, 2010; Huynh et al., 2010; Harrison et al., 2012; McNamee et al., 2012). This chapter provides a more detailed case study of Chinese entrepreneurship in the city of Johannesburg. The aim of the chapter is twofold: first, to provide an outline of the business activities of Chinese shops in the city and, second, to provide an overview of the Chinese shop entrepreneurs' perceptions and opinions of their surroundings, with specific emphasis on the constraints they experience.

CHINESE MIGRATION TO SOUTH AFRICA

South Africa has the largest Chinese population in Africa. While the number of Chinese migrants in South Africa has increased significantly in recent years, it is difficult to determine precisely how many are living in South Africa. Irregular migration (facilitated by corruption within Chinese and South African government departments), poor record keeping, and the constant flow of migrants and workers between South Africa and China make accurate estimates very difficult (Mohan and Kale, 2007; Park, 2009b).

The Chinese population of South Africa migrated to the country in three distinctive phases, each group leaving behind a very different China and each entering a very different South Africa (Laribee, 2008; Huynh et al., 2010). The first group (Chinese South Africans) consisted mainly of men who emigrated between 1870 and 1970 from China's Guangdong Province (Park, 2010). Most settled in Johannesburg to work in mining, while others worked on plantations and in railway construction. Some started small-scale export and trading businesses to service local Chinese communities, resulting in the establishment of the first Chinatown in Johannesburg in Commissioner Street in the CBD and the Cyrildene Chinatown, consisting of general stores, eating houses, bars, butcheries, laundries, social clubs and gambling dens (Mohan and Kale, 2007; Laribee, 2008; Park, 2009a).

The second group arrived from Taiwan between the 1970s and 1990s, as a result of the strong political relationship forged between the apartheid South African government and the internationally marginal Taiwanese government. Taiwan provided grants and projects in construction, agriculture and health to South Africa, while South Africa enticed Taiwanese industrialists to invest in remote areas through generous investment and incentive schemes in an effort to stop black Africans from moving to urban areas (Wilhelm, 2006; Mohan and Kale, 2007; Laribee, 2008; Huynh et al., 2010). The incentive schemes attracted a group of opportunistic capitalist Taiwanese entrepreneurs who opened import/export firms, restaurants and other small businesses and settled in South Africa (Park, 2009a, 2009b).

The arrival of the third group from the People's Republic of China overlapped with the second group. Three major subgroups can be distinguished. The first subgroup arrived between 1989 and 1992 via Hungary, the Ivory Coast and Lesotho and started small-scale businesses with few resources that eventually grew into profitable import and wholesale businesses, while others worked as employees in Taiwanese businesses (Park, 2009b, 2010). The second subgroup arrived from the mid to late 1990s and comprised wealthy, well-educated and experienced business professionals who settled in Johannesburg and the port cities to focus on import/export, retail and wholesale trading businesses. This subgroup was responsible for the expansion of the Chinatowns in Johannesburg and Cyrildene by adding facilities to cater specifically for the Chinese community. These included schools, a Chinese newspaper, medical practices such as doctors, acupuncturists and herbalists providing traditional Chinese medicine, massage parlours, hair salons, small shops, restaurants, liquor stores and stores selling Chinese medicines and herbs. Many later expanded to mining, the manufacturing of consumer goods (especially textiles, shoes, bags and other light industrial products) and property development, while others invested back in China (Wilhelm, 2006; Park, 2009a, 2009b; Huynh et al., 2010). The third subgroup arrived in South Africa in the post-2000 period; their numbers continue to grow and they make up the largest segment of the current Chinese population in South Africa.

The third sub-group consists of small traders and peasants mostly from Fujian, one of the poorest provinces in China. Many Fujians have immigrated to other countries as well in the hope of improving their lives (Laribee, 2008; Park, 2009a; Huynh et al., 2010). The Fujians speak limited English, are poorly educated and lack business networks and capital, and many are forced to run small shops with very limited profits in the more remote towns of South Africa (Laribee, 2008; Park, 2009a; Huynh et al., 2010). Most Chinese employ family members in their shops although *guanxi* networks are also used to recruit Chinese employees through informal arrangements or formally written contracts. A new arrival's first few years in South Africa are considered an apprenticeship, in which employees learn the local languages and business skills. Local residents are also often employed to assist customers in their local languages (Haugen and Carling, 2005; Gadzala, 2009).

Chinese trading networks are established on the practice of *"guanxi"*, defined as "a special kind of personal relationship [between people] in which long-term mutual benefits are more important than short-term individual gains" (Gadzala, 2009, p. 205). *Guanxi* trading networks consist of absolute trust among family members, obligated trust between friends and business partners, and mistrust of people outside the network. *Guanxi* networks give the Chinese a competitive advantage by sharing cost information, contacts, information about qualified labourers and producers, joint training initiatives and finance through credit or investment associations (Brautigam, 2003; Gadzala, 2009). *Guanxi* supply chain networks are also used to source goods directly from China, which keeps prices as low as possible. Goods are either imported by phoning contacts in China to place an order, or shop owners may visit China once or twice a year to arrange the bulk import of goods including clothes, shoes, travel accessories, furniture, kitchenware, household appliances, electronic goods, toys and Chinese medicines. Long-standing *guanxi* supply chain networks decrease the likelihood of losing shipments or paying fines because of the incorrect goods being inside the container (Haugen and Carling, 2005; Laribee, 2008; Phan and Luk, 2008; Dobler, 2009). Trading networks are important for transmitting information and resources to ensure a competitive advantage.

The limited purchasing power of their customer base forces the Chinese to keep their prices low. Many Chinese shops capture a niche in local markets by importing a variety of goods directly from China (Ma, 2008; Park, 2009b; Dittgen, 2010; Liu, 2010). Although some local entrepreneurs try to compete by selling Chinese products, the Chinese still have the advantage of sourcing their products more cheaply through *guanxi* networks. The Chinese also have the ability to adapt their supplies quickly in reaction to consumer demand (Laribee, 2008; Gadzala, 2009; Kohnert, 2010). South Africans are generally pleased to pay lower prices for Chinese goods but also claim that successful Chinese businesses cause local business failures and unemployment. For example, according to the Southern African Clothing & Textile Workers Union, over 800 firms were liquidated and 60,000 workers were left unemployed between 2001 and 2005 because of the excessive presence of cheap Chinese goods in South Africa (Alden and Davies, 2006; Wenping, 2007; McNamee et al., 2012).

South Africans harbour mixed feelings about the impact of the Chinese on their lives. The Chinese presence is certainly seen by some in a positive light, especially their efforts in creating jobs, increasing the purchasing power of South Africans, providing cheaper consumer goods, investing and participating in local construction and infrastructure projects, improving local education systems, enhancing the tourism potential of South Africa and stimulating trade and import/export relations with China (Dobler, 2009; Gadzala, 2009; Park, 2009a). On the other hand, the Chinese presence has various negative connotations. First, there is the perceived threat of "China, Inc.", a feeling that Chinese shops are collaborating to better themselves socially and economically at the expense of local communities (Laribee, 2008). Second, some feel that the Chinese are not investing their money locally but in more stock or transferring it to China as savings or remittances (Dobler, 2009). Third, the Chinese are accused of treating their employees poorly by paying them very low wages and making them work very long hours (Park, 2009a). Fourth, the Chinese are blamed for putting locals out of business because locals do not have the same strong supply chains that can provide goods at cheaper prices (Gadzala, 2009). Certainly, competition between local and Chinese businesses has increased significantly due to the cheaper consumer goods offered by the latter, triggering business failures and increased unemployment among South Africans (Mohan and Kale, 2007; Laribee, 2008).

Despite the fact that Chinese migrants do help South African economic development through job creation and the provision of cheap consumer goods, Chinese migration is increasingly viewed as a cultural invasion and responsible for society's ills. Xenophobic attacks, crime and protests against foreign nationals are common with an increasing number of incidents relating directly to the Chinese economic presence in the country. Chinese businesses are targeted not only because of general negative perceptions, but also because shopkeepers are known to carry large amounts of money on their person. Those in the country without proper documentation cannot make use of formal banking facilities and, instead, deal exclusively in cash. Documented attacks on the Chinese include break-ins, theft, car hijackings, murders, police brutality and demands for bribes by corrupt government officials (Laribee, 2008; Ma, 2008; Park, 2009a; Liu, 2010). Anti-Chinese sentiment may be exacerbated by South African perceptions that potential employment opportunities are given to the Chinese at their expense. Some believe that all Chinese will benefit from and qualify for black economic empowerment legislation and consequently fear that this may lead to South Africa being flooded by goods from China (Laribee, 2008).

The Chinese use two strategies to fit into the societies where they have settled. First, they establish Chinese associations to give themselves a voice in the local economic, political and social arena. These associations help them to send remittances to China, borrow money through the associations' rotating credit mechanisms, fight legal battles to defend their rights, mitigate the impact of discrimination, enforce contracts with employees and developers, and provide camaraderie and entertainment (Yeoh and Kong, 1994; Yip, 1995; Dittgen, 2010). Second, they make regular use of Chinatowns to maintain their Chinese culture and traditions. As Sales et al. (2009, p. 21) remark:

> Chinatown is a meeting-place to buy Chinese products and eat Chinese food, a familiar space within the vast anonymity of the city. It is a hub, providing multiple connections with the Chinese 'community' and its associations and businesses; with friends and acquaintances who may live in different parts of the city or outside; and with 'home'.

Many Chinese who have established themselves and their families in South Africa retain links with extended family in China. They remain sojourners with one foot in South Africa and the other still in China, working hard to earn a living and assimilate with local cultures, traditions and languages. Conversely, their links to China isolate them from local cultures and traditions. They continue to make regular calls and visits to China, send money to family, invest in projects, and assist in emergency relief efforts in China (Mohan and Kale, 2007; Sales et al., 2009; Park, 2010).

METHODOLOGY

A survey questionnaire was administered in person to 500 Chinese entrepreneurs in Johannesburg in 2011. The interviewees were randomly selected, based on their willingness to participate in the study. Questionnaire interviews were specifically conducted in areas in the city of Johannesburg where most Chinese businesses congregate, including the first Chinatown area in Commissioner Street and other Chinatowns such as China City, Dragon City and China Mart; the Chinatown located in Cyrildene; and smaller Chinese shops located in Bruma Lake flea market and Ormonde Mall (Figure 6.1). The questionnaire consisted of seven sections and collected information on the demographic profile of the respondents, general business profile, the economic and product profile of the businesses, physical characteristics and locational factors of the businesses, the opportunities and constraints faced by the respondents and their perceptions and opinions of their business surroundings.

Figure 6.1: Location of Study Area

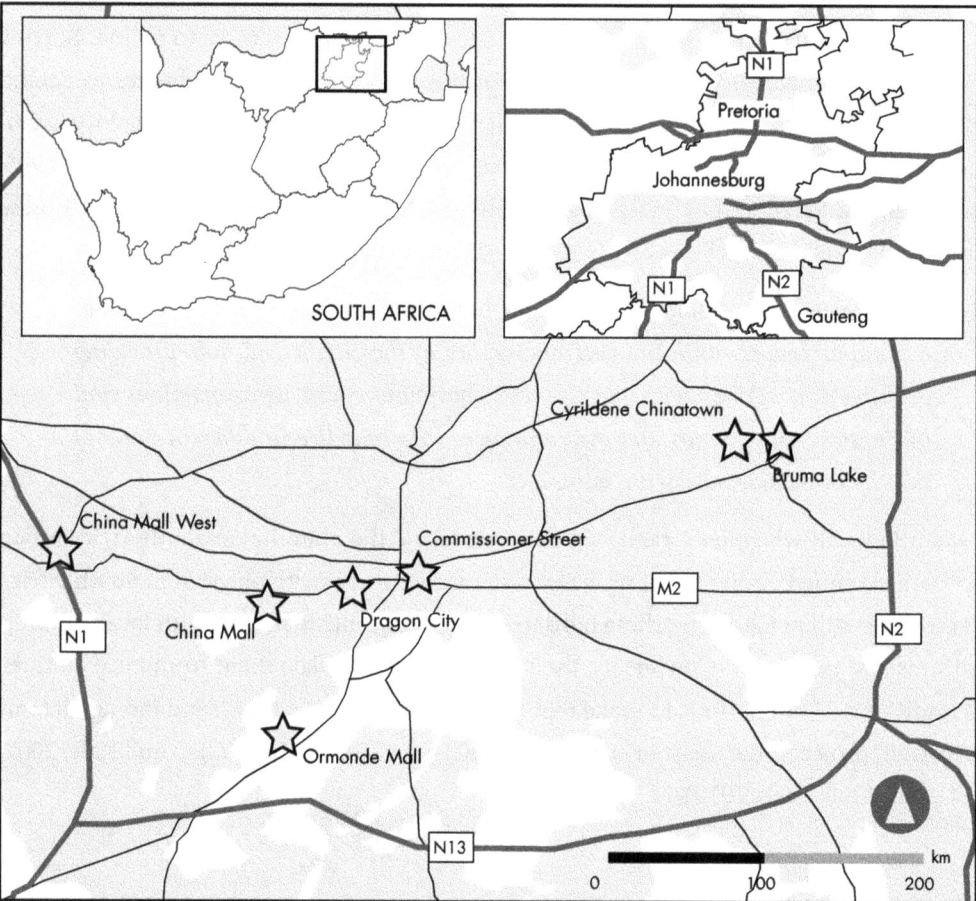

DEMOGRAPHIC PROFILE OF RESPONDENTS

Almost three quarters of the respondents owned their own businesses, while the remainder were employees. While some studies have found that Chinese entrepreneurs are usually young, in their late teens or early 20s (Haugen and Carling, 2005; Gadzala, 2009), only a third of the Johannesburg respondents were younger than 30. Approximately 11 per cent were over 50 (Table 6.1). Most respondents came to South Africa during the first and second waves of Chinese migration; primarily from the Guangdong Province and Taiwan (Laribee, 2008; Park, 2009b). Men were generally the first to migrate, with women and children joining them later (Yip, 1995; Phan and Luk, 2008; Dobler, 2009; Park, 2010).

Table 6.1: Demographic Profile of Chinese Respondents

	Percentage
Age	
<18	0.6
18-30	33.4
31-50	55.3
>50	10.7
Gender	
Male	57.8
Female	42.2
Dependants*	
None	19.0
One	26.3
Two	20.0
Three	10.8
Four or more	23.8
Education*	
None	1.0
Primary	9.0
Some secondary	30.8
Completed secondary	37.9
Tertiary	21.2
* Results may not total 100 per cent due to rounding	

Chinese culture places a strong emphasis on family ties through *guanxi* networks (Haugen and Carling, 2005; Mohan and Kale, 2007; Gadzala, 2009), which could explain why approximately 35 per cent of respondents have large household sizes with three or more dependants (Table 6.1). However, slightly more than 25 per cent of respondents had only one dependant. There are two possible reasons why one in five of the respondents had no dependants at all. First, they could be younger immigrants, between the ages of 18 and 30, who migrated to improve their living conditions. Second, employees (especially the younger generation) might be obligated to repay their migration fees to their employers by working for a very small salary (or none) for a predetermined time, which would make it difficult to settle down and start a family (Gadzala, 2009). Generally, the respondents were well educated, with almost 60 per cent having completed secondary and tertiary education. Approximately 30 per cent had completed some secondary education, while only 10 per cent had completed only primary education or had no education.

Most of the respondents live in the Cyrildene area, followed by Bruma and Bedfordview in Johannesburg's southern suburbs (Figure 6.2). Chinese business owners and employees in Johannesburg tend to live relatively close to their businesses. However, none of the respondents lived in the Observatory/Bellevue and Berea/Hillbrow areas, probably because they are considered unsafe or, in the case of Observatory specifically, because housing is expensive.

Figure 6.2: Areas of Residence of Chinese Respondents

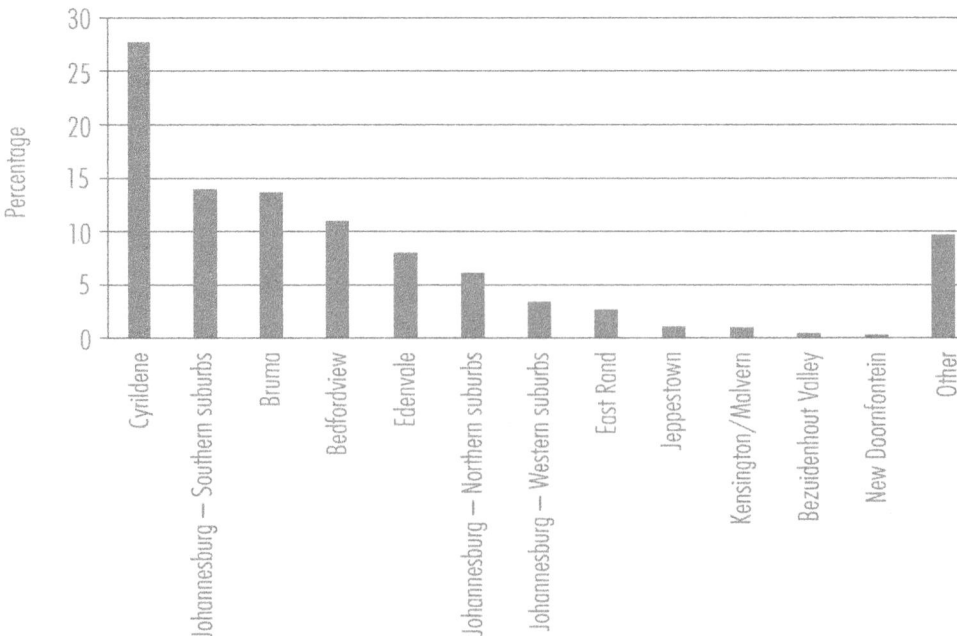

GENERAL BUSINESS PROFILE

Roughly two thirds of the entrepreneurs indicated that they had started their businesses to earn an income, to increase their income or to seize a business opportunity as an entrepreneur. The Chinese practice of *guanxi* ensures that chain migration occurs through extended family lines, with the younger generation following in the footsteps of the older by continuing the family business in foreign countries or starting their own businesses there (Haugen and Carling, 2005; Phan and Luk, 2008; Dobler, 2009; Gadzala, 2009). The majority of entrepreneurs (53 per cent) have only one business, almost a third have two businesses, while 14 per cent own three or more businesses. The businesses are all relatively new: approximately a third have been operating for less than two years and another third between two and five years. About a quarter of entrepreneurs have had their businesses between five and 10 years, while less than 10 per cent have run theirs for longer than that.

In this study, 71 per cent of respondents chose their business location, while the local municipality allocated business sites to the remainder. Almost 96 per cent of respondents were accommodated in shops designated by the local municipality or the owners of the shopping malls of which 75 per cent are located in the Johannesburg CBD core area, and 14 per cent are within shopping malls. This suggests that the traditional Chinese shop houses as found in Singapore and North America are not present in South Africa, where formal stores are used to do business.

Market factors are usually the most important consideration when choosing the optimum business location to ensure sustainable livelihood opportunities (Phan and Luk, 2008; Gadzala, 2009; Dittgen, 2010). Just over half of the respondents chose a business location in close proximity to their clientele, while 16 per cent worked in close proximity to cultural associations and their support services (Figure 6.3). Just over 9 per cent of businesses were also located in areas that provide high security and surveillance. Respondents were asked if they wanted to relocate their business: of those who want to relocate, 27 per cent identified the CBD core area and 18 per cent shopping malls.

In terms of sources of start-up capital, almost two thirds of the respondents used their own or household members' savings to start their businesses (Figure 6.4). *Guanxi* networks allowed 27 per cent of respondents to borrow money from relatives or friends to start their businesses and 7 per cent to obtain funds from manufacturers or suppliers. The networks thus play an important role in creating opportunities to access credit or investment mechanisms (Brautigam, 2003; Gadzala, 2009).

Figure 6.3: **Reasons for Choosing Current Business Location**

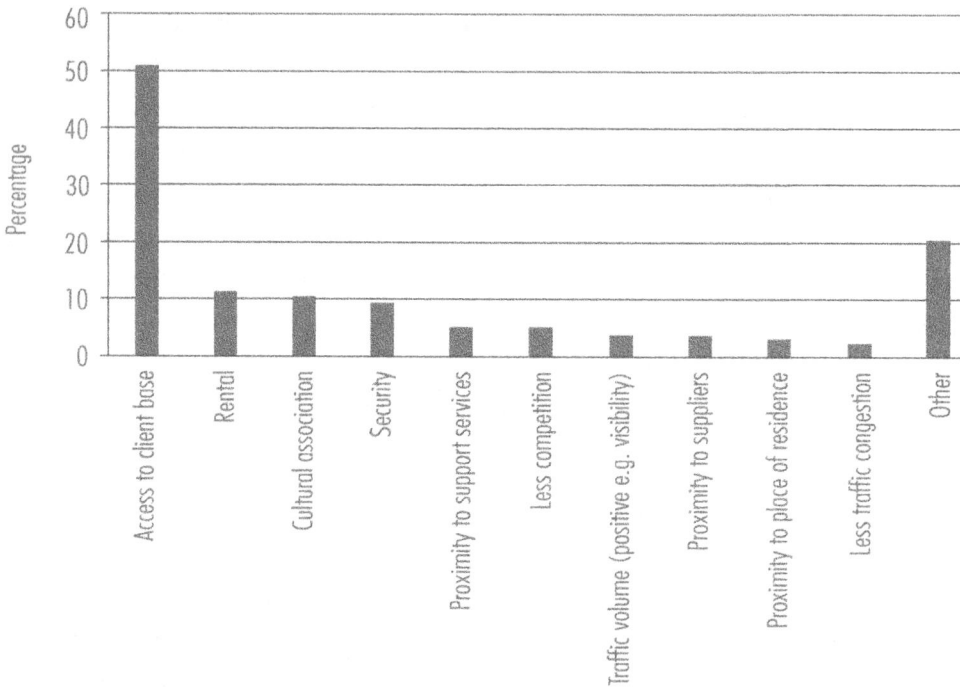

Note: Multiple response question

Figure 6.4: **Sources of Start-Up Capital**

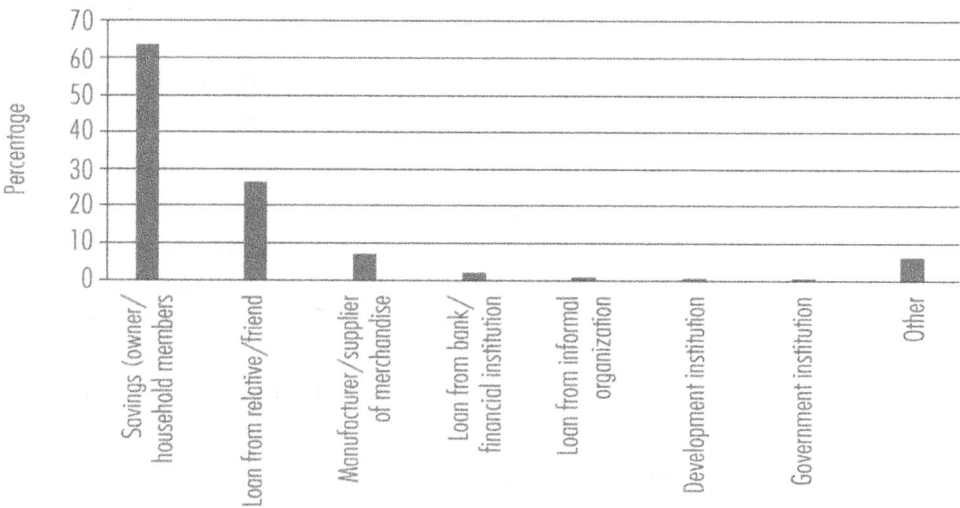

Note: Multiple response question

Many respondents spent large amounts to start their businesses: 42 per cent spent between ZAR100,000 and ZAR500,000 and 15 per cent spent well over ZAR1 million (Figure 6.5). There are two possible reasons why so much capital is required. First, three quarters of the respondents source their products directly from China, and a third also obtain them from wholesalers in South Africa. Bulk purchasing of stock from these suppliers increases start-up costs (Haugen and Carling, 2005; Laribee, 2008; Dobler, 2009). The products are mostly sold on a wholesale or retail basis and include textiles, clothing, footwear, personal and household goods, cosmetics, jewellery, carpets/rugs, food products, take-away foods, electrical household equipment, photographic and multimedia products, computer hardware and tobacco. Second, initial and operating costs are driven up by the way in which the respondents recruit their employees. Approximately 75 per cent of respondents have between two and five employees, around 8 per cent have between six and 10, and 5 per cent have more than 11. Some Chinese entrepreneurs recruit employees directly from China through *guanxi* networks, by paying their migration fees and offering them accommodation, health care and, in some cases, a monthly salary, all of which increases their business start-up costs.

Figure 6.5: Amount of Business Start-Up Capital Required

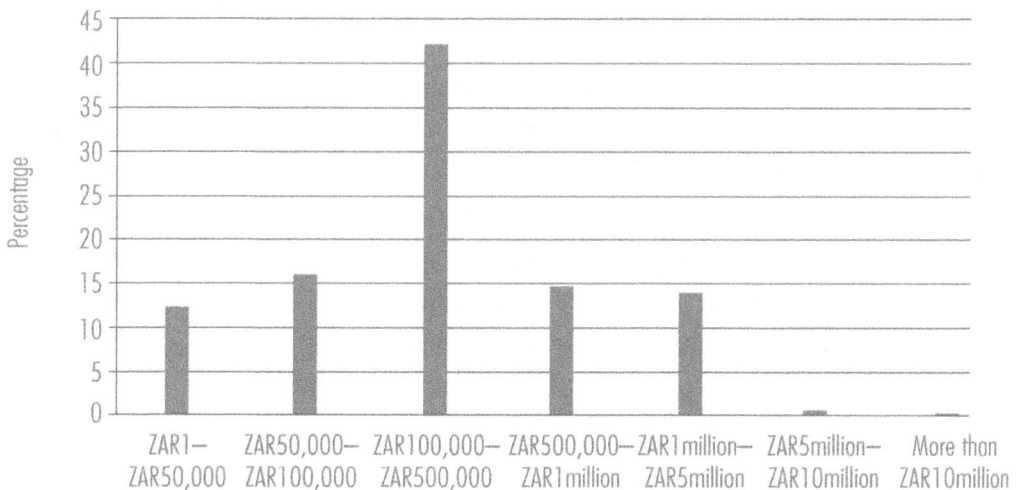

The Chinese entrepreneurs were generally reluctant to talk about income and costs, which complicates the accurate estimation of profit levels. At the same time, only 14 per cent said they earn another income, mostly in the form of other self-employment (9.5 per cent), permanent employment (4 per cent) and financial support from family and/or friends (1 per cent). Proxies for undisclosed income include the number of customers served per day and the amounts of money customers spend per visit. A total of 58 per cent said that they served between 11 and 50 customers daily, 15 per cent between 51 and 100, and 8 per cent more than 100. The customers spend relatively significant amounts of money on their purchases with almost half spending between ZAR100 and ZAR1,000 per visit, and 29 per cent between ZAR1,000 and ZAR10,000 per visit.

PERCEPTIONS AND OPINIONS OF BUSINESS CHALLENGES

Three questions were asked relating to respondents' perceptions of their business surroundings. An overwhelming 95 per cent regard the city of Johannesburg as unsafe. Areas designated as particularly unsafe include the CBD, Chinatowns, areas outside Chinatowns, and townships. Overall, 59 per cent of respondents were optimistic about the business climate in Johannesburg as a whole, 38 per cent saw it as average, and only 4 per cent were pessimistic. However, the respondents were not quite as positive about the business climate where they were actually located: 42 per cent were optimistic, 59 per cent average and 6 per cent pessimistic.

Among the factors identified by respondents as influencing day-to-day business operations, two stood out. The police were mentioned by 70 per cent and crime by 63 per cent. The fact that the police, whose job it is to protect businesses from crime, are seen as a bigger problem than crime itself is highly instructive. Chinese entrepreneurs are clearly targeted by corrupt police, government officials, security guards and angry citizens. First, they are regularly confronted by police, traffic and immigration officers who attempt to extort bribes from them in return for not making their illegal status known. Second, Chinese entrepreneurs do not make use of formal banking facilities and consequently carry significant quantities of cash. Many business premises also lack adequate security systems. All of this leaves them vulnerable to break-ins, looting and car hijacking.

Some entrepreneurs employ security guards to protect their businesses from threatening and criminal behaviour. While 29 per cent said that private security had a positive impact on their businesses, 11 per cent saw it as a negative force, because some guards instigate the same corrupt activities as government officials, police and traffic officers. Other negative factors include parking problems (11 per cent), traffic congestion (6 per cent) and crowding

(6 per cent), which all relate to the fact that Johannesburg is the most densely populated city in the country. Poor services were also mentioned by some respondents, who complained about litter (7 per cent) and dirt (5 per cent) in their business areas.

To obtain a better understanding of the general difficulties faced by Chinese businesses in Johannesburg, respondents were asked to indicate their most serious operational constraints and the ways in which those problems might be improved (Table 6.2). The language barrier was the most significant issue, faced by almost a third of respondents. The problem is more pronounced for the older generation that struggles to learn local languages and relies on employing locals to assist local customers (Gadzala, 2009; Huynh et al., 2010). While Chinese entrepreneurs often provide cheaper goods of somewhat inferior quality to cater for poorer local communities, they face their own competitive challenges. About 11 and 6 per cent of respondents complain that competition from South African formal and informal businesses, respectively, influences their businesses negatively. This suggests that many locals also sell cheap Chinese products in their stores.

Other economic challenges mentioned by respondents include stocking problems (11 per cent), difficulties in financing start-ups and business expansion (9 per cent), cash flow problems (8 per cent) and inadequate business infrastructure (7 per cent). Stocking problems relate mainly to importing goods in bulk from China, which is costly and difficult because most *guanxi* suppliers demand an immediate transfer of money before they will ship their goods. Chinese entrepreneurs risk paying a fine or losing the entire shipment when customs officials check the containers for discrepancies between the ordered goods and the goods in the containers (Haugen and Carling, 2005; Laribee, 2008; Dobler, 2009; Park, 2009a). Among the "other issues" that negatively affect 43 per cent of respondents were safety and security concerns, including a fear of crime, hijackings and robberies, and unjust and ruthless treatment by police officers.

Not surprisingly, the most important strategies to resolve the problems faced by businesses were the mirror image of the most significant constraints. Setting competitive pricing standards (36 per cent), improving security (16 per cent) and store structure or shelter (12 per cent) and expanding stock (12 per cent), financial assistance (11 per cent) and basic management skills (8 per cent) were seen as the most important ways to address the issues that they faced. Other ways to improve their businesses included courses to learn the local languages of South Africa (especially English), expanding stock to provide more high-quality and fashionable goods, building better relations with South Africans through increased knowledge of local customs and traditions, and cementing a place for themselves in the South African economy by earning higher incomes.

Table 6.2: Business Problems Experienced by Chinese Entrepreneurs

	Percentage
Problems faced by respondents	
Language	32.0
Competition from other formal businesses	11.4
Problem to maintain stock levels	11.2
Unavailability of funding sources to support start-up and expansion of business	9.4
Cash flow problems	8.0
Insufficient structure/shelter	7.0
Location of business	6.4
Competition from informal businesses	6.2
Staff	4.4
Insufficient service from suppliers	1.8
Unavailability of transport	1.4
Insufficient infrastructure (e.g. water, waste bins, etc.)	0.6
Unavailability of equipment	0.2
Other	43.2
Ways to resolve the problems	
Competitive pricing	36.4
Improved security	15.6
Improvements to structure/shelter	12.4
Ability to maintain sufficient stock	11.8
Availability of financial assistance	11.2
Basic management skills	8.6
Availability of labour	1.6
Availability of better equipment	1.2
Access to more affordable transport	0.8
Availability of basic services	0.2
Other	23.8
Note: Multiple response question	

CONCLUSION

Chinese entrepreneurship in Johannesburg is influenced and shaped by economic factors and *guanxi* networks, which are intimately connected to why and how businesses start and the choice of business location. The ideal business location is in close proximity to clientele and in relative proximity to cultural associations and support services, which provide respondents with a voice in the local economic, political and social arena. *Guanxi* networks further influence the everyday operation of Chinese businesses by providing money to start and grow an enterprise, ensuring increased accountability in the supply of stock and aiding in the procurement of employees from China. Despite operational challenges such as crime, police corruption, language barriers and competition from formal and informal businesses, Chinese business owners are innovative entrepreneurs who use their economic resourcefulness and *guanxi* networks to adapt quickly to local conditions, maintaining a competitive edge over local entrepreneurs. Respondents will stock anything that will sell, allowing them to maintain an income flow in relatively difficult circumstances.

The Chinese presence in Johannesburg has increased over the years, as seen by the Chinese products that are now sold in most stores. It is thus important for the City of Johannesburg to improve its planning and protection of Chinese communities and businesses. There certainly needs to be a better understanding of Chinese business activities and greater efforts at integration, instead of stereotyping and treating them as outcasts. To date, they have received little institutional support through participation in government SMME programmes (Rogerson, 2008). There is also a lesson for South African entrepreneurs in terms of the business advantages conferred by social networks such as *guanxi*.

ACKNOWLEDGEMENT

With kind permission from Springer Science+Business Media: *Urban Forum*, The role of economic factors and Guanxi networks in the success of Chinese shops in Johannesburg, South Africa, 25(1), 2014, pp. 105-123, Lodene Willemse.

REFERENCES

Alden, C. and Davies, M. (2006) Profile of the operations of Chinese multinationals in Africa. *South African Journal of International Affairs*, 13: 83–96.

Brautigam, D. (2003) Close encounters: Chinese business networks as industrial catalysts in Sub-Saharan Africa. *African Affairs*, 102: 447–467.

Dittgen, R. (2010) From isolation to integration? A study of Chinese retailers in Dakar. Occasional Paper No. 57, South African Institute of International Affairs, Johannesburg.

Dobler, G. (2009) Chinese Shops and the formation of a Chinese expatriate community in Namibia. *China Quarterly*, 199: 707-727.

Gadzala, A. (2009) Survival of the fittest? Kenya's *jua kali* and Chinese businesses. *Journal of Eastern African Studies*, 3: 202–220.

Harris, K. (1999) Accepting the group, but not the area: The South African Chinese and the Group Areas Act. *South African Historical Journal*, 40: 179–201.

Harrison, P., Moyo, K. and Yang, Y. (2012) Strategy and tactics: Chinese immigrants and diasporic spaces in Johannesburg, South Africa. *Journal of Southern African Studies*, 38: 899–925.

Haugen, H. and Carling, J. (2005) On the edge of the Chinese diaspora: The surge of baihuo business in an African city. *Ethnic and Racial Studies*, 28: 639–662.

Huynh, T., Park, Y. and Chen, A. (2010) Faces of China: New Chinese migrants in South Africa, 1980s to present. *African and Asian Studies*, 9: 286–306.

Ip, D. (2005) Contesting Chinatown: Place-making and the emergence of 'ethnoburbia' in Brisbane, Australia. *GeoJournal*, 64: 63–74.

Jacobsen, M. (2006) Doing business the Chinese way? On Manadonese Chinese entrepreneurship in North Sulawesi. *Copenhagen Journal of Asian Studies*, 24: 72–104.

Kohnert, D. (2010) Are the Chinese in Africa more innovative than the Africans? Comparing Chinese and Nigerian entrepreneurial migrants' cultures of innovation. Working Paper No. 140, German Institute of Global and Area Studies, Hamburg.

Lai, D. (1990) The visual character of Chinatowns. *Places*, 7: 28–31.

Laribee, R. (2008) The China shop phenomenon: Trade supply within the Chinese diaspora in South Africa. *Africa Spectrum*, 13: 353–370.

Liu, J. (2010) Contact and identity: The experience of 'China goods' in a Ghanaian marketplace. *Journal of Community and Applied Social Psychology*, 20: 184–201.

Ma, H. (2008) Chinese traders in Primorsky Krai in 2007. *Far Eastern Studies*, 7: 81–98.

McNamee, T., Mills, G., Manoeli, S., Mulaudzi, M., Doran, S. and Chen, E. (2012) Africa in their words: A study of Chinese traders in South Africa, Lesotho, Botswana, Zambia and Angola. Discussion Paper No. 2012/03, Brenthurst Foundation, Johannesburg.

Mohan, G. and Kale, D. (2007) The invisible hand of South-South globalisation: Chinese migrants in Africa. Report for Rockefeller Foundation by Development Policy and Practice Department, Open University, Milton Keynes.

Park, Y. (2009a) Chinese enclave communities and their impact on South African society. In S. Marks (ed.), *Strengthening the Civil Society Perspective: China's African Impact* (pp.113–127). Cape Town: Fahamu Emerging Powers in Africa Programme.

Park, Y. (2009b) Recent Chinese migrations to South Africa: New intersections of race, class and ethnicity. In T. Rahimy (ed.), *Representation, Expression and Identity: Interdisciplinary Insights on Multiculturalism, Conflict and Belonging* (pp. 153–168). Oxford: Inter-Disciplinary Press.

Park, Y. (2010) Boundaries, borders and borderland constructions: Chinese in contemporary South Africa and the region. *African Studies*, 69: 457–479.

Phan, M. and Luk, C. (2008) I don't say I have a business in Chinatown: Chinese sub-ethnic relations in Toronto's Chinatown West. *Ethnic and Racial Studies*, 31: 294–326.

Rogerson, C. (2008) Tracking SMME development in South Africa: Issues of finance, training and the regulatory environment. *Urban Forum*, 19: 61–81.

Rogerson, C. (2009) The locational behaviour of foreign direct investment: Evidence from Johannesburg, South Africa. *Urban Forum*, 20: 415–435.

Sales, R., Hatziprokopiou, P., Christiansen, F., D'Angelo, A., Lian, X., Lin, X. and Montagna, N. (2009) London's Chinatown: Diaspora, identity and belonging. Working Paper No. 3, Social Policy Research Centre, School of Health & Social Sciences, Middlesex University, UK.

Selvarajah, C. and Masli, E. (2011) Ethnic entrepreneurial business cluster development: Chinatowns in Melbourne. *Journal of Asia Business Studies*, 5: 42–60.

Wang, S. (1999) Chinese commercial activity in the Toronto CMA: New development patterns and impacts. *Canadian Geographer*, 43: 19–35.

Wenping, H. (2007) The balancing act of China's Africa policy. *China Security*, 3: 23–40.

Wilhelm, J. (2006) The Chinese communities in South Africa. In S. Buhlungu, R. Southall, and J. Lutchman (eds.), *South Africa 2005-2006: State of the Nation* (pp. 350–368). Cape Town: HSRC.

Yeoh, B. and Kong, L. (1994) Reading landscape meanings: State constructions and lived experiences in Singapore's Chinatown. *Habitat International*, 18: 17–35.

Yip, C. (1995) Association, residence, and shop: An appropriation of commercial blocks in North American Chinatowns. *Perspectives in Vernacular Architecture*, 5: 109–117.

Chapter Seven

On the Move: Cameroonian Migrants in Durban

Akwa Tafuh and Pranitha Maharaj

INTRODUCTION

The country of Cameroon, situated between Central and West Africa, has a population of approximately 22 million and two major language communities: Francophone and Anglophone. In recent decades it has witnessed various migration trends: people in the rural areas moving to the cities, those in the cities moving to other countries within Africa, and those moving to other continents, particularly Europe; in each case with the objective of improving their living conditions and livelihoods (Mberu and Pongou, 2012). The main African destinations for migrants include Chad, Gabon, Nigeria, the Central African Republic and Congo-Brazzaville, all of which border Cameroon. The main non-African destinations include France, the United States, Germany, Italy, the United Kingdom, Switzerland, Belgium, Canada, Pakistan and Spain. Even though South Africa is not a preferred or major destination, the Cameroonian population in South Africa has been growing rapidly. The UNDESA (2013) database shows that the number of Cameroonians living in South Africa rose from 978 in 2000 to 2,454 in 2013.

Against this backdrop, this chapter aims to explore the personal experiences of Cameroonian migrants in South Africa, with particular reference to their entrepreneurial activities. More specifically, it investigates the reasons for their migration to South Africa, and their livelihood strategies once there. Research was conducted with Cameroonian migrants living in the South Beach area of Durban, also called "The Point". Known for its high concentration of Cameroonians and other African migrants, this area is close to Durban's harbour. The South Beach area is popular with African migrant groups and continues to attract people who share the common experience of migration to post-apartheid South Africa. They either live and work in the South Beach area, or live there and work in other parts of the city. Many Cameroonians coming to Durban for the first time go straight to the South Beach area and end up staying there because of its proximity to the city centre, where most informal business is conducted. The study on which this chapter is based involved in-depth qualitative interviews with Cameroonian migrants and two focus group discussions. All of those selected for interview had resided in Durban for at least five years.

REASONS FOR MIGRATING TO SOUTH AFRICA

The respondents gave a variety of reasons for leaving Cameroon and moving to South Africa. Common to most accounts was that they had been encouraged to do so by Cameroonians who were already in South Africa. As one female respondent recounted:

> I really did not know much. I never thought of where could be best for me since I had very little or no knowledge about life out of Cameroon. I then thought of a friend of mine who had left Cameroon the previous year. When I communicated with her, she told me that she was doing well in South Africa and that life here was quite good. She said if I travelled to join her, I was going to make a lot of money. It was then that I told myself that I was going to South Africa. I could not think of somewhere else, because I only had a friend in South Africa who could tell me how to join her. If I had chosen another country, I would not know how to get there or where to even stay if I eventually got there (Interview No. 9, 21 May 2011).

Another male respondent stated:

> I left home because my friends who were already here were sending much money and very expensive goods to their families. I also believed that if I came to the

country, I would be doing the same as them. Unfortunately when I arrived here, I was first robbed of everything I had, and then finding my way out became my main challenge. Also, the community members were not friendly and sociable enough to allow me to integrate with them (Interview No. 2, 5 May 2011).

These accounts provide insights into the way in which social networks play an important role in decisions to move from Cameroon to South Africa. Both were persuaded to migrate to South Africa by friends and relatives. One was influenced by the fact that there was a "lot of money" to be made in South Africa. The other saw that friends already in South Africa were remitting considerable sums and expensive goods to their family members in Cameroon and wanted to do the same. The reality was somewhat different for the second respondent who was robbed of all his possessions soon after arrival and found that the community he joined was unfriendly.

The existence of transnational social networks and the information (and misinformation) that they generate about migration and migrant destinations are topics of everyday conversation in Cameroon (Pelican, 2013). This helps explain why South Africa has become an increasingly popular destination for Cameroonian migrants but not necessarily why people were disposed to leave Cameroon in the first place. In this regard, most respondents spoke of the hardships of life in their home country. As one male respondent observed:

I finished college and could not get a job in the private sector. My parents also did not have money to bribe for a position with the Government and I had no 'godfathers' in high places. Life was so bad and I could not continue staying at home and begging money from my parents. I felt sorry for them because they had tried so hard to give me a college education which was kind of useless in Cameroon. I decided to leave Cameroon in search of greener pastures for me and my parents (Interview No. 3, 8 May 2011).

According to this respondent, the employment situation in Cameroon was unpromising, even for highly qualified young people. Rather than being an isolated and possibly exceptional case, Pelican (2013: 237-8) notes that the literature depicts the situation of Cameroonian youth "as overshadowed by general feelings of disappointment and disillusionment; disappointment with the economic and political situation in Cameroon, and disillusionment about the (im)possibility of a decent future in their home country. As a result...aspiring Cameroonians consider migration to the US, Europe and the Near and Far

East, as well as within Africa, to be a preferable alternative to social immobility and failure at home" (see also Pelican, 2010; Alpes, 2014). These perceptions push many young people out of the country in search of opportunity elsewhere. A recent study by the African, Caribbean and Pacific (ACP) Observatory on Migration found that the search for employment, the desire for a better income and study were the three main reasons for leaving Cameroon (Table 7.1).

Table 7.1: Reasons for Departure

Reason	%
Search for a steady job	45.2
Studies	38.4
Hope for a better income	26.2
Left for marital reasons	9.9
Acquiring skills	8.8
Joining family members abroad	6.6
Left to succeed as others have	2.4
Learning another language	2.1
Following the decision of other family members	0.5
Security reasons	0.5
Victim of discrimination	0.3
Other reasons	5.4

Note: Multiple response question
Source: Zourkaleini et al. (2013: 42)

With regard to the second most important reason for migration (study), Mberu and Pongou (2012: 10) argue that the higher education sector in Cameroon suffers from "long-term decay." As a result, the high emigration rates of the highly skilled "hide a much larger human capital loss – the outflow of dynamic, intellectually engaged young people who go abroad to study and often remain there upon completing their coursework, as a consequence of the depressing economic and political situations in their country of origin." South Africa has become a preferred African destination for students from Cameroon and some Cameroonians in Durban originally came to South Africa to further their education.

The country is seen as an attractive alternative to Europe because the cost of study is considerably lower:

> I travelled to South Africa for educational reasons. When I finished my first degree in the University of Yaoundé, I could not find a job in the private sector or the Government. I wasted two years of my life trying to find a job. When I failed to find a job, I decided to look for a Master's degree programme in Europe. I was lucky to get admission, but there was too much money involved. My parents could not afford it and I was very disappointed. I spoke to my friend who was studying in South Africa and he told me that cost was not as high here. I was excited and immediately begged him to help me with my application (Interview No. 7, 17 May 2011).

There are also opportunities in South Africa to support oneself economically while studying:

> I am working and am grateful to the [academic] institution for the opportunities they are giving to post graduate students. I have benefitted a lot and I am still benefitting from the good structures set up by the university that empower postgraduate students. It is not about my experience because I only got experience as a high school teacher back home, not at a tertiary level, so I will not really say it is that. I therefore think that it is due to the opportunities offered by the system and not solely experience. I am an academic in the making and that is why I so much value opportunities of this nature as they empower me to face my dreams and earn a monthly living (Interview No. 7, 17 May 2011).

Family reunification was given as a reason for leaving Cameroon by nearly 20 per cent of the migrants in the study by the ACP Observatory on Migration (Zourkaleini et al., 2013: 42). Some of the migrants in Durban, especially the female respondents, felt compelled to migrate to South Africa if they wanted to remain or reunite with their male partner:

> I moved to South Africa after marrying my husband. I was living in England before we got married and he was living here. I left a good job in England for South Africa as a housewife. My reason for leaving England was not in search of better opportunities but to be together with my husband as he was not ready to relocate to England. However, it's not like I am complaining; I guess it is all part of being a woman (Interview No. 5, 16 May 2011).

I did not choose South Africa. I just had to come to South Africa because my husband was already here, and I guess I would have gone wherever he was, if it was not South Africa. If I had a chance to choose where I wanted to settle, it would not have been South Africa. I always dreamt of travelling abroad, but South Africa never crossed my mind as an option. I thought of Europe and America. But then when I got married to my husband, he was already a South African citizen, I had to adjust my plans to fit into his (Interview No. 4, 12 May 2011).

The implication of these accounts is that women sometimes have little influence over the decision to migrate if they want to maintain their social and familial relationships.

A few migrants said they came to South Africa with the explicit intention of establishing a business in the country. These migrants were drawn by what they perceived to be new or unparalleled entrepreneurial opportunities. As one well-travelled respondent commented:

I had no other reason for coming to South Africa other than business. It was the search for better economic opportunities because I knew I could do better outside the country based on what friends told me. After being in 22 countries, I decided to move to South Africa because it was regarded as a 'virgin' country as far as business is concerned. In terms of competition, opportunity and creativity here, people are still trying to establish their own stuff, unlike in Europe where it seems all has been done and there are few opportunities and in most cases you have to work for someone. In South Africa, if you have money, the next day you can get your own shop. In Europe, you cannot just do that, but you have to follow a process and it is difficult (Interview No. 11, 20 May, 2011).

South Africa, then, was perceived as a land of opportunity for small business enterprise, particularly when compared with destinations such as Europe.

Looking just at the numbers of Cameroonians who apply for asylum in South Africa, one might conclude that many migrants also leave Cameroon as refugees. Between 2004 and 2013, a total of 5,539 Cameroonians lodged claims for political asylum in South Africa (Table 7.2). However, Cameroon receives far more refugees than it ever sends and less than 1 per cent of migrants in the ACP Observatory on Migration study left the country for security reasons or because they felt victimized. The Department of Home Affairs in South Africa tends to agree that Cameroon is not a refugee-generating country. Of the over 5,500 claims for asylum submitted by Cameroonians, only 104 had been granted refugee status by the end of 2013 (a success rate of less than 2 per cent). Given the difficulty of obtaining work and residence permits in South Africa, and the large backlog in the adjudication of refugee claims, most of the claims for asylum are clearly strategic since they ensure that a migrant can stay well beyond the 90 days that most visitors to the country are permitted. This is only a temporary reprieve, however, since as many as 2,660 had been adjudicated and rejected. In effect, this means that there were still over 2,700 Cameroonian migrants in the country with valid asylum-seeker permits at the end of 2013.

Table 7.2: Applications for Refugee Status by Cameroonians in South Africa, 2004-2013

	Applied during year	Total accepted	Total rejected
2004	395	9	2
2005	226	11	8
2006	219	27	11
2007	311	22	36
2008	1,050	–	–
2009	667	9	429
2010	494	22	593
2011	531	4	206
2012	1,072	1	725
2013	574	0	650
Total	5,539	105	2,660
Source: UNHCR (2014)			

An additional strategy to remain in South Africa adopted by some male migrants is to marry South Africans so that they can obtain the documentation that allows them to stay and find employment (Pineteh, 2015). While some of these relationships are genuine, others are financial transactions involving marriages of convenience:

> There are different types of marriages and I do not know if I can say I am married because inside I know I am not. Marriages are arranged in South Africa for the purposes of getting documents and I have such a marriage. For real, I am not married, but on paper, I am married. It was just a contract arrangement between me and the person that stood in as a wife. Initially you could pay that

person about R2,000 or R3,000 or even less, depending on your agreement. It is strictly a business transaction as we do not act or behave as a couple in any sense. It is hard to get a permit to stay in the country so we look for ways to obtain our permits (Interview No. 1, 3 May 2011).

LIVELIHOOD STRATEGIES

When they arrive in the country, Cameroonian migrants depend on fellow Cameroonians, either friends or family, for support. These social networks are very useful because they are a means of quickly securing employment and an income. In the context of a high level of formal unemployment in South Africa and the difficulties of obtaining employment as non-South Africans, Cameroonian migrants are forced to use a variety of livelihood strategies. During the initial period in South Africa, they are most likely to work in the informal businesses of other Cameroonians already settled in Durban. This gives them time to become familiar with the new environment and to decide on the best way forward.

Many noted that the difficulty of finding formal sector employment led them to create employment opportunities for themselves. They started their own small businesses to provide a source of income. Some were involved in street trading while others had small shops where they employed South Africans and new arrivals from Cameroon. Almost all reported that when they first arrived in the country they did not have the necessary finances to start their own business and ended up working informally. However, as one man reported, this did not really do any more than provide enough to live on and even that was not assured:

I work in a computer maintenance shop owned by another Cameroonian. There have been lots of challenges due to my lack of resources to further my studies and I am unable to complete, therefore I cannot access better opportunities. I will say it in two words: difficult and strenuous. Life has been extremely difficult. I was unable to pay the rent, let alone feed myself. The salary allowed me to live hand-to-mouth and it took me three years to be able to save one rand from the job I had. I have been trying to associate myself with colleagues and also to save some money so that I can be able to go to school and compete with the growing society, but it is difficult still. Life here is really hard as compared to Cameroon where you might not work very hard but still have food to eat; here there is no food for lazy men. I would say life here is fast and that in Cameroon it is laid-

back. You might not have a very good job, but have food to eat, and you can visit
family and have food to eat, whereas here there is no free lunch (Interview No.
3, 8 May 2011).

Only those with sufficient finances are able to start their own businesses. Once they do so, they often make a success of their enterprise:

When I arrived in this country, my husband was already a big business man. He
set up his own business and had bought himself a big house then. Now I am the
one who is in charge of his business and he decided to go and further his studies
(Interview No. 5, 16 May 2011).

Others struggle along, not least the students who enter the informal economy to generate some income to help support their studies and their families:

I do some kinds of small businesses to help sustain myself while I study. One
would hardly know I am a student because I run around a lot, trying to earn
a living. I go to the shops, get clothes from them at a cheaper rate and sell it to
get something additional. I then pay the shopkeeper and keep the balance. My
biggest challenge is capital (Interview No. 4, 12 May 2011).

While some migrants struggle to make an honest living in the country, others engage in more clandestine activities. They blame this on the fact that they do not have the proper documents that would allow them to obtain formal, legal employment and insist that they did not come to the country with these intentions:

There is no other way for me to survive...I really wanted to go to school,
unfortunately I could not afford the fees and my parents could not support me. I
had seen my seniors in the university in Cameroon making counterfeit money. I
make fake money and I am also a sangoma *[traditional healer] providing* muti
[traditional medicine] to the citizens who are in need. Through this I have done
well for myself and I am happy. Although my business is illegal, it is not very
criminal as I do not steal from anyone. I do not kill people. I am only trying to
make ends meet. I make a lot of money which is what every businessman wants.
The local people do not know how to detect a counterfeit, plus I have people
who buy the money I make so I do not have to deal with it. I am doing well, I
take proper care of my family and I visit home when I feel like it, which lots of
Cameroonians in South Africa cannot afford. People must understand life is all
about risk (Interview No. 12, 22 May 2011).

Activities such as counterfeiting and pretending to be traditional healers become a means of survival. These migrants came to South Africa with the impression that they would be able to find employment but the reality is different. This case was certainly not typical, however. Most of the respondents insisted that their businesses were legal and that they did not engage in illegal or criminal activity.

BUSINESS CHALLENGES

Apart from the obstacle of securing sufficient start-up capital, entrepreneurs from Cameroon face several other business challenges. The majority of respondents stated that they remit money to support family members back home. Some migrants do not earn enough to be able to send remittances. One respondent said that he did not send remittances as he was earning a meagre income that could only be used to ensure his own survival. Even those who are not in a position to send money are under pressure to fulfil their financial obligations to their household:

> I send money home to my family. Once you migrate, you are expected to cater for the family left back regardless of whether you are working or not. No one bothers how you are faring; the thinking is usually that once you are out of a country, you are rich and thus responsible for those left behind. It is sad because this is not true but it is hard to convince your family that things are hard. When you fail to meet their demands, you are considered greedy (Interview No. 10, 17 May 2011).

Migrants often have to make major sacrifices to secure funds to remit. One female respondent indicated that at times she borrows money from friends to send remittances home and has to repay this money as soon as she gets paid, which often means that she has little left for herself to cover rent and other basic necessities. Remittances do have a positive impact on households back in Cameroon. However, the responsibility to take care of household members left behind means that funds that could be used to grow the informal business enterprise are unavailable:

> I do send money home, but this I do with tears in my eyes. It is a big sacrifice as I sometimes find myself lacking after sending money to my family. I have to borrow from friends sometimes, because someone cannot cry back at home that they need assistance and I just ignore them. I usually feel like helping out so I

have to push myself too hard, which leaves me with debts (Interview No. 6, 11 May 2011).

The other major challenge faced by informal entrepreneurs from Cameroon is the hostility they face from South Africans in the city. There are obvious language barriers to overcome but even when there is a common language, migrants are often spurned:

I face some problems of language barriers when I meet some potential buyers. Some do not know how to speak English and I do not know how to speak the local language. On the other hand, others who even speak English just act like they do not when they realize that I am a foreigner. Even though I manage by the grace of God, I am not looking for money to feed a family, but just enough to take care of myself. I sell to those I can and those who do not want to buy from me, because I am a foreigner, I walk away when I get that tone.

Cameroonians in Durban report that they make a huge effort to adapt to the host country in the face of criticism and ridicule:

It is not easy living in South Africa as a Cameroonian as one has to try and copy the ways of the people. The accent of Cameroonians is different from the accent of South Africans and one has to try to talk like the locals in order to integrate and be understood by the people. This is not an easy task as I grew up talking like this and now I have to imitate a foreign accent so as to relate with the people. It is even more difficult as the locals are not supportive; some of my colleagues will laugh at the way I pronounce certain words. They do not understand I also find their accent weird (Interview No. 10, 18 May 2011).

Yet despite these negative attitudes, they are not ready to leave the country. Asked whether they would encourage others to come and live in South Africa, the responses were more guarded, with most insisting that they would only do so if someone agreed to come and study in South Africa.

CONCLUSION

Migration is one of many challenges facing South Africa. The steady influx of migrants from the rest of Africa has been accompanied by widespread opposition and hostile sentiments towards foreigners culminating in xenophobic outbreaks in major cities including Durban. In South Africa, unemployment is high, affecting almost a quarter of the labour force. As the unemployment rate rises, more and more people are moving into the informal sector. Migrants from other countries often have no choice but to work in the informal economy to secure a livelihood. Research suggests that this is a source of tension because of the widely-held local perception that they are more entrepreneurial than their South African counterparts as well as the concern by locals that economic opportunities would have to be shared with migrants (Rogerson 1997; Palmary 2002).

In the past two decades, the areas of origin of migrants to South Africa have extended to countries outside the Southern African region. The findings of this research are consistent with other studies that suggest that the reasons why Cameroonians decide to leave their home country are multiple and far from unique. Though most migrants are said to be mainly motivated by economic incentives, this study has shown that different reasons combine to lead people to migrate. Respondents reported coming to South Africa in search of economic opportunities and the hope of securing a better life. Education was another key reason cited for why Cameroonian migrants choose to come to South Africa.

The findings of this study suggest that the longer migrants stay in South Africa, the more integrated they become and this makes it easier to survive economically. Most Cameroonians do not come to South Africa with the intention of starting a business, formal or informal (Fomunyam, 2010). Few have any entrepreneurial experience or training before they arrive. However, their inability to access formal employment opportunities pushes them into informality. Initially they tend to work for other Cameroonians in the sector as they do not have sufficient funds to start their own businesses, which is their ultimate goal. Initially, they start small by selling a few items and then expand as opportunities arise. However, the gains are low and the challenges many.

REFERENCES

Alpes, M. (2014) Imagining a future in 'bush': Migration aspirations at times of crisis in Anglophone Cameroon identities. *Global Studies in Culture and Power*, 21: 259-274.

Fomunyam, N. (2010) Migrant adjustment and regrouping: The case of Cameroonians in Durban. MA Thesis, University of KwaZulu-Natal, Durban.

Mberu, B. and Pongou, R. (2012) Crossing boundaries: Internal, regional and international migration in Cameroon. *International Migration* DOI:10.1111/j.1468-2435.2012.00766.x.

Palmary, I. (2002) Refugees, safety and xenophobia in South African cities: The role of local government. Centre for the Study of Violence and Reconciliation, Johannesburg.

Pelican, M. (2010) Local perspectives on transnational relations of Cameroonian migrants. In T. Grätz (ed.), *Mobility, Transnationalism and Contemporary African Societies.* Newcastle: Cambridge Scholars Publishing.

Pelican, M. (2013) International migration: Virtue or vice? Perspectives from Cameroon. *Journal of Ethnic and Migration Studies,* 39(2): 237-258.

Pineteh, E. (2015) The challenges of living here and there': Conflicting narratives of intermarriage between Cameroonian migrants and South Africans in Johannesburg. *African and Black Diaspora: An International Journal,* 8: 71-85.

Rogerson, C. (1997) International migration, immigrant entrepreneurs and South Africa's small enterprise economy. SAMP Migration Policy Series No. 3, Cape Town.

UNDESA (United Nations, Department of Economic and Social Affairs) (2013) Trends in International Migrant Stock: Migrants by Destination and Origin. (United Nations database, POP/DB/MIG/Stock/Rev.2013). UNDESA, New York.

UNHCR (2014) UNHCR Statistical Online Population Database. Geneva: UNHCR.

Zourkaleini, Y., Mimche, H., Nganawara, D., Nouetagni, S., Seke, K., Chouapi, N., Hamadou, S. and Tjomb, J. (2013) Shedding light on the South: Migrant profiles and the impact of migration on human development in Cameroon. Research Report ACPOBS/2013/PUB12, ACP Migration Observatory, Brussels.

Chapter Eight

Refugees and Asylum Seekers in Cape Town's Informal Economy

Madeleine Northcote and Belinda Dodson

INTRODUCTION

Refugees and asylum-seekers who come to South Africa from elsewhere on the African continent engage in a number of different occupations and forms of employment to earn a livelihood. Although some are in formal employment, many earn their living in insecure, informal employment – such as casual labour in construction or domestic service – or through entrepreneurial activities as traders, artisans or providers of various personal services. Refugees and registered asylum-seekers are legally permitted to work in South Africa, but even with valid documents, formal employment is difficult to secure given prevailing anti-immigrant attitudes and South African employers' suspicion of documents such as asylum-seekers' permits (Handmaker et al., 2008; Landau and Segatti, 2009). Forced migrants thus commonly resort to marginal informal economic activity such as street trading, tailoring and the creation and sale of curios and beadwork, often in co-ethnic networks. Forced migrants' livelihoods commonly straddle, and indeed challenge, the division between formality and informality. We find that many migrants combine formal and informal employment, or use gains from one to attain entry to the other. For some, working in the informal sector can be a stepping stone to more formal and secure employment, while for others it remains a survivalist trap from which they are unable to escape.

After a brief discussion of methodology, this chapter considers the four prominent self-employment sectors that emerged in interviews with forced migrants in Cape Town. Through participants' stories, it is clear that factors such as social support, education and, above all, gender determine which sectors individuals choose, and their success within them. The chapter explores these individual narratives to provide insight as to why some migrants are able to make the transition into steady employment and others are not. A complex amalgam of factors structures the range of livelihood strategies available to migrants, and their choices must be understood within the context of personal history, local and transnational social connections, and the legal and political frameworks of South African society. The final section of this chapter discusses the effect that robberies have on migrant businesses, as well as the physical and emotional well-being of the traders affected.

RESEARCH METHODS

The findings are drawn from interviews with 32 refugees and other forced migrants who live and operate in the Cape Town area. The interviews were arranged and conducted by the primary author between May and September of 2013 in Cape Town. While not intended to be a representative sample, effort was made to include a range of participants, representing six countries: the Democratic Republic of the Congo (DRC) (16), Zimbabwe (7), Somalia (4), Congo-Brazzaville (2), Malawi (1) and Nigeria (2). To qualify for the study, participants had to be over 18, engaged in non-formal or non-regular work, self-identify as a forced migrant, and feel that they had to emigrate for their own security. Although their precise legal status was not determined, owing to its sensitivity, all identified themselves as forced as opposed to voluntary migrants, and included recognized refugees and formal asylum-seekers as well as migrants outside the formal asylum and refugee determination system.

In order to locate a range of participants from different countries, different economic niches and a relatively equal gender balance, a variety of recruitment strategies were used. Interviews were conducted with, among others, staff at a refugee service organization, the Agency for Refugee Education, Skills Training & Advocacy (ARESTA, located in Athlone), and the Fundi Network, a non-profit employment agency in Mowbray. These early inter-views were essential in providing introductions to the first set of forced migrant partici-pants. In order to locate additional participants, directed snowball sampling was used from this group – particularly to find more female participants. Snowball sampling, however, did not prove entirely effective in producing a diverse body of participants with differ-ent occupations, countries of origin or, for that matter, many women, and so the final few participants were identified and recruited through small talk in the course of transactions, such as buying vegetables, souvenirs or mobile phone airtime in spaza shops.

Among the forced migrants interviewed for this study, four broad categories of occu-pation were identified. First, there was employment as casual or day labour, notably in construction and gardening for men and domestic work for women. Second, there were various forms of trading and hawking, from roadside stalls and itinerant trading to more fixed establishments known as spaza shops. Third, there were various forms of artisanship in the manufacture of crafts such as beadwork, wire and metalwork, woodcarvings and paintings. Fourth, there were services such as hair braiding and barbering, often to clients who are themselves migrants. The sections below detail each of these livelihood categories, drawing on the experiences of individual migrants to highlight the strategies adopted and the opportunities and obstacles encountered.

CASUAL LABOUR LIVELIHOODS

The term "casual labour" is used to refer to informal work that is performed for an employer without the rights associated with formal employment, such as sick leave, paid leave, or a formal contract (Devey et al., 2006). "Day labour" is used to describe a job-seeking practice in which workers search for work on a day-to-day basis, in both the formal and informal sectors (Krugell and Blaauw, 2014). These search strategies include posting personal adver-tisements on public notice boards and private mailboxes, using employment agencies, ask-ing door to door and, most visibly, standing at roadside labour recruitment sites. Casual and day labour is an important source of income for many South African nationals as well as international migrants. A previous study in Cape Town showed that employers picking up labour at roadside sites tend to prefer foreign nationals (Sharp, 2012). Similarly, a study in Pretoria found that Zimbabweans, who on average had higher levels of human capital and English language skills, were able to earn more on a day-to-day basis than their South African counterparts (Blaauw et al., 2012).

Certainly, day labour was or had been a major source of income for many of the participants in this study. While some were able to move from casual and day labour into more secure and formal employment, the ability to make this transition was heavily mediated by an individual's social position. One migrant from Congo-Brazzaville, for example, first came to South Africa as a refugee more than 12 years ago. Beginning by retrieving shopping trolleys at a grocery store, he moved on to work as a car guard and eventually a security guard while going to college in Cape Town to get a qualification in electrical engineering. After graduating, he worked for an electrical company and then, through the Fundi Network, built an independent electrical contracting business. The turning point came when he was able to buy a truck:

> *Three years ago...I had a small car - and that car was giving me a lot of problems. And the guy said to me, "like this you can't make it. In order to make it, you must get a truck. But to get a truck is not easy, so the money that you make, you must keep it away, because you are living in my place, so don't pay rent, and that money you can save, and then, until you can get the money that will allow you to buy the truck"* (Interview No. 17, 19 July 2013).

The generosity of his friend, along with substantial remittances from family in Brazzaville, thus allowed him to save up to buy a truck, a key step in the transition to self-employment and even becoming an employer himself. At the time he was interviewed, he was making use of the casual labour system to hire employees for his own business.

By contrast, a single father of three from Goma, DRC, had failed to secure even a subsistence wage since his arrival in South Africa in 2005. At the time of the interview, he was still earning less than the bare minimum to support his family. A key means of survival was the generosity of fellow Congolese – one woman in particular allowed him and his young daughters to live with her family and contribute what he could to the rent whenever possible. He continued to have little success obtaining formal employment based on his office work experience. Furthermore, the casual jobs he did obtain as a painter never translated into longer-term projects. Since painting is a job that utilizes common skills, he competed with a large pool of applicants for each job. Painting is a low-paying occupation – about ZAR250 per day compared to an electrician or carpenter's ZAR350 per day. Finally, as a refugee from war-torn eastern DRC, he had endured considerable trauma at home, having lost most of his immediate family to a combination of war and illness. The effect of this loss, paired with the strain of caring for his young daughters, was extreme mental anguish, which undoubtedly interfered with his ability to find and secure work.

A 28-year-old participant from Kinshasa, DRC, had come to South Africa the previous year, in 2012, with only a basic understanding of English. He occasionally received remittances from his sisters, who live in Europe, in the form of cologne, electronics and cash. When he was first interviewed, he had steady employment as a painter and general labourer, and attended free English classes in the afternoons at a local refugee aid organization. In the following year, he went through a series of jobs but in an upward trajectory. He had found work in a private security firm, which eventually led him to a hospitality training programme. He was able to do the programme because the owner of the house where he worked as a security guard gave him a lump sum of ZAR1,500 for tuition, an amount he would otherwise have had difficulty obtaining. That programme resulted in him finding work as a waiter in a high-end restaurant in Cape Town's southern suburbs where he had been fully employed for several months.

A 20-year-old mother from eastern DRC had one of the most precarious work situations in this study. A survivor of rape while still in the Congo, she came to South Africa to join her sole remaining family member, and supports her two-year-old daughter out of the money she earns working two days a week as a domestic worker in Woodstock and Paarl, each for ZAR150 per day. She shares a room in a rented apartment with eight other individuals and pays rent monthly. Unlike the previous male respondent with three children, she did not receive much support from community members in looking after her daughter. This difference in community support may be gender-based – while single parenting as a father is seen as an aberration, hers, despite resulting from an unwanted pregnancy, is not. A sentiment expressed by many of the Congolese women interviewed was that "to be a woman, you have to learn how to suffer." The lack of support had a direct effect on her employment prospects. At the time of the interview, she had recently turned down a job washing dishes in a restaurant because transportation and child-care costs would have outweighed the additional income.

What these individual stories illustrate is the considerable heterogeneity of experience among this group of "refugee" labourers. While two were able to build and then leverage their social and kinship networks financially, and successfully move from insecure or undesirable work into more secure and higher-earning jobs, the others had so far been unable to move beyond casual, low-status employment, and seemed trapped in precarious labour.

Those who arrived in South Africa without dependants, and were well-educated, urban and middle-class, could draw on family members for financial support. Each also had a "lucky break" through a generous friend or employer providing a "rent holiday" or financial assistance for skills development or business investment. The others lacked the same social capital or connections that could provide a launching point into formal employment.

Further, there is a clear gender bias in how success is attained. In contrast to the casual jobs that the men were able to secure, work as a domestic labourer was comparatively socially isolating for the women involved. Male participants commonly worked as part of a team, such as on a construction site, thereby allowing them to build their language skills and open up a web of possible social and business connections. Domestic labour, such as washing dishes, doing laundry and cleaning homes, does not offer these same possibilities. Particular home country experiences are also an important consideration, as some had experienced severe personal trauma related to the conflict in eastern DRC. Although the stories above are all drawn from refugee narratives, casual labour is used by individuals to varying effect, based upon the other resources on which they are able to draw. The evidence suggests that it can, in conjunction with social capital, individual ambition and sheer good luck, act as a stepping stone to more secure, formal employment.

HAWKING AND TRADING: STREET-SIDE STALLS TO SPAZA SHOPS

Perhaps the most visible livelihood strategy in which forced migrants engage is hawking and various forms of street-side selling. This is undertaken either on foot or out of stalls that line roadsides carrying heavy pedestrian traffic, such as near taxi and bus ranks. Passers-by have access to a series of hawkers' stands that sell an ever-changing combination of sweets, cigarettes, and fruit and vegetables, as well as cosmetic and hygiene products, clothing and shoes. Artisanal craft traders operate from various sites including traffic intersections, tourist destinations, or in markets that have themselves become tourist destinations, such as Greenmarket Square located in central Cape Town.

Another common migrant trading enterprise is the spaza shop, the small convenience store found in informal and low-income residential areas of South African cities. These forms of retail activity are variously complementary, collaborative, or in competition with those of South African nationals. This has sometimes made the migrants targets of xenophobic violence (Crush, 2008; Charman and Piper, 2011, 2012; Gastrow, 2013). Other constraints include the pressure to remit money to family members in their countries of origin and the extra time required to keep their refugee papers and asylum-seekers' permits up to date. As with the casual labour livelihoods described above, factors such as family relations, gender roles and sheer good (or bad) fortune also affect the success or otherwise of their businesses.

Outside a Shoprite supermarket in Mowbray – a neighbourhood near the University of Cape Town – are a series of hawker and vegetable stands. Two Zimbabwean women in their late 20s who operate vegetable stalls were doing a brisk trade during the early afternoon when they were interviewed. Their livelihoods are based on low-margin trading: buying bunches of various greens for six rands and selling them for seven, thus making a one rand profit on each transaction. Because the margin is so slight, ensuring a high number of sales each day is crucial. As one explained, "when you don't open, you lose money." The need for a high daily sales volume is threatened by the bureaucratic requirement for refugees and asylum-seekers to return regularly to the Department of Home Affairs where they initiated their claim in order to renew their permits. The length of time between renewals depends on the individual case, and can range between one day, in extreme cases, to just once a year, as determined at the discretion of the immigration officer.

The majority of participants renew their papers every two to six months. This has a serious impact on income earning, as each day spent queuing at Home Affairs means a day not spent working, and thus not earning any income. The two women also spoke about the long hours, high expense and hard labour involved in acquiring their produce: a twice-weekly event which involves travel by train, bus and by foot to transport the sizable bags of greens from the local markets in Ottery and Epping to Mowbray. Both women had found their vendor locations through word-of-mouth networking, and rental of the space was managed through verbal agreement with the "owner" of the space, who rents the space from the City in his own name. They store their produce nearby which, along with rental of the space, costs them ZAR550 every month – a considerable amount, given that each woman estimated she made only ZAR2,000 after expenses each month.

Asked where they would like to be in five years, both women said they hoped to be doing something other than selling vegetables. Although it provided an income, it was not a "good job." For many migrants, running a marginal stall or a shop is still preferable to being an employee. One of the women had left her previous job working at a guesthouse in order to deliver and look after her second child and was optimistic about her new trade as a vegetable seller:

> *Here is better... it's better to get my three hundred or two hundred a day... than to get three-fifty a week... they don't want to increase the money – that's why this is better for me* (Interview No. 24, 25 July 2013).

The freedom of self-employment is compromised by the inherent uncertainty of running a business. While earning two or three hundred rands a day may seem to be a healthy income, day-to-day income fluctuates widely. Most participants highlighted that at the beginning of the month, when paycheques are received, sales are high and business is good, but by the end of the month, when earnings have been spent, sales taper downward until the next month's pay period.

The need to work in order to survive in South Africa, but also to remit money home, is an intense pressure that trumps everything else. An illustrative example is a 26-year-old Somali woman who sent her young son back to Somalia so that she could open up a shop and start remitting money to relatives:

> *[My husband] told me, you can't work if you have a small kid – you can't work outside [but] he doesn't have enough money to give me – he's paying rent, and then he's paying Pampers, milk, food. Whatever he had he gave me, but I don't have money to send to my family, and so the family suffered in Somalia. I sent [my baby] to Somalia. My baby is now staying in Somalia. My mom took the baby and then I can work hard. I'm a strong woman, I get everywhere to buy stuff, I have money to survive, and then I will rent house. But now I am living in only room, by myself* (Interview No. 3, 13 June 2013).

The pressure to support her family in Somalia, including her mother and eight younger siblings, was sufficient for her to ignore cultural expectations that a young mother should stay home and care for her children and instead open up a shop. Her decision came at a price. Not only was her young child back in Somalia, but her marriage eventually ended over continued disagreements between her and her husband over her decision to work. Her situation not only demonstrates the strongly gendered ideas about work and social roles in many migrant communities, it shows the significance that migrants attach to earning sufficient income to remit money back home. This is something for which they are prepared to endure considerable personal sacrifice and self-exploitation.

Her hard work and entrepreneurship were evident as she described how she had built up her business from a ZAR3,000 investment, given to her by her husband, by buying and reselling items in the Bellville business district, gradually expanding the scale and scope of her trading:

> *I asked him for R3,000 and I bought socks, sunglasses, and earrings, and then I put them in big plastic [carton] outside in the taxi rank, in Bellville. People come and say "Hey, how are you" and picked earrings and sunglasses. With the small money I got, I made this stand. And then when I made a stand, I bought two tables, and put them this side. And then I worked and got enough money - I put in clothes, I put this side jackets, this side clothes. It is now three years [since I started the business]* (Interview No. 3, 13 June 2013).

In economic terms alone, she might be considered a refugee success story. Another successful entrepreneur was a Congolese woman who makes her living operating a small grocery stall in Cape Town's main bus terminal, where she had been selling for over 10 years. Unlike the others, who sell local produce, she sells imported food products from the DRC. Though her trade is based on selling foreign goods, she acquires her stock through an in-country process whereby money changes hands (via intermediaries) several times in South Africa before the products reach her shop. This is noteworthy for two reasons. First, a variety of individuals are employed in South Africa in transporting the goods; and second, she is not overtly competing with South African counterparts, as they are unlikely to sell Congolese products.

One major form of competition between foreign traders and their South African counterparts is for physical space in trading sites, whether formally or informally managed and controlled (Hunter and Skinner, 2003). This scramble for space emerged again and again in the interviews with hawkers and traders. One extreme example concerns a young Somali woman who was working as an itinerant clothes seller. Because she could not secure a permanent place to sell her goods, she was travelling between Cape Town, Port Elizabeth and Johannesburg and walking door to door in Somali neighbourhoods to sell clothing, finding places to stay as she went. The Congolese woman discussed above who operates her own imported foods stand, noted with some resentment that South Africans get preferential access to the City's trading sites in Cape Town's bus terminal. The difficulty of accessing retail space not only happens in the central business district, but also in neighbourhoods outside of the city core. One spaza shop operator in Mitchell's Plain described how his rent continued to rise as his landlord threatened to find a new tenant who was willing to pay more.

Most of the individuals engaged in street and spaza shop trading can be classified as survivalists rather than successful entrepreneurs. Their businesses have low market entry costs, but also low profit margins, and very little possibility for significant growth or advancement. Family networks can be both an asset and a liability, supplying start-up capital but also pressuring them to remit money which they might otherwise save or reinvest in their businesses. Although some respondents had managed to establish themselves with a degree of long-term security, the livelihoods of many remained highly precarious despite their hard work and considerable personal sacrifice, often at the cost of a stable family life and their own personal safety.

ARTISANS, WIREWORKERS AND ARTISTS

The artisan industry, which caters primarily to tourists visiting Cape Town, is an important form of self-employment among migrants (Visser and Rogerson, 2004). Among the items associated with this form of business are wire-beaded and metalwork sculptures, carvings of animals and wooden utensils, and various kinds of art, including paintings as well as potato-print and tie-dye cloth, which are made and sold for a profit. This informal industry, which clusters geographically around tourist attractions, includes a diversity of actors from different countries. Certain sectors are associated with particular nationalities. The local cost and availability of materials, which can differ significantly between cities, also affects artisans' choice of media. In Johannesburg, Zimbabweans are known for their stone and wood sculptures, which are carved from materials sourced in Zimbabwe. Due to the geographical distance, Zimbabwean artisans in Cape Town choose to specialize in wire and beadwork as the materials are easier to source and the margins are greater (Interview No. 1, 25 May 2013).

The artisanal craft trade is complex, with a series of internal rules and conventions. As with street traders and hawkers, space is at a premium and competition fierce. Newcomers have to fight and negotiate to gain a place on the street to sell their goods, a process that can take several weeks or even months. Sellers range from individuals, normally migrants, selling crafts they have made themselves to established South African business owners selling bought pieces in brick and mortar shops. Some migrants act as intermediaries selling a variety of items sourced from artisans within Cape Town or from other artisans across

South Africa and other parts of the continent. Several vendors interviewed for this study said that they travelled back and forth, buying goods such as items made of malachite or wooden masks in their home countries (for example, Senegal and the DRC) and then selling them at a profit in South Africa.

Two of the Zimbabwean artisans in this study were interviewed in Kalk Bay and Camps Bay, respectively. They had come to South Africa with the specific intention of pursuing their art as a business in South Africa. Both had studied various art techniques in Zimbabwe and acquired these skills while still in high school. While these skills have translated into a steady revenue stream in Cape Town, both men had previously worked in other industries, and in other countries (Namibia, Botswana and Swaziland) before coming to South Africa. This had given them a chance to further improve their skills through practice and instruction from peers with more refined techniques. Both men showed considerable business acumen and skill – for instance, by making contact with organizations for commissioned works, and constantly searching for new venues and outlets through which to display and sell their crafts. Both participants employed web searches and word-of-mouth networks to secure tables at weekly markets or larger events. One noted that although the cost to rent a table at the National Arts Festival in Grahamstown was expensive – over ZAR4,000 for 10 days in addition to transport and other expenses – when shared between four friends, it was "worth it" because of the considerable profit to be made. One described how his artistic decisions are mediated by his business practice as follows:

> I taught myself after school. [I do] paintings, bead and wire, metal…at the moment, I like these townships [paintings], because they're cheap, cheap material. I don't buy anything, only the paint, which is very cheap, compared to the beads and wire, which is very expensive. Like this [painting], the production cost is R5 or maybe even less but I can sell it for R80. I would have gone for work in a restaurant or somewhere here in Cape Town, but art is better for me (Interview No. 2, 8 June 2013).

The wire-working industry is heavily male-dominated, perhaps because among young men in the trade, wire working is "an esteemed trade, a masculine domain" (Matshaka, 2009: 73). Asked why the artisan trade was almost exclusively male, one man responded:

> The only thing is with the craft you have to be strong. You have to be patient – you sit at home, like a week, you produce, then maybe on the weekends you come out, you come to Camps Bay, and you don't sell anything. I've seen a lot

of people trying to do crafts – they tried, at first they were patient, but later on, they're like, "ah no." And they're doing something else now. To be a crafter? You need to be patient and work hard. Like for me...I paint until two a.m., then I sleep maybe four hours or so, and then I get up and dry things and then I come here (Interview No. 2, 8 June 2013).

In her fieldwork on Cape Town's wire workers, Matshaka (2009) notes that she encountered only two women engaged in the sale of these crafts. The implication of the above opinion – that women do not sell crafts because they lack patience and a good work ethic – is disproved by the many successful female entrepreneurs interviewed for this study. Rather, the imbalance of female artisans and sellers probably has more to do with factors such as willingness to approach tourists repeatedly, in English, to make a sale; access to mentors willing to train women in the craft; and their ability to contend successfully – verbally and sometimes physically – with other artisans for a space to sell their wares. For the men involved, selling wire crafts was not only a means of securing an income, but also a path to self-employment. One participant expressed this as the freedom of self-determination – to decide what to sell, and when, and not to have to be beholden to a boss.

The artisanal sector spans survivalist, entry-level participants right through to successful craft entrepreneurs. In general, this sector appears to accord higher status and generate greater earnings relative to other forms of trading, despite having similarly low entry costs. Although the basic form of the artisans' livelihood is similar to that of street traders and hawkers, their income is based less on numerous low-margin transactions and more on a smaller number of more lucrative transactions, primarily with tourists. There seemed to be a wide range of income levels, but most of the artisans indicated that they were working in the sector because the income was steady enough to make it worthwhile. It was also preferred to casual labour or even formal employment in the service sector.

HAIR SALONS AND HAIR BRAIDING

Despite the widespread presence of migrant-operated hair salons in South Africa, there is very little research literature on this particular kind of migrant entrepreneurship. An investigation into the types of foreign workers in Durban found that 32 per cent were involved in cutting hair as a primary activity (Hunter and Skinner, 2003). In areas such as Mowbray and Claremont in Cape Town, there are several brick and mortar hairdresser and barber shops clustered together in order to draw students from the University of Cape Town as well as passing shoppers. In the main minibus stations, women advertize their hairdressing services with placards displaying the various styles available to passing commuters. Two aspects of this industry make it particularly interesting: first, it offers a low-cost entry-level job for self-employed women; and second, it has a reputation for being a business with a high proportion of non-South Africans.

Many women from the DRC and Congo-Brazzaville are to be found working and running hair-braiding salons across the city of Cape Town. One hair salon owner said that when she arrived in 2002 from Kinshasa, few South African women were braiding their hair. As more Congolese women migrated to South Africa and opened shops, South African women started having their hair braided in salons. In Cape Town, the hair-braiding salons represent a significant industry and source of income for migrant women. All the braiders interviewed for this study had non-professional experience braiding hair before coming to South Africa and, for this reason, considered it a suitable job for them to undertake. With flexible hours of work, and the possibility of bringing their children to work with them, working as a hair-braider accommodates women's childcare duties better than other kinds of work.

There is also a clear progression in the sector. Hair-braiders typically begin working as apprentices, making an incremental amount of money to help the salon owner or other braiders complete a job. Despite the small amounts, this money still plays a vital role in some families. One Congolese braider whose husband had postponed cataract surgery until he became blind, was supporting her family of two adults and five children on their dwindling savings and the money she was making as a hair-braiding apprentice. Although her older children mocked the meagre earnings of around ZAR200 per week, she pointed out that it was able to cover part of the weekly grocery budget.

As apprentices progress, they start bringing in their own clients and pay commission to the salon owner:

> For the beginning, I was working outside. After that, I met my husband here, and then my man. He was the one who looked for a place for me because he said I could not work because it's winter. I was working and getting just forty per cent. You do something for R100 and the boss pays you R40. Imagine for the month how much you're going to get! After that, I started to think about having my own place. To have the shop here is really difficult. I learned about this place my friend was renting here. She told me, "you cannot continue working for the

people – you can take my place." And then I came here – it's been one year already (Interview No. 21, 23 July 2013).

Asked whether business was good, she replied in the negative, saying that sometimes she got enough money to eat and to pay the rent even though she was also renting chairs to others. She said that she was "going to start selling my body" so that she could continue to rent a place to stay. Asked how much she made from a typical job, she responded:

> *It depends – you can braid for R150, R200, R80, R100. It depends what the person wants. And also, I'm not going to plait alone, I'm going to plait with my sisters – you need to share the money. You see like now, it's quiet, no one [is] here. Sometimes you can have customers, like three, four customers here, it depends. Like now it's the month end, it's supposed to be busy, but it's quiet.*

Over the course of the study, it became clear that working in a salon was considered a "natural" job by and for migrant women. Women working as hair-braiders and running salons do not actively frame themselves as self-employed, but rather describe this work as better than the alternative of sex work. For the male artisans, in contrast, being self-employed was a way of publicly asserting their agency through self-employment. Two separate Congolese ethnic organizations interviewed for this study were already either involved with or in the planning stages of a programme that would help migrant women start their own hair salons. The fact that both organizations appeared to be run almost exclusively by men suggests that hair-braiding is seen as a job that is appropriate for a woman, perhaps because it is a service that is largely performed by women for other women.

Hair-braiding salons are places where migrants employ other migrants, and a rare example of an industry where, by and large, women train and employ other women. As with hawking and trading, some hair-braiders had received financial or other assistance from a friend or family member to establish themselves, but they in turn helped others. Migrants are also able to achieve upward mobility, unlike the low-level trap of domestic service.

BUSINESS ROBBERIES

An extremely common theme that emerged in the study was the amount of violence that many experience, particularly in township areas of Cape Town. Two of the men – both spaza shop owners originally from Somalia – described armed robberies that were considerably more violent than those related by other respondents. Both men described multiple occasions when they, or those they were with, had been threatened and physically attacked in the course of armed robberies. One had large scars on his leg and stomach from when he was shot while operating his shop. After being attacked and having the stock from his shop plundered, he was hospitalized for 23 days for complications related to the attack.

The other, who had previously operated a shop in Khayelitsha and was operating one in Mitchell's Plain at the time of the interview, had also experienced multiple armed robberies. His shop assistant had also been critically wounded after being stoned by a group of youths. He summed up his experience as follows:

> As for safety, it is very bad in South Africa for refugees, especially for Somalians. If they see [a] Somalian, they think they've got money. But money is very difficult – if you sell sweets and what-what, and small groceries, if you sell that stuff, maybe, plus minus, you can get more than R2,000 or R3,000 per month. Then, early in the morning, you wake up, you try and buy some stock. The people, they see this money and they think that you've got a lot of money (Interview No. 6, 24 June 2013).

Both men's experiences reflect a common pattern in which Somali traders operating businesses in townships are disproportionately affected by some kinds of crime – particularly business robberies that include looting, arson and murder (Gastrow and Amit, 2012). Many migrant shop owners sleep in their shops to try and prevent theft. Not only is the level and frequency of such crimes alarming, it has serious consequences for the livelihoods of traders. Robberies from shops, often of mobile phone airtime credits or other valuable items, cut sharply into their monthly earnings and represent a considerable strain on their livelihood. Furthermore, given the difficulty of accessing the free health care to which refugees and asylum seekers have a right (Landau, 2006), injuries sustained while working in dangerous areas constitute a further financial drain on shop operators.

CONCLUSION

This chapter has investigated various forms of livelihood practised by forced migrants living in Cape Town, using individual narratives to draw out the diversity of their experiences. The reasons why an individual fails or succeeds involve an intersection of personal, structural and contingent factors. In addition to acquiring skills, training, and experience, improved livelihoods frequently depend on access to social and kinship networks and the kindness or generosity of others, especially for establishing an informal enterprise and in enabling movement from informal to more formal employment. Pre-migration experiences and particular family circumstances also play a role in determining the opportunities and constraints that migrants encounter. Pressure from family members in the home country to remit earnings can impede migrants' economic progress, but personal networks can also be sources of financial and other forms of support to engage in entrepreneurial activity in the first place.

Gender is another important factor. As several of the women's narratives in this chapter have shown, encouragement or opposition from a spouse or other family members can determine livelihood pathways, and influence whether they can embark on any form of income-earning occupation at all. In addition, certain migrant occupations are heavily gendered, such as women in hair braiding and men in craft production and sales, or construction work for males and domestic service for females engaged in casual labour. Within trading and hawking activities, the women in this study were engaged in more marginal and less secure forms of trade, such as itinerant selling or roadside stalls, whereas it was men who ran spaza shops. While this does not mean that men's livelihoods are necessarily easier to secure, it does demonstrate the importance of gender in determining migrants' incorporation into the labour market, whether formal or informal.

A rigid distinction between formal and informal sectors is not especially helpful in understanding the livelihood strategies and pathways of forced migrants. Self-employment or small enterprise is a better description of some occupations, such as running spaza shops or hair-braiding salons. Even the trading and artisanal production systems are embedded in complex procurement and value chains that extend beyond South Africa, intersecting with the formal wholesale and retail sectors in multiple ways. Seemingly unorganized casual employment is connected to labour recruitment agencies and can in practice be more regular and quasi-formal than at first appears. What is also apparent is that refugees and other forced migrants are restricted in their labour options and economic mobility, whether by exploitative employers, bureaucratic and legal hurdles, or hostility from South African nationals. This matches findings from other studies of urban refugee livelihoods, both in other South African cities and elsewhere in the world. As Buscher (2011, p. 25) has concluded: "Regardless of the economic coping strategies employed, the majority of urban refugees, while demonstrating a high level of resilience, remain on the fringes of the economies in which they live. For many their survival is day-to-day, hand-to-mouth subsistence joining the ranks of the urban poor."

REFERENCES

Blaauw, P., Pretorius, A., Schoeman, C. and Schenck, C. (2012) Explaining migrant wages: The case of Zimbabwean day labourers in South Africa. *International Business & Economics Research Journal*, 11: 1333-1346.

Buscher, D. (2011) New approaches to urban refugee livelihoods. *Refuge*, 28: 17-29.

Charman, A. and Piper, L. (2011) Conflict and cohesion in the informal economy: A reassessment of the mobilization of xenophobic violence in the case of spaza shops in Delft South, Cape Town, South Africa. African Centre for Citizenship and Democracy, University of the Western Cape, Cape Town.

Charman, A. and Piper, L. (2012) Xenophobia, criminality and violent entrepreneurship: Violence against Somali shopkeepers in Delft South, Cape Town, South Africa. *South African Review of Sociology*, 43: 81-105.

Crush, J. (2008) The perfect storm: The realities of xenophobia in contemporary South Africa. SAMP Migration Policy Series No. 50, Cape Town.

Devey, R., Skinner, C. and Valodia, I. (2006) Second best? Trends and linkages in the informal economy in South Africa. Working Paper 06/102, School of Development Studies, University of KwaZulu–Natal, Durban.

Gastrow, V. (2013) Business robbery, the foreign trader and the small shop: How business robberies affect Somali traders in the Western Cape. *SA Crime Quarterly*, 43: 5-15.

Gastrow, V. and Amit, R. (2012) Elusive justice: Somali traders' access to formal and informal justice mechanisms in the Western Cape. African Centre for Migration & Society, University of the Witwatersrand, Johannesburg.

Handmaker, J., De La Hunt, L. and Klaaren, J. (eds.) (2008) *Advancing Refugee Protection in South Africa*. New York and Oxford: Berghahn Books.

Hunter, N. and Skinner, C. (2003) Foreign street traders working in inner city Durban: Local government policy challenges. *Urban Forum*, 14: 301-319.

Krugell, W. and Blaauw, P. (2014) Micro-evidence on day labourers and the thickness of labour markets in South Africa. *South African Journal of Economic and Management Sciences*, NS17: 484-500.

Landau, L. (2006) Transplants and transients: Idioms of belonging and dislocation in inner-city Johannesburg. *African Studies Review*, 49: 125-145.

Landau, L. and Segatti, A. (2009) Human development impacts of migration: South Africa case study. Human Development Research Paper No. 2009/05, UNDP, New York.

Matshaka, N. (2009) "Marobot neMawaya" – Traffic lights and wire: Crafting Zimbabwean migrant masculinities in Cape Town. *Feminist Africa*, 13: 65-85.

Sharp, M. (2012) Day labour and xenophobia in South Africa: The need for mixed methods approaches in policy-orientated research. *Urban Forum*, 24: 251-268.

Visser, G. and Rogerson, C. (2004) Researching the South African tourism and development nexus. *GeoJournal*, 60: 201-215.

Chapter Nine

The Role of Migrant Traders in Local Economies: A Case Study of Somali Spaza Shops in Cape Town

Vanya Gastrow and Roni Amit

INTRODUCTION

Much recent anti-foreigner violence in South Africa has targeted migrant-owned shops. The antagonism toward these shops is twofold: first, there is a belief that migrant entrepreneurs engage in unfair trade practices that disadvantage South African-owned shops; and second, there is the related notion that the very presence of migrant-owned businesses is illegitimate, and that local South Africans are therefore entitled to take action to remove these businesses. The tensions stemming from the view that migrants are engaged in unfair competition and that they have no legitimate right to compete in local economies has encouraged interventions by local and national governance structures, both formal and informal, that have sought to regulate and curb foreign business activities. At the local level, mediators have drafted informal agreements limiting the operation of migrant-owned businesses, setting prices, and barring entry into a number of township markets in the Western Cape and Eastern Cape provinces (Gastrow and Amit, 2012; Mkentane, 2011). Nationally, the draft 2013 Licensing of Businesses Bill sought to restrain the business activities of migrants in South Africa.

Public discourse around migrant-owned businesses fails to acknowledge the complexity of both their trading activities and their role in local economies. This chapter therefore examines the business practices of migrant informal entrepreneurs and their role in local economies through a case study of Somali spaza traders in Cape Town. Spaza shops are informal grocery stores operated from private residential properties in low-income neighbourhoods. They sell a variety of products including basic food items such as bread, maize meal and milk, as well as mobile phone airtime, cosmetics and toiletries. Through this case study, the chapter aims to provide a better understanding of the economic dynamics of migrant-run businesses, which can inform the South African informal business sector and help craft interventions that contribute to business development and local economic growth. It also challenges perceptions of migrant business practices as inherently unfair and harmful to local economies in general.

METHODOLOGY

The chapter is based on qualitative field research conducted for the African Centre for Migration & Society at the University of the Witwatersrand between 2010 and 2012 (Gastrow and Amit, 2012, 2013). The research focused on access to justice for Somali traders who were victims of crime and included 188 qualitative interviews with Somali traders, South African residents, police, prosecutors, landlords, South African traders, non-governmental organizations, local government officials and legal aid workers (Table 9.1). The field sites consisted of three township neighbourhoods in Cape Town: Khayelitsha, Philippi East, and Bloekombos and Wallacedene in Kraaifontein. More limited interviews with Somali traders took place in small towns in the Western Cape: Vredenberg, Velddrif, Laingville, Hopland, Tulbagh, Prince Albert Hamlet, Ceres and Caledon. A focus group with 10 Somali traders in Khayelitsha was also conducted, supplemented by an additional six interviews with Somalis specifically on their supply practices.

According to a 2011 police audit of migrant-owned spaza shops in Philippi, Somalis held 69 per cent of the migrant-owned shops (Interview with Philippi East police sector managers, 8 November 2011). Other international migrants involved in the spaza trade in Cape Town include Ethiopians, Pakistanis, Bangladeshis, Burundians and Chinese.

Table 9.1: Location of Study Interviews

Area	Somali traders	South African residents	South African traders	Police	Landlords	Legal Aid	Prosecutors	Other
Khayelitsha	15	14	0	11	1	1	0	3
Kraaifontein	10	10	3	5	2	2	0	2
Philippi	15	35	5	4	4	1	4	3
Small towns	17	0	0	0	0	0	0	0
Other areas	9	6	1	0	0	0	0	5
Total	66	65	9	20	7	4	4	13

SOMALIS IN SOUTH AFRICA

Most Somalis in South Africa have asylum-seeker permits or refugee status. Somalis are one of the most highly represented nationalities in the country's asylum and refugee system (Table 9.2). Between 2001 and 2014, a total of 46,640 asylum applications were recorded from Somalis in South Africa. Of these, a total of 23,057 were adjudicated and 19,287 yielded positive outcomes, giving an acceptance rate of 83.6 per cent. This shows that Somalis are generally seen as credible applicants by the South African asylum system.

Most of these Somalis have fled their country's civil war or political repression in the Somali region of Ethiopia, also known as the Ogaden (HRW, 2008). As asylum seekers and refugees, they are entitled to work, which includes engaging in informal trade. Although some Somali migrants come to South Africa with prior business experience, many others were teachers, civil servants, electricians, learners, herders or in the fishing industry before they left. Yet, the vast majority of Somali migrants in South Africa turn to informal trade and small business to support themselves. In the words of one Somali shop owner:

> That's my shop, where I lost my elder brother [killed by robbers in 2010]. But I have no choice - I have to carry on. Should I be a beggar? Coming to your house and knocking and say 'sister I need a bread'. No. I have more great dignity than becoming a beggar (Interview with Somali trader, 5 June 2012).

Somali businesses include clothing shops, homeware shops, fabric shops, restaurants, laundry services, taxi services, travel agencies, guest lodges, coffee shops, internet cafes, and wholesale or "cash and carry" shops. But by far the most popular form of Somali business is the spaza shop. These shops are set up in the front room of a house or in converted garages while some operate from shipping containers set up in residential front yards.

Table 9.2: Somali Asylum Applications in South Africa

	Applied during year	Total decisions	Total positive	Total rejected	Closed	Recognition rate (%)
2001	359	648	530	64	54	81.8
2004	3,893	238	236	2		99.2
2005	3,774	586	447	122	17	76.3
2006	3,024	299	275	24		92.0
2007	2,041	765	747	18		97.6
2008	8,520	n.d.	n.d.	n.d.	n.d.	n.d
2009	3,580	1,851	1,213	638		65.5
2010	5,959	6,623	5,563	1,060		84.0
2011	9,986	4,308	3,639	669		84.5
2012	3,453	3,640	3,058	582		84.0
2013	2,051	4,099	3,579	520		87.3
Total	46,640	23,057	19,287	3,699	71	83.6

Note: Data for 2002 and 2003 was missing
n.d = no data available
Source: UNHCR Statistical Online Population Database

SOMALI BUSINESS PRACTICES IN THE SPAZA MARKET

Somali spaza shops reflect a high degree of diversity, especially in size and ownership structure. Shops may be solely or severally owned. Some shops operate from small cramped spaces in dilapidated houses. Others are relatively spacious, brightly coloured, and resemble small superettes (or small supermarkets) with space for customers to walk around. There are also Somali wholesalers, not included in this study, who supply smaller spaza shops. A key feature of Somali business practices is that of concurrent cooperation and competition, or what has been termed "coopetition" (Brandenburger and Nalebuff, 1996). Individual shops compete to get the best prices through individual purchasing and bargaining with wholesalers. But they also cooperatively share transport to wholesalers and jointly invest in shops. While these practices represent deliberate choices, other practices are a function of necessity. Almost all Somali traders rent their shop premises because social and financial barriers prevent them from purchasing. Many also feel compelled to sleep in their shops to guard their contents.

Investing in a shop is usually beyond the means of a single Somali entrepreneur. Somalis often address this financial barrier by investing in shops as co-owners. In a study in Motherwell, Port Elizabeth, for example, Hikam (2011) found that only 12 per cent of businesses had sole owners while 87 per cent had co-owners with shares in their business. On average, each Somali shop was co-owned by 2.45 people. Many Somali owners and co-owners interviewed by ACMS first worked for two to three years, saving between ZAR5,000 to ZAR15,000 to co-invest in a shop with other employees. Shop owners also sometimes gave enterprising shop employees a share in a shop to retain them in the business and further incentivize them. Additionally, some entrepreneurs relied on loans from relatives or paid the shop seller in instalments. However, according to Hikam (2011), personal savings from earnings in South Africa provided the most common source of business investment.

Somali entrepreneurs often hold a share in more than one shop. Co-owners set aside shop profits to invest in a second or third shop and then appoint one of the co-owners to manage the new shop, sometimes with the help of an employee. Some co-owners eventually decide to separate and become sole owners of the shops they established together. Among multiple shop owners, most invest in two or three shops, although one respondent owned a small percentage of as many as five shops. His minority shareholding enabled him to spend less time in townships, where he felt unsafe (two of his brothers had been murdered in their shops in separate incidents). Most of his time was devoted to buying sweets in bulk and supplying various spaza shops (Interview with Somali trader, 22 March 2013).

Somali shops depend on high turnover, which leads their owners to locate in areas with a lot of pedestrian traffic. This makes townships and informal settlements appealing areas, as low car ownership means higher pedestrian numbers. Residents in more affluent neighbourhoods are more likely to own cars and drive to distant supermarkets, although some Somalis have set up shops in affluent areas and inner city locations that also have high pedestrian traffic. Somali spaza shops have long operating hours, opening as early as 6am and closing after 10pm. Traders adopt these hours to be more competitive, both with supermarkets and with other spaza shops, as well as to cater to customers on their way to and from work.

Somali entrepreneurs rarely own the properties from which they trade, preferring to rent. They cite a number of reasons for this practice. Many cannot afford to buy immovable property and lack access to state housing subsidies. They also express little interest in purchasing immovable property due to "insecurity" (Focus group with Somali traders, 16 September 2012; Interview with Somali trader, 8 August 2013). They worry about being run out of the area in xenophobic attacks and also fear a local backlash if they tried to purchase houses in the townships. Many also anticipate leaving South Africa to return to Somalia or to settle in a third country.

Somali shops are usually owner-operated, sometimes with the help of employees who are relatives or members of the same sub-clan. Because of high crime rates, shop owners or their employees often sleep on the premises, either in the shop itself or in an adjacent room. Their families generally live elsewhere, mostly in Somali neighbourhoods in Bellville or Mitchell's Plain which have lower crime rates than the townships. Somali women often find work in restaurants, shops and stalls in the central business districts of these areas. In Cape Town, it is unclear what proportion of those working in the shops are owners as opposed to employees. Hikam's (2011) study of spaza shops in Motherwell found that 63 per cent of respondents were shop owners, while 36 per cent were employees.

In sourcing their goods, Somali spaza shopkeepers prioritize obtaining the lowest prices. There is a common perception that most Somalis do this through collective bulk purchasing (see, e.g., Charman et al., 2011). However, the Somali respondents in this study stated that they never engaged in bulk purchasing arrangements and did not know any Somali spaza shop traders who did. Instead, they negotiated and purchased their goods individually, comparing the prices of competing wholesalers from advertising leaflets and information obtained from other traders. Because wholesalers may discount different items (for example, one wholesaler may sell discounted sugar, while another sells discounted maize meal), traders generally divide their purchases among a number of wholesalers and do not make bulk purchases at one wholesaler. Although purchasing was done individually, Somali respondents did say that they coordinated the transport of their goods to reduce costs, either by renting or relying on traders who owned vehicles. They suggested that it is this practice that has given rise to the mistaken perception of collective bulk buying.

Respondents discounted the feasibility of collective bulk buying because of their variable stock requirements that needed to be met quickly and regularly. Collective purchasing arrangements would only delay and complicate their ability to re-stock. Joint purchasing would also create confusion over amounts paid and the division of stock. Respondents did not view the discounts from collective buying as sufficient to justify the effort it would take to separate and re-account for goods. A Somali trader in Franschhoek said that such discounts amounted to less than one per cent of his total purchases (Interview with Somali trader, 30 March 2013). A Somali translator who worked at Philippi Cash & Carry said that the wholesaler offered a two per cent discount on non-promotional items to traders who purchased a minimum of ZAR6,000 in stock (Interview with Somali translator, 6 May 2013). Faced with such low payoffs, respondents opted to negotiate individually with wholesale managers by referencing the prices of competing stores and emphasizing their customer loyalty.

Some respondents who held a stake in multiple shops did report purchasing stock for all of their shops from a single wholesaler to benefit from bulk discounts (Interview with Elsies River trader, 30 May 2013). However, not all of them combined purchases in this way, particularly when co-owners were responsible for managing one particular shop. Joint purchasing for co-owners posed similar inventory and management problems as joint purchasing for single shop owners. Somali supply practices therefore reflect both collective and individual dimensions. While they share pricing information and transport, they negotiate and purchase goods separately. These competitive and collective practices enable them to source low prices for their goods, a benefit that is then passed on to consumers.

Somali shop owners place relatively low mark-ups on their goods and cite both commercial and religious reasons for this practice. Commercially, low mark ups encourage higher turnover. Additionally, respondents noted that Islam forbade selling goods above their market value. Where Somalis' prices were comparable to those in South African-owned shops, respondents attributed this to factors such as their greater variety of stock (entailing higher transport costs), shop rental overheads (usually not experienced by South Africans), and buying from the same wholesalers as South Africans.

Somali shops not only draw customers through competitive prices, they also focus on customer service and demand. The South African respondents consistently ranked customer service at Somali shops as superior to that of South African shops. Somali shops offered wider product ranges, consistent stock, shorter queues, correct change, small discounts to accommodate insufficient customer funds, and flexible quantities (such as a single egg rather than a box of eggs, or a small plastic pouch of sugar as opposed to a whole kilogram). They also sold hampers or bulk packages of goods at a discount. Flexible selling terms also drew customers. Pensioners, for example, often bought goods on credit and paid for their purchases at the end of the month when their pension payments came through. Additional competitive practices included end-of-month sales and special offers to draw customers to their shops. South African shops, by contrast, were generally seen by customers as inferior. They opened later in the morning and closed in the early evening, so residents could not shop there on their way to and from work. Respondents also complained that they were unable to find the goods they needed at South African shops, which regularly ran out of stock and had a narrower product range.

Somali business practices have facilitated both the growth of their shops and their continued sustainability in difficult market circumstances. Key to this success is the ability to draw on the efficiencies of individual as well as cooperative practices. While individual management fosters competition and a degree of flexibility and autonomy over each shop, cooperative practices enable traders to leverage finance and lower transport costs. The success of the Somali spaza shops has inevitably led South African entrepreneurs to blame them for their own decreasing profits.

IMPACT ON THE SOUTH AFRICAN SPAZA SECTOR

South African spaza shops have certainly declined in number and profitability. At the same time, many Somali spaza shops have continued to prosper, contributing to unfounded accusations of unfair practices. However, the Somali entrepreneurs not only run their businesses in a way that is legal and fair, their example could easily be emulated by South African competitors wishing to achieve an equal measure of success. Indeed, South African spaza shop owners possess substantial competitive advantages over their Somali counterparts. Many do not have the added overhead cost of rent, and their shops are less frequently targeted by criminal and xenophobic attackers (Gastrow and Amit, 2012). Additionally, their shared background with their clientele increases their familiarity with customer needs.

While Somali competition does play a role in the declining fortunes of South African-owned spaza shops, it is not the sole factor contributing to South African business struggles in the spaza market. Other challenges include the lack of basic business skills, increasing food prices and the expansion of supermarket chains. In 2009, for example, the City of Cape Town commissioned a comparative survey of 214 migrant and 138 South African spazas in Khayelitsha (KLS, 2009). Among its findings was that the majority of South African spaza shop owners lacked basic business skills. While 93 per cent of migrant respondents kept business records, for example, only 28 per cent of South African respondents did so. Additionally, 94 per cent of migrant respondents utilized cashbooks compared to only 58 per cent of South African respondents.

Another factor that has hit South African spazas particularly hard is food price inflation, which has outpaced standard inflation in recent years, increasing the proportion of income that South Africans spend on food (LRS, 2012; National Agricultural Marketing Council, 2014). The decreased affordability of food is likely to be felt more acutely in poorer communities - where many spaza shops are located – thus reducing consumer demand (Jacobs, 2012; Frayne et al., 2010). One spaza shop owner identified food price increases as a key business challenge:

> Everything is going up up up... In 2005 when I started having a shop in Khayelitsha oil was R9 and I'd sell for R12 or R13. Flour was R20 in 2005 and now it's R51. Now Sasko flour is R65. Snow Flake flour is R63 (10kg). Oil in 2005 was R9, now it is R30... Sugar was about R40 or R50 at that time, now it's R76.99. Expensive sugar now (the best brand) is R84 for 10kg. So what do you see here - everything is going up... Everything is going up, everything is going up. So everything is going down. People are not employed, where are they going to get the money? (Interview, 6 November 2011).

Somali-owned shops' wider range of products helps to offset the impact of price increases and maintains their competitiveness with both local spaza shops and supermarkets. Longer operating times also enables them to draw customers when supermarkets and local spazas are closed.

South African spaza shops that fail to adjust their prices, services and operating times are less competitive with supermarkets. In the last several years, supermarkets have increasingly entered Cape Town's township market (Battersby and Peyton, 2014). In 2009, for example, the Gugulethu Square shopping centre opened in central Gugulethu. The shopping centre contains a Shoprite and Superspar and is easily accessible by foot from surrounding residential areas. Khayelitsha now has six supermarkets - three Shoprites, two Spars and one Pick n Pay. The low prices and wide product ranges at these shops draw customers away from less competitive spaza shops. Residents weigh the prices and services at spaza shops against those of supermarkets. Somali owners were keenly aware of this practice and worried that adopting the higher prices charged by South African spaza shops would cause them to lose customers to nearby supermarkets.

A study conducted by the Sustainable Livelihoods Foundation points to other factors that have also hurt South African spaza traders (Charman et al., 2011). The study surveyed 50 South African households in Delft South, Cape Town, including 11 respondents who had run a spaza shop in the previous five years. Of these, seven had been forced to close for reasons unconnected to competition from migrant entrepreneurs including the transfer of the business to relatives, debt stemming from outstanding customer credit, drug addiction, and witchcraft. Only four former spaza owners attributed their exit from the market to competition from migrant entrepreneurs.

Nevertheless, Charman et al. (2011) claim that migrant entrepreneurs (mostly Somalis) are predominantly responsible for the decline of South African spaza shops. They argue that the ability of migrant entrepreneurs to negotiate bulk discounts through collective procurement enables them to outcompete South African traders who cannot adopt the practice due to a lack of trust. In addition, the authors argue that migrant traders are "wealthy entrepreneurs" who have an economic advantage over South African spaza traders (Charman et al., 2011: 2). According to them, migrant traders invest between ZAR25,000 and ZAR35,000 in starting up shops, and "each buying collective" can "afford to maintain a vehicle permanently on the road" (Charman et al., 2011: 19).

Charman et al. (2011) do not explain the origins of this specific information on buying collectives. However, this study's own field observations and interviews with Somali traders provide an alternative picture of Somali trade practices and call into question the claim that bulk buying collectives and personal wealth constitute widespread phenomena among them. The Somali spaza traders interviewed for this study purchased goods on an individual basis. Rather than operating as wealthy entrepreneurs, many set aside personal savings over several years of work and invested jointly with other shareholders. Many did not own their own vehicles, and coordinated transport and other costs with other traders. Further research is therefore needed to determine the extent of Somali buying collectives in the spaza market and their influence relative to simpler collective practices (such as sharing transport) in increasing competitiveness.

The fate of South African traders is also not necessarily that of "quiet surrender" (Charman et al., 2011: 23). Many South African traders have chosen to exit the spaza market because the entrance of Somalis into the sector has created a new economic opportunity: becoming a landlord. The 2011 study of 129 spaza shop owners in Motherwell found that the previous users of the properties of 47 per cent of the Somali traders were South Africans. Eighty nine per cent of these properties were either operational or dormant business premises when acquired by Somalis (Hikam, 2011). By renting out their shops, former South African spaza owners were able to tap into a passive monthly income stream. This regular income enables them to engage in other businesses, take on extra work, or simply devote their time to personal or community affairs. This is not a form of "quiet surrender," but rather of active collaboration and mutual economic advantage.

Some South African traders adopted other competitive strategies and reported business growth as a result. A shop owner in Kraaifontein, for example, attributed increased profits over the previous year to shop renovations and the adoption of practices used by nearby Somali shops (Interview, 16 November 2011). These included offering bulk discounted hampers of products to customers, offering a wide product range, and maintaining adequate stock. A Gugulethu shop owner had experienced growth by adopting practices that drew customers to his shop, such as selling items in differing quantities (using a "save-rite machine" that weighed products such as sugar and flour) and selling electricity vouchers (Interview, 10 February 2012).

SOUTH AFRICAN BENEFICIARIES OF SOMALI ENTREPRENEURSHIP

The vocal dissatisfaction of South African traders with their migrant entrepreneur competitors has led to the framing of migrant-run businesses as generally harmful to local economies. The presence of migrant entrepreneurs is repeatedly portrayed as the primary cause of South African spaza business difficulties (Davies, 2013; Sapa, 2013; Mtyala 2011; Johns, 2011; Styan, 2012). An examination of the broader economic landscape does not support this view. South African spaza shop owners are also hampered by increased supermarket competition, rising food prices, and inadequate business training, none of which are given much attention in explaining their business problems.

Moreover, consumers, wholesalers, landlords, and South African employees in Somali shops (particularly in the connected economy of Bellville) have all reaped economic benefits from Somali shops. These shops also provide potential entry points for small-scale suppliers and manufacturers. The list of economic benefits departs from the negative portrayal that emerges from an exclusive focus on South African shop owners and their interests.

As mentioned above, Somali shop owners usually rent their shops from South African landlords, many of whom were spaza shop owners themselves. Rental amounts ranged from ZAR900 to ZAR1,500 per month for front yard container shops in Philippi, and from ZAR2,000 to ZAR4,000 for a portion or the whole of a small brick house. According to the police, landlords in all three field sites (Kraaifontein, Philippi East and Khayelitsha) were generally pleased with these arrangements (Interviews with Harare police sector managers, 20 December 2011; Kraaifontein police officer, 24 April 2012; Philippi East sector managers, 8 November 2011).

Two cases are illustrative of this trend. In Philippi East, a former South African spaza shop owner sold his struggling spaza business to Somali traders in 2003 for ZAR70,000 and rents the property to them for ZAR4,000 per month. Selling his shop and renting the property enabled him to focus solely on his second business, a shebeen that was doing well financially (Interview, 22 November 2011). The wife of another former South African spaza shop owner in Philippi East also described the economic gain achieved by renting out her husband's shop after he became too ill to continue operating it. The shop rental has provided the couple with a continued source of income since the husband can no longer work (Interview, 22 November 2011). Other beneficiaries of renting include single mothers and community volunteers with no other sources of income.

Anecdotal evidence suggests that the growth in migrant-owned spaza shops has opened up opportunities for small-scale suppliers and manufacturers. These small businesses are typically unable to access larger supermarkets. Small fruit and vegetable suppliers interviewed in Kraaifontein sourced fruit and vegetables from nearby farms and sold the produce directly to spaza shops. Somali shop owners also mentioned buying cosmetics from South African door-to-door sellers, selling locally made "*vetkoek*" (a type of fried dough) and fudge, and locally sourced traditional medicines.

Wholesale businesses have also benefitted from the growth in Somali spaza shops, potentially increasing employment opportunities for South Africans in the sector. Somali spaza shops in Cape Town source most of their products from large wholesalers such as Makro, Metro Cash & Carry, and Philippi Cash & Carry. Somali wholesalers also make bulk purchases at large South African wholesalers to sell to the spaza market. As business increases, these wholesalers increase their workforce. Philippi Cash & Carry employed 103 South Africans and two migrants (the manager, and a Somali translator who was employed to facilitate communication with the wholesaler's large Somali customer base). According to the manager, the growth of migrant-owned shops had expanded his customer base and they made up approximately half of his customers. This led directly to increased sales and an expanded workforce (Interview, 12 July 2012). In addition to these large wholesalers, smaller-scale Somali wholesalers found near townships or in Somali neighbourhoods in Bellville and Mitchell's Plain employ South Africans.

More formal Somali businesses in Bellville and Mitchell's Plain are connected with and benefit from the spaza market. Somali spaza shop owners visit Somali neighbourhoods to socialize or meet with colleagues. While there, they frequent Somali businesses such as internet cafes, restaurants, coffee shops, wholesalers, international call centres, guest lodges and laundry services. Some Somali spaza shop owners later invest in these kinds of businesses. Two respondents with spaza shops in townships, for example, later opened businesses in Cape Town's city centre: an internet cafe at the Golden Acre shopping centre, and a small convenience store on Long Street.

Somali businesses in CBD areas employ many South Africans as shop assistants, cleaners, waiters or cooks. The spaza market thus contributes indirectly to South African job creation in connected CBD economies in Bellville and Mitchell's Plain. Some Somali spaza shops also employ South Africans to clean shops and stack shelves. Somali traders explained that owing to security concerns these employees are almost always women.

South African consumers are the greatest beneficiaries of Somali spaza businesses. Most of the township resident respondents who frequented Somali shops believed that these shops had made a positive contribution to their communities. They mentioned a range of beneficial features of Somali shops, including their low prices, long operating hours, product range, stock availability, bulk hampers of goods, flexible quantities, shorter queues, availability of credit and proximity. The most common complaint they had concerned hygiene and the fact that Somalis slept in their shops. Some residents noted that Somali traders bathed with a cup, bucket or 1.5 litre water bottles. Somali traders attributed concerns over bathing to ignorance of Islamic prayer ablution practices. Prayer ablution entails washing one's hands, face, head and feet. Somalis frequently performed prayer ablution outside their shops in view of local residents who believed that they were bathing, and hence that they bathed improperly.

There is no data available on the tax contributions of Somali spaza shops in Cape Town. However, the Motherwell study found that 74 per cent of Somali respondents were registered for income tax, in contrast to a mere 17 per cent of South African respondents. Twenty four per cent of Somali, but only 14 per cent of South African respondents were registered for VAT (Hikam, 2011), although businesses with less than ZAR1 million annually in sales are not required to register for VAT. Most spaza shops do not claim back VAT paid to wholesalers. The Motherwell study calculated that, on average, each Somali spaza shop paid ZAR38,740 in VAT annually (Hikam, 2011). While spaza shops may register for tax, the informal nature of the spaza market makes tax collection and assessment very difficult. The difficulties that refugees and asylum seekers face in opening bank accounts further compound this problem.

CONCLUSION

This chapter has examined the role of migrant-owned spaza shops in broader economic context. From this perspective, the argument that they pose a threat to economic growth and job creation becomes less convincing. They are invariably blamed by South African traders for their own declining businesses, but the latter are not only competing against migrant-owned shops, they are also contending with supermarket entry into the township market, increasing food prices and skills shortages. At the same time, a range of parties benefit – or stand to benefit – from the trading activities of migrant entrepreneurs. These include poor consumers, South African shop owners and residents renting their premises, wholesalers, job seekers, and small-scale suppliers and manufacturers. The inclusion of these parties in economic assessments may lead to the conclusion that, contrary to popular perceptions, these shops are in fact benefitting local economies.

This chapter has also addressed some of the common misperceptions about migrant-owned businesses that play a large role in xenophobic violence against them. While migrant-owned shops do compete with South African-run shops, they neither engage in unfair trade practices, nor is their very presence in low-income areas illegitimate. Their role in the local economy suggests that, rather than constituting a net drain on the local economy, they are in fact providing economic benefits to the residents in these neighbourhoods. Moreover, Somali spaza trading practices show how small operators can survive, compete and grow in a market increasingly dominated by corporate retail. A better understanding of spaza market dynamics and the role of these shops can inform strategies targeting South

African small business growth. Such understanding may also encourage policy makers to leverage – rather than restrain - the full potential benefit of migrant entrepreneurship for local economic growth. Finally, it can help craft a response to xenophobic violence that does not rely on unfairly restricting these migrant-owned businesses.

ACKNOWLEDGEMENTS

This chapter is a revised and updated version of a research report released by the African Centre for Migration & Society (ACMS) at the University of the Witwatersrand, with support from Oxfam and the Atlantic Philanthropies.

REFERENCES

Battersby, J. and Peyton, S. (2014) The geography of supermarkets in Cape Town: Supermarket expansion and food access. *Urban Forum*, 25: 153–164.

Brandenburger, A. and Nalebuff, B. (1996) *Co-opetition*. New York: Doubleday.

Charman, A., Petersen L. and Piper, L. (2011) Spaza shops in Delft: the changing face of township entrepreneurship. Working Paper No. 6, African Centre for Citizenship and Democracy, University of the Western Cape, Cape Town.

Davies, R. (2013) Address to Orange Farm small businesses. At: http://www.youtube.com/watch?v=BGTvJWlTSFg

Frayne, B. et al. (2010) The state of urban food insecurity in Southern Africa. AFSUN Series Report No. 2, Cape Town.

Gastrow, V. and Amit, R. (2012) Elusive Justice: Somali traders' access to formal and informal justice mechanisms in the Western Cape. African Centre for Migration & Society, University of the Witwatersrand, Johannesburg.

Gastrow, V. and Amit, R. (2013) Somalinomics: A case study on the economic dimensions of Somali informal trade in the Western Cape. African Centre for Migration & Society, University of the Witwatersrand, Johannesburg.

Hikam, A. (2011) An exploratory study on the Somali immigrants' involvement in the informal economy of Nelson Mandela Bay. MA Thesis, Nelson Mandela Metropolitan University, Port Elizabeth.

HRW (2008) Collective punishment: War crimes and crimes against humanity in the Ogaden area of Ethiopia's Somali regional state. Human Rights Watch, New York.

Jacobs, P. (2012) Protecting food insecure households against rapid food price inflation. Policy Brief, Human Science Research Council, Pretoria.

Johns, L. (2011) Myriad laws on foreigners 'must change.' *Cape Argus*, 22 September.

KLS (Knowledge Link Services) (2009) An audit of spaza shops in Khayelitsha, Cape Town. Report for City of Cape Town, Cape Town.

LRS (Labour Research Service) (2012). Inflation monitor February 2012. Labour Research Services, Salt River, Cape Town.

Mkentane, L. (2011) Somalis to register with spaza body. *Herald*, 25 March.

Mtyala, Q. (2011) Cele's xenophobic outburst. *Cape Times*, 7 October.

NAMC (National Agricultural Marketing Council) (2014) Food Price Monitor May 2014. National Agricultural Marketing Council, Pretoria.

Sapa (2013) Foreign-owned businesses hampering rural growth – DTI. *City Press,* 10 October.

Styan, J. (2012) ANC calls for regulation of illegal shops. *Witness*, 27 June.

The Role of Networks and Herd Behaviour in the Entrepreneurial Activity and Success of African Migrants in South Africa

Robertson K. Tengeh

INTRODUCTION

The geographical clustering of immigrants from the same source region, background or language has been reported in several migrant destination countries. Epstein and Gang (2010), for example, have noted that migrants choose to live together in enclaves, forming ethnic communities, and tend to carry out a significant proportion of their transactions among themselves. The associated concentration of migrant businesses in certain geographical spaces raises two main questions: first, why has migration resulted in concentrations of populations with particular characteristics in certain areas and not others? and second, why do migrants from a specific background tend to dominate certain entrepreneurial activities?

The prevailing explanation for migrant clustering is the existence of beneficial network externalities (Bauer et al., 2002; Epstein, 2008). According to Epstein and Gang (2010), these externalities are generated when earlier generations of migrants provide shelter, work and assistance in obtaining credit or generally reduce the stress of relocation to a foreign country. Simply put, network externalities imply that migrants will go where they are likely to receive assistance from other migrants (Bauer et al., 2002). Thus, the number of migrants in a certain location directly affects the utility a migrant will receive by joining the ethnic community. According to Fukuyama (2001) and Elfring and Hulsink (2003), the downside of social networks is that strong in-group moral bonding and solidarity reduces the ability of a group's members to cooperate with others not in the group. Another downside of network externalities identified by Epstein (2008; 2010) is that an increase in the number of foreign migrants in the host country inflates competition for jobs available to migrants, thus decreasing their wages. Furthermore, as the number of migrants increase, the native population may become xenophobic (Epstein, 2008).

An alternative explanation for clustering is what is known as the "herd behaviour" hypothesis. According to Bauer et al. (2002), herd behaviour involves new migrants opting to go where they have seen earlier generations go, primarily because they believe the earlier migrants have information that they lack. Thus, herd behaviour is driven less by individual information and preference than by the decisions taken by previous migrants (Epstein, 2008). Although several studies have underscored the importance of networks in migration (Wentzel et al., 2006; Muanamoha et al., 2010; Ryan, 2011), the argument that migrant clustering might be explained by herd behaviour is a recent addition to the migration literature (Bauer et al, 2002). Epstein (2008) notes that the extent to which the clustering of migrants can produce network externalities depends on their numbers, although it is not clear how or why large numbers of people arrive at a particular location or dominate certain entrepreneurial activities. Herd behaviour may also help us to understand the creation of the critical mass of migrants that produces the network externalities large enough to attract others to join.

In South Africa, migrants from similar backgrounds do tend to cluster in certain entrepreneurial activities and geographical locations (Crush, 2008; Harrison et al., 2012; Nyamnjoh, 2013). The country therefore provides a useful case study for examining the relative importance of network externalities and herding behaviour in the choice of migration destination and the decision to engage in entrepreneurial activity. This chapter examines the role played by migrant networks and herding behaviour in shaping the migration intention and entrepreneurial activities of the current generation of African migrant entrepreneurs in Cape Town, South Africa. The main questions addressed in the first part of the chapter are: What role do migrant social networks play in the choice of migration destination? What role do migrant social networks play in the decision to engage in self-employment and entrepreneurial activity? Does herd behaviour play a role in influencing the choice of migration destination and entrepreneurial activities of African migrants in South Africa?

The chapter then examines the business success of migrant entrepreneurs in Cape Town and questions whether social networks are an important factor in that success or whether migrants are able to build their businesses without reference to the material assistance and guidance of others. Following Epstein (2008), the chapter argues that herd behaviour may play a significant role in an individual's decision to migrate to South Africa and to start a business once there. Although there are differences between migrants from different countries, the majority make individual decisions about these matters, without direct advice, input or encouragement from others. However, these decisions do appear to be based on the example provided by previous generations of migrants. Such herd behaviour does not explain why migrant entrepreneurs in South Africa are relatively successful both in growing their businesses and in generating employment for others. The second part of the chapter therefore examines the growth of migrant businesses over time and the role played by social networks in establishing a successful business.

METHODOLOGY

This chapter is based on information from a study of migrant entrepreneurs in Cape Town. The sample population comprised migrants from Cameroon, Ghana, Ethiopia, Senegal and Somalia. Using snowball methods, 135 migrant-owned businesses (27 from each country) were selected. The businesses all operated within the Cape Town Metropolitan Area and had been in existence for three or more years. The majority of those interviewed (66 per cent) were involved in various kinds of trading or retailing activity (Table 10.1). As many as 12 per cent were in mobile phone repairs and the rest were involved in a wide variety of businesses. The businesses surveyed for this study were drawn from three sites: Khayelitsha (site C), Bellville and the Cape Town Central Business District (Table 10.2).

A questionnaire consisting of over 40 closed and open-ended questions was administered face-to-face or telephonically to each respondent. The questionnaire took approximately 45 minutes to answer. Two focus groups of six and seven participants were also held. Participants in each 90-minute session shared their experiences, which were recorded and supplemented by note taking. An abridged transcript was then prepared and the data summarized and coded by identifying idea clusters and key themes. The survey data was analyzed using the Statistical Package for the Social Sciences (SPSS).

Table 10.1: Types of Informal Businesses Surveyed

Business activity	No.	Percentage
Trading	89	65.9
Cellphone repairs	17	12.6
Shoe repairs	4	3.0
Mechanic	3	2.2
Panel-beating	3	2.2
Clothing	2	1.5
Crafts	2	1.5
Electrician	2	1.5
Restaurant	2	1.5
Fridge repair	1	0.7
Manufacturing	1	0.7
Nightclub	1	0.7
Other	8	5.9
Total	135	100.0

Table 10.2: Location and Ethnic Composition of Respondents

	Bellville	CBD	Khayelitsha	Frequency
Cameroon	10	12	5	27
Ethiopia	18	9	0	27
Ghana	0	2	25	27
Senegal	10	17	0	27
Somalia	10	4	13	27
Total	48	44	43	135

The survey and focus groups revealed the clustering of migrants in certain entrepreneurial activities. Ghanaians, for example, dominate in the hair salon and shoe repair businesses. Somalis cluster in clothing, general trading and grocery businesses. Cameroonians are more visible in furniture, general trading, car repairs, and panel beating businesses while Ethiopians prefer clothing businesses, both retail and wholesale. The study results also showed that most Somali businesses were clustered in specific suburban districts such as Bellville in Cape Town and nearby townships. A significant proportion of Ghanaians seem to cluster in these townships too. Entrepreneurs from Cameroon and Senegal preferred street trading and shops in urban and suburban centres.

MIGRATION MOTIVATORS

What motivated these migrants of African origin to move to South Africa and, more importantly, to choose self-employment as an economic activity once there? Just over two-thirds of the respondents said that their primary reason for coming to South Africa was political in nature (Table 10.3). Many of the migrants therefore left their country to seek political asylum as refugees. Just under a third said their main reason for migrating was economic. The main reason for migrating varied considerably from group to group (Table 10.4). All of the migrants from Ethiopia and Somalia (and almost all of those from Ghana) said their motivation was political. In contrast, all of the migrants from Senegal said their reason was economic. Only migrants from Cameroon were divided between those who came for economic (56 per cent) and political (44 per cent) reasons. Very few had originally come to study or to re-unite with family in South Africa.

Table 10.3: Reasons for Migrating to South Africa

	% Agreed	% Disagreed	% Unsure
Political	68.2	31.0	0.8
Economic	31.1	68.9	0.0
Study	0.7	99.3	0.0
Re-unite with family	2.2	70.0	28.0

Table 10.4: Reasons for Migrating to South Africa by Country of Origin

	Cameroon % Agreed	Ethiopia % Agreed	Ghana % Agreed	Senegal % Agreed	Somalia % Agreed
Political	44.4	100.0	96.3	0.0	100.0
Economic	55.6	0.0	13.7	100.0	0.0

Given that distant South Africa would not be the "first country of refuge" for people leaving any of these countries, it is important to know if social networks played any role in their decision to go to South Africa. Similarly for economic migrants, why choose South Africa rather than another country? Most respondents said that they were not directly encouraged or influenced by anyone at home or in South Africa to migrate to the country. Family members in the country of origin played little or no role in motivating most of the respondents to migrate to South Africa (Table 10.5). Likewise, friends in the home country had little influence (3 per cent). Very few were encouraged by family members already in South Africa (only 4 per cent). The most important source of influence was friends already in South Africa (but still only 36 per cent).

Table 10.5: Sources of Encouragement to Migrate to South Africa

I was encouraged to immigrate to South Africa by:	% Strongly agree	% Agree	% Unsure	% Disagree	% Strongly disagree
A family member back home	0.0	0.0	6.7	19.3	74.1
A family member living here in South Africa	4.4	1.5	0.0	33.3	60.7
A friend back home	2.2	0.7	0.0	35.6	61.5
A friend living here in South Africa	25.9	9.6	0.0	47.4	17.0
No one	32.6	28.9	0.7	11.9	25.9

There were significant differences between the different groups in terms of the influence of friends already in South Africa (Table 10.6). The influence of social networks in the decision of the one-third of respondents who were encouraged to migrate to South Africa by friends therefore varies considerably. The influence was greatest in the case of Ethiopians, all of whom had been encouraged by friends to come. At the other end of the spectrum were Somalis, none of whom had been encouraged by friends, and Ghanaians (only 4 per cent). In between were the migrants from Senegal (56 per cent) and Cameroon (18.5 per cent). These variations are confirmed by the majority (two-thirds) of respondents who said that no one had encouraged them to come to South Africa and that the decision was their own. This group mainly consisted of migrants from Somalia, Ghana and Cameroon with smaller numbers from Senegal and no Ethiopians.

Based on these results, it can be concluded that most migrants were not directly encouraged or motivated by other individuals to go to South Africa, and that they were largely self-motivated. Only migrants from Ethiopia and about half of those from Senegal did not fall into this category. The herd behaviour thesis would therefore appear to fit the decision-making process of most migrants who decided on South Africa because they were generally aware that this was a desirable destination for previous emigrants from their country. The focus group discussion suggested that migrants who go to South Africa do not see it as their final destination. As one participant from Ghana observed: "My intentions have not changed. To me South Africa was just a means for me to go to Europe." Again, this would fit within decision-making motivated by herd behaviour.

Table 10.6: Sources of Encouragement to Migrate to South Africa by Country of Origin

I was encouraged to immigrate to South Africa by:	Cameroon % Agree	Ethiopia % Agree	Ghana % Agree	Senegal % Agree	Somalia % Agree
A friend living here in South Africa	18.5	100.0	3.7	55.6	0.0
No one	74.1	0.0	96.3	37.0	100.0

SELF-EMPLOYMENT MOTIVATORS

When and why did the African migrant entrepreneurs interviewed for this study take up self-employment activities in South Africa? On the advice of an older generation of migrants already in the country, many newly-arrived migrants did not bother to seek employment. As many as 56 per cent of the migrants decided to enter self-employment because they were told it was a waste of time looking for a job (Table 10.7). As one Cameroonian man observed: "I was told to keep my qualifications in a safe place as I would not need them any time soon. I did as I was told and was initiated into the hawking business." An even greater number of respondents (61 per cent) said that they chose self-employment because they could not get a job, although this group probably consisted of many who did not bother to look. Again there were notable differences in the way the different groups answered the question. Somalis (at 100 per cent) were most likely to be advised by members of their community not to waste time looking for a job. Others receiving similar advice included Ghanaians (81 per cent), Cameroonians (55 per cent) and Senegalese (44 per cent). Only Ethiopians did not give this as a reason for entering self-employment.

Table 10.7: Self-Employment Motivators

I ended up starting my own business upon arrival in South Africa because:	% Strongly agree	% Agree	% Unsure	% Disagree	% Strongly disagree
I was advised not to waste my time looking for a job	55.6	0.0	0.0	4.4	40.0
I could not get a job	60.7	6.7	0.0	9.6	23.0
I got fired	3.0	1.5	0.7	2.2	92.6
My initial travel plans changed	16.3	14.1	0.0	2.2	67.4
I wanted to be independent	20.0	5.9	5.2	23.7	45.2

Only 26 per cent of the respondents said that they started their own business because they wanted to be independent. This suggests that the majority of respondents did not come to South Africa with a view to establishing a small business but chose self-employment either because their first preference (obtaining a job) was not open to them or because they were advised by others that there was no point in looking for one. Nearly two-thirds of the respondents (64 per cent) said that their first occupation in South Africa was self-employment. Less than 2 per cent said their first occupation was wage employment. Participants in the focus group sessions confirmed that formal employment was virtually unobtainable by new migrants. Many noted the role of an earlier generation of migrants, based on their own experiences and knowledge of the labour market in South Africa, in influencing a new migrant's decision not to look for employment.

Did anyone encourage these entrepreneurs to start their own business or did they simply "follow the herd"? A review of the general literature points in the direction of friends, family and co-ethnics as influencing factors (see, for example, Aldrich and Cliff, 2003; Bagwell,

2008; Barrett et al., 2001; Renzulli et al., 2000). As many as three-quarters of the respondents in this study said that no one had encouraged them to start their own business (Table 10.8). This suggests that the decision to start the business was made independently by the migrants with little input from friends, relatives or members of the same ethnic group. It seems, therefore, that the main influence of previous generations of migrants is a pessimistic outlook on job prospects but that they do not necessarily encourage the new migrant to turn to self-employment as a solution. The fact that starting a business was the route taken by earlier migrants was undoubtedly a big motivator. The new migrants may not have been encouraged by those in their social networks to become entrepreneurs but they did tend to follow the example of others; a conclusion validated by the focus group discussions.

However, around half of the respondents also agreed that they were encouraged to start their own business by friends and 41 per cent mentioned relatives as an important influence. Only a quarter said they were encouraged by other people of similar ethnic background. All of the respondents from Ethiopia, 96 per cent of those from Ghana, 48 per cent of those from Cameroon, and 7 per cent of those from Senegal cited the influence of friends. None of the respondents from Somalia said they were encouraged by a friend to start the business. Only a quarter said that they were encouraged by a member of their own ethnic background. This suggests that at least half of the migrants were influenced in some way by friends and relatives. Exactly what form that encouragement took is difficult to say but it suggests that many migrants were not blindly following the herd but took advice from those in their family and social networks.

Table 10.8: Encouragement to Start Own Business

I was encouraged to start my own business by:	% Strongly agree	% Agree	% Unsure	% Disagree	% Strongly disagree
No one in particular	68.9	6.7	5.2	3.7	15.6
A friend	25.9	24.4	0	12.6	37.0
A relative	21.5	19.3	0	3.0	56.3
A member of my ethnic community	7.4	17.0	0	13.3	62.2

SOCIAL NETWORKS IN BUSINESS OPERATIONS

Support in starting a business may take various forms, other than simply financial, and come from a variety of sources, including family and ethnic networks. A total of 80 per cent of the respondents in the study said that they had used their own resources in starting their business in South Africa. Not many identified family as the source of that support. Only 10 per cent said that most of the assistance came from immediate and extended family in South Africa. Around 20 per cent said that the idea for their type of business came from family.

In terms of start-up capital, most of the entrepreneurs surveyed began with small amounts of less than ZAR5,000: 71 per cent started with between ZAR1,000 and ZAR5,000 and another 18 per cent with between ZAR5,000 and ZAR10,000. Given the difficulties that migrants encounter in raising capital from the formal banking sector (who will not lend to asylum-seekers and refugees), it is of interest how and where they raised that capital and whether they relied on themselves or others (Table 10.9). An overwhelming majority (83 per cent) used their personal savings as a source of start-up capital. Much less important were funds and credit from other family members (25 per cent), goods on credit (23 per cent), and informal money-lenders (4 per cent). However, when it came to acquiring additional funding after start-up, the picture changes in favour of greater reliance on others (Table 10.10). The two most important sources of additional funding are friends (98 per cent) and other migrants from the same country (84 per cent), many of whom are probably also friends. Around 20 per cent turn to family members either in South Africa or in their home country or other countries. Very few can access funding from formal lending institutions even once their business is established (4 per cent).

Table 10.9: Sources of Start-Up Capital

	No.	%
Personal savings	112	83.0
Business credit (goods on terms)	31	23.0
Personal savings from family member	21	15.6
Loan from family member	7	5.2
Loan from informal sources (e.g. stokvel)	6	4.4
Note: Multiple response question		

Table 10.10: Sources of Additional Funding

When I need additional funding I turn to:	% Strongly agree	% Agree	% Neither	% Disagree	% Strongly disagree
My friends	95.6	2.2	0.7	0.7	0.7
People from my country in South Africa	82.2	1.5	0.7	0.0	15.6
My family in South Africa	20.0	0.7	0.7	13.3	65.2
My family back home or abroad	20.0	0.0	0.0	12.6	67.4
The bank	4.4	0.0	0.0	2.2	93.3

These results suggest that although start-up capital comes mainly from personal sources, once the business is established (and presumably flourishing), they can turn to their networks of friends and/or associates from their home country for additional financing. The critical role played by ethnic networks was confirmed across a range of different kinds of support (Table 10.11). The greatest support from fellow migrants from the country of origin came in deciding which line of business to follow and exactly where in the city they should operate. They also provided important assistance in starting the business and advising where to obtain supplies. Friends were particularly important in providing information about new business opportunities.

Table 10.11: Types and Sources of Business Support

	% Strongly agree	% Agree	% Disagree	% Strongly disagree
People from my home country assisted me in choosing my line of business	90.4	1.5	3.0	5.2
People from my home country guided me in choosing where to trade	86.7	5.2	0.0	8.1
If I need information about new business opportunities I turn to my friends	86.7	9.6	3.0	0.7
If I need information about new business opportunities I turn to my ethnic network	80.0	2.2	6.7	11.1
Most of the assistance in starting my business came from my ethnic network	74.1	3.0	10.4	12.6
People from my home country guided me in choosing where to buy or supplier contacts	69.6	20.7	0.0	8.9

INFORMAL BUSINESS SUCCESS

The number of years a business has existed and its sales volume (reflected in the growth of business capital) are good indicators of success (Fertala, 2006). The second criterion of business success was measured by the increase in the value of the businesses from start-up to the time of the interview. The third measure of success is the contribution of the business to employment creation in the country. By selecting businesses that had existed for three years or more for this study, the first criterion of success was satisfied. With regard to the second measure of success, most of the entrepreneurs (71 per cent) started their business with less than ZAR5,000 (Figure 10.1). Another 18 per cent had between ZAR5,001 and ZAR10,000 at start-up. Only 10 per cent had more than ZAR20,000. By the time of the interview at least three years later, virtually all of the businesses had increased in value. None of the businesses were worth less than ZAR10,000 and 64 per cent were worth over ZAR50,000. The greatest group success was among Ethiopians, all of whom had started with ZAR1,000-ZAR5,000 and were worth ZAR50,000-ZAR100,000 at the time of the interview (Figure 10.2). Migrants from Cameroon had the most mixed success although all had increased the value of their businesses to some degree. The Cameroonians also had the greatest number of very successful enterprises (with values of between ZAR100,000 and ZAR500,000). Several Somalis had achieved similar levels of success.

Figure 10.1: Growth of Business Capitalization

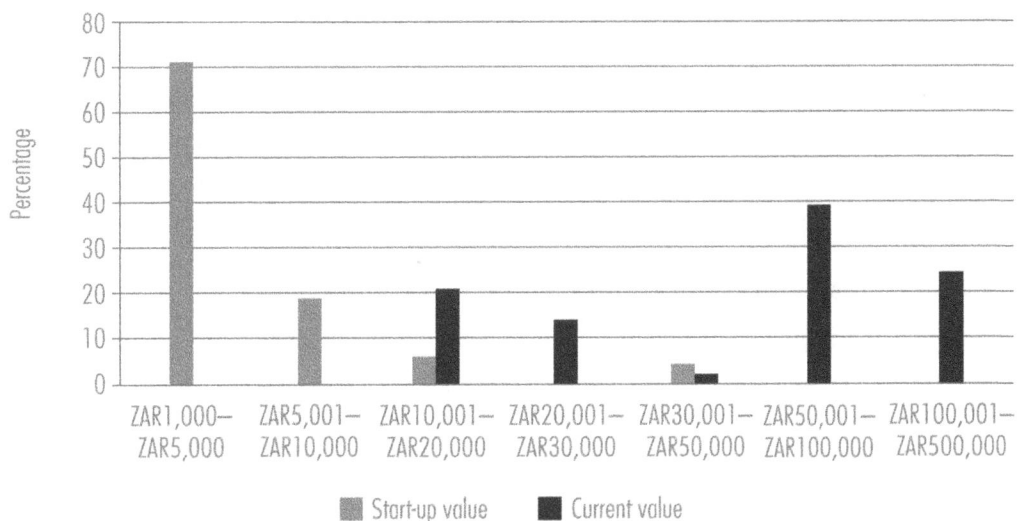

Figure 10.2: Increase in Value of Business Over Time by Country of Origin

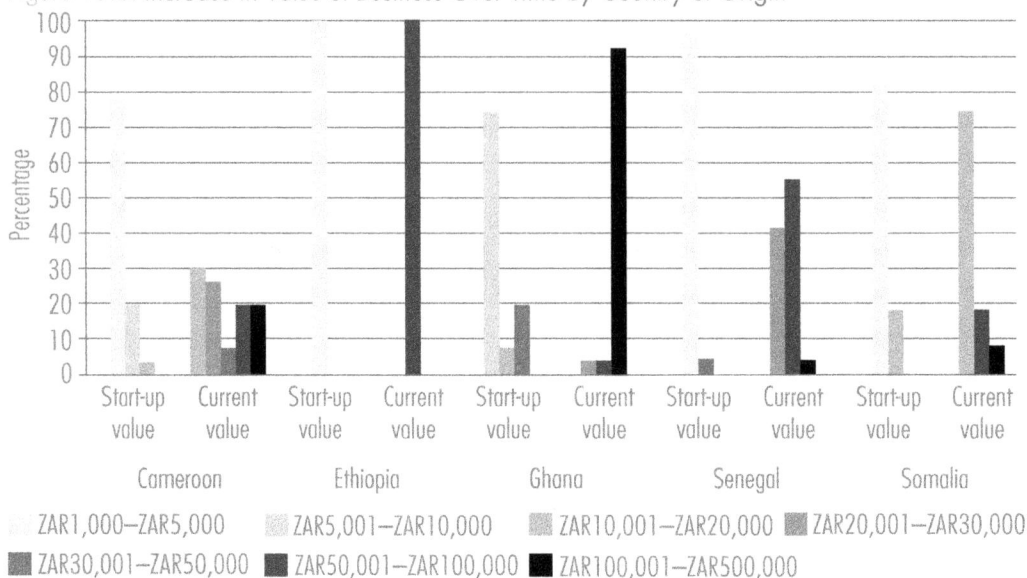

The survey also provided valuable information on the employment creation potential of migrant entrepreneurs. Far from the popular belief and perception that migrants take jobs away from South Africans, the research supports insights from emerging literature that migrant entrepreneurs create employment in South Africa (Kalitanyi and Visser, 2010; Radipere, 2012). Out of the 135 migrant entrepreneurs surveyed, a total of 70 (or 52 per cent) had paid employees while 30 (or 22 per cent) had unpaid employees. The unpaid employees were either children or spouses of the entrepreneur. However, the composition of the paid employees varied widely (Table 10.12). Parents, children and spouses of the entrepreneurs made up around half (53 per cent) of the paid employees, while a significant proportion were migrants from the same country as the entrepreneur (46 per cent).

Table 10.12: Paid Employees of the Enterprise

	No.	%
Father/mother	20	28.6
Wife/partner's relatives	16	22.9
Children	1	1.4
Other relative	1	1.4
Co-ethnics	32	45.7
Total	70	100.0

One important issue that emerged was the change in employment patterns since the establishment of the business. Specifically, the study sought to investigate whether there had been changes in preferences for employing family members, people from the country of origin or South Africans. Interestingly, most of the entrepreneurs did not turn to their family members or to people from their country of origin when they initially established their business. Rather they employed mostly South Africans to help them run their business operations (Table 10.13).

Table 10.13: Source of Workers at Business Start-Up

	Family members	People from my country of origin	South Africans
Strongly agree	0.7	11.9	48.1
Agree	1.5	20.0	21.5
Disagree	41.5	32.6	21.5
Strongly disagree	56.3	35.6	8.9
Total	100.0	100.0	100.0

Clearly, the migrant entrepreneurs prefer employing South Africans during the start-up phase of the business. This is essentially seen as a strategy to overcome some of the barriers they face in running their business, such as language and communication skills. As they become more familiar with the business environment, they gain the confidence to employ their family members or co-ethnics. However, they continue to employ some South Africans. As an entrepreneur from Somalia noted: "When I just started, my stock was so small and employing someone was not an option. But as my stock grew, I employed a South African to sit in for me as I hawked around. Today, I have a South African, a distant relative and my wife assisting in the business."

CONCLUSION

This chapter has examined the role of networks in explaining the migration intentions, geographic and entrepreneurial clustering of African migrants to South Africa. The study questioned the role that migration networks play in shaping the migration intentions and decision to engage in self-employment in the informal economy among the current generation of African migrant entrepreneurs in South Africa. The study of migrant entrepreneurs in Cape Town found that for the majority, migration and self-employment decisions cannot be fully attributed to the influence of social networks. Instead, the chapter has suggested that these aspects of the road to entrepreneurship are characterized more by individual decisions that closely approximate the herd behaviour thesis of migrant decision-making (Epstein, 2008). While the study suggests intergroup differences as far as the role of social networks and herding behaviour is concerned, this can be attributed to mitigating factors not limited to host country conditions, the composition of the ethnic group, time, level of rivalry and activities. The stronger the network ties that characterize an ethnic group, the less likely they will adopt the herding behaviour and vice versa.

Even though there is some evidence that supports the idea that networks play a role in the decision to migrate to South Africa and the choice of self-employment rather than formal employment, it is not a sufficient explanation. However, while most migrants emphasize that their choices were made without encouragement, input or persuasion from others, further research would be necessary to prove that the decisions they made were actually herdlike. What is clear, however, is that once the decision is taken to become an entrepreneur in the informal economy, and the migrant has the capital from their own resources to begin operations, social networks play an extremely important role in the running of the business and therefore in its success. In particular, ethnic and friendship networks, which often overlap, are relied upon by the vast majority of migrants for a variety of types of support, financial and other.

REFERENCES

Aldrich, H. and Cliff, J. (2003) The pervasive effects of family on entrepreneurship: Toward a family embeddedness perspective. *Journal of Business Venturing,* 18: 573-596.

Bagwell, S. (2008) Transnational family networks and ethnic minority business development: The case of Vietnamese nail-shops in the UK. *International Journal of Entrepreneurial Behaviour & Research,* 14: 377-394.

Barrett, G., Jones, T. and McEvoy, D. (2001) Socio-economic and policy dimensions of the mixed embeddedness of ethnic minority business in Britain. *Journal of Ethnic and Migration Studies,* 27: 241-258.

Bauer, T., Epstein, G. and Gang, I. (2002) Herd effects or migration networks? The location choice of Mexican immigrants in the U.S.. Discussion Paper No. 551, Institute for the Study of Labor (IZA), Germany.

Crush, J. (2008) Mean streets: Johannesburg as an emergent gateway. In M. Price and L. Benton-Short (eds.), *Migrants to the Metropolis: The Rise of Immigrant Gateway Cities* (pp. 255-282). Syracuse: Syracuse University Press.

Elfring, T. and Hulsink, W. (2003) Networks in entrepreneurship: The case of high technology firms. *Small Business Economics*, 21: 409-422.

Epstein, G. and Gang, I. (2010) Migration and culture. Discussion Paper No. 5123, Institute for the Study of Labor (IZA), Germany.

Epstein, G. (2008) Herd and network effects in migration decision-making. *Journal of Ethnic and Migration Studies*, 34: 567-583.

Fukuyama, F. (2001) Social capital, civil society and development. *Third World Quarterly*, 22: 7-20.

Harrison, P., Moyo, K. and Yang, Y. (2012) Strategy and tactics: Chinese immigrants and diasporic spaces in Johannesburg, South Africa. *Journal of Southern African Studies*, 38: 899-925.

Kalitanyi, V. and Visser, K. (2010) African immigrants in South Africa: Job takers or job creators? *South African Journal of Economic and Management Sciences*, 13: 376-390.

Muanamoha, R.C., Maharaj, B. and Preston-Whyte, E. (2010) Social networks and undocumented Mozambican migration to South Africa. *Geoforum*, 41: 885-896.

Nyamnjoh, H. (2013) *Bridging Mobilities. ICTs Appropriation by Cameroonians in South Africa and the Netherlands*. Leiden: African Studies Centre and Langaa Publishers.

Radipere, N. (2012) An analysis of local and immigrant entrepreneurship in the South African small enterprise sector (Gauteng Province). PhD Thesis, University of South Africa, Pretoria.

Renzulli, L., Aldrich, H. and Moody, J. (2000) Family matters: Gender, networks, and entrepreneurial outcomes. *Social Forces*, 79: 523-546.

Ryan, L. (2011) Migrants' social networks and weak ties: Accessing resources and constructing relationships post-migration. *Sociological Review*, 59: 707-724.

Wentzel, M., Viljoen, J. and Kok, P. (2006) Contemporary South African migration patterns and intentions. In P. Kok, D. Gelderblom, J. Oucho and J. van Zyl (eds.), *Migration in South and Southern Africa* (pp. 171-204). Cape Town: HSRC Press.

Chapter Eleven

The *Malayisha* Industry and the Transnational Movement of Remittances to Zimbabwe

Vusilizwe Thebe

INTRODUCTION

In the migrant labour societies of Southern Africa, remittances have played a central role in the consumption, accumulation and survival of migrant-sending households. In the context of the complex urban-rural linkages and centrality of "combinations of wage and hoe," in colonial and postcolonial Zimbabwe the dominant form of remittances was the consumer goods that moved from cities and smaller towns to the rural hinterland (Duggan, 1980; Bush and Cliffe, 1984; Potts and Mutambirwa, 1990; Bernstein, 2004). The 1990s and 2000s witnessed major shifts in the movement of remittances after the relocation of urban-based livelihoods from cities such as Bulawayo to various South African cities, especially in the province of Gauteng. The informal transnational movement of remittances and people became big business. This informal industry, which acquired the tag "*malayisha*", was mostly dominated by Johannesburg-based migrants. While the term "*ukulayisha*" literally means "to transport", for many people in migrant-sending communities *omalayisha* came to mean livelihood and hope (Thebe, 2011, p. 648).

In rural south-western Matabeleland, *omalayisha* began to take over the role of the rural bus service, which for over a century had been the epitome of worker-peasant survival. The rapid same day or overnight service that they offered bridged the geographical gap between Johannesburg and even the remotest rural areas. By moving people, goods and cash remittances, they provided an apparently sustainable and seamless exchange between labour and its earnings (Thebe, 2011). Normally identifiable through vehicles and trailers packed precariously high, *omalayisha* have become a visible and ubiquitous feature on the road networks of South Africa, Botswana and Zimbabwe. The traffic continued to increase despite the challenges associated with informality and perceptions of impropriety.

After 2009, the future of *omalayisha* as an industry and informal channel of remittances came under threat. Events in both Zimbabwe and South Africa combined to create an environment ill-suited for the surreptitious repatriation and expatriation of goods and people. In Zimbabwe itself, the adoption of a multiple currency policy and the subsequent return of goods to shop shelves made the transnational movement of remittances in the form of consumer goods increasingly unnecessary. In South Africa, the regularization of Zimbabwean migration through the Zimbabwe Documentation Project (ZDP) and related immigration reforms led to two important developments (Amit, 2011; Derman, 2013). First, one of the reasons for the popularity of *omalayisha* as a channel for remittances was avoidance of formal and official ways of doing business (Maphosa, 2010). By granting migrants legal status, the policy not only formalized diaspora livelihoods but also led to greater use of formal remittance channels. Second, the ZDP, along with the earlier lifting of entry visas, reduced the barriers to cross-border movements for Zimbabwean citizens and made people-smuggling, another core activity of *omalayisha* after the post-2000 crisis, less important.

This chapter highlights the changing role of *omalayisha* and their importance to both the households in migrant-sending areas and migrant entrepreneurship. The chapter is based on the findings from two separate studies of the *malayisha* industry. The first was conducted at the height of the Zimbabwe crisis from 2007 to 2009. This wide-ranging study examined the origins of the industry and its operations and significance to migrants and households in Zimbabwe. The second was a follow-up study, carried out between 2010 and 2013, following the policy changes in both Zimbabwe and South Africa.

METHODOLOGY

The 2007-2009 study involved the collection of accounts from 16 transport operators (*omalayisha*) and 147 Ndebele migrants who had patronized *omalayisha* as a channel of remittances, as passengers or to smuggle relatives into and out of South Africa. This study was biased towards the pioneer transport operators who were privy to the development of the industry. They were purposively identified and engaged in extended conversations that were shaped by set questions as well as transporters' knowledge and recollection of events. The 147 interviews with migrants focused mainly on passenger clients but also on individuals in Johannesburg who have maintained strong linkages with their places of origin and could illuminate not only the significance of the industry but also the nature of the relationship with the transport operators. The 2010-2013 study focused on the future of *omalayisha* as a channel of informal remittances and a source of livelihood for migrant entrepreneurs in the context of policy changes in both countries. Every effort was made to follow up with the same group of *omalayisha* who participated in the earlier study, but where they were no longer available, substitutes with similar characteristics were interviewed. The study adopted an ethnographic approach, drawing heavily on the experiences of 24 *omalayisha* on both the inbound and outbound routes and passenger migrants. Discussions were conducted with 124 migrant clients – 61 males, 52 females and 11 children – either en route home or going to South Africa or those who sponsored the expatriation process in Johannesburg. Thirteen of these clients were sickly and being taken home while 47 were travelling from Zimbabwe to South Africa.

FROM PART-TIME SOCIAL ACTIVITY TO LIVELIHOOD BUSINESS

Transport entrepreneurs involved in the movement of remittances and people between cities and rural hinterlands have a long pedigree in Southern Africa, and are often linked to the migratory labour regimes that characterized the region (Potts, 2000; Bernstein, 2004). The origins of *omalayisha* are usually traced to the late 1980s and early 1990s when migrants returning for holidays would take home goods, money and letters from relatives and neighbours (Thebe, 2011). The *malayisha* industry as we now know it was initially an informal remittance channel linking Johannesburg to rural Matabeleland in the 1980s initiated by migrants of Ndebele/Kalanga ethnic origin, mostly from the Kezi, Matopo, Plumtree and Tsholotsho regions of Matabeleland. However, the industry actually built on the decades-old practice of moving goods, letters and money between cities and the rural hinterland in Zimbabwe. Men working in Bulawayo and visiting rural homes would take goods, money or letters from relatives, neighbours and friends to families in the rural areas. Thus, the movement of remittances in earlier years was not business so much as a gesture based on kinship and neighbourhood relationships.

These transport operators were often part of the community – they were sons, husbands, home owners, and members of the wider kinship system (Thebe, 2011). The remittance system thus afforded households a livelihood lifeline and additional income for vehicle owners. It also greatly influenced later migration flows, which in turn transformed the movement of remittances into a full-time activity and *omalayisha* into a complex network of entrepreneurs. The demand for a regular and efficient informal channel for remittances grew with increased migration, forcing the system to adapt. The pioneers of the new system were mostly the same migrants who now started engaging in full-time transportation, but the residue of the old system remained. The main means of transportation was still small cars with trailers in tow. More importantly, the communal orientation was maintained. What stood out about this new system was the frequency of home trips and the home-to-home "pick up and deliver" service, which was convenient for both migrants and families in rural Matabeleland. The service was unique and operated entirely on trust - earned through reliability, neighbourliness, friendship, kinship relations and good references (Solidarity Peace Trust, 2009; Maphosa, 2010; Thebe, 2011).

The system was to change in the 1990s after the effects of Zimbabwe's Economic Structural Adjustment Programme (ESAP) began to be felt in urban areas. ESAP increased household vulnerability and reduced coping strategies, forcing more people to seek livelihood opportunities elsewhere (Tevera and Zinyama, 2002). For most of Matabeleland, the destination was South Africa, where new migrants had established social networks (Rutherford and Addison, 2007; Maphosa, 2010; Sibanda, 2010). With increased migration from Bulawayo and other Ndebele areas, *omalayisha* expanded their operations into these areas. But unlike the rural service that had a community orientation, these transport operators delivered anywhere and for anybody. Goods transported across the border were mostly those unavailable locally, like agricultural products and electronic appliances. But, in time, it became cheaper and more fashionable for migrant households to receive almost all of their requirements from South Africa. Transport operators also engaged in people-smuggling activities but not on the scale of syndicates outside the formal and informal transport systems.

By the 2000s, political unrest, continued loss of employment, food insecurity and soaring food prices in Zimbabwe led to a massive increase in migration to South Africa (Tevera and Zinyama, 2002; Crush and Tevera, 2010). This shifted both the outbound and inbound cargo, and human smuggling became a core business for *omalayisha*. The period also brought more subtle changes to the concept of *ukulayisha*. The fact that certain laws and processes could be circumvented through the exchange of money enabled both cross-border transport systems (*omalayisha* and the formal passenger taxi service) to move anything across the two borders (Thebe, 2011). *Ukulayisha* was now big business and the industry became notorious for anything on the margins of the law – overloading, people smuggling and unroadworthy vehicles – and the challenges they presented on the road network. The system could transport anything, including consumables, household furniture, building material and people (in health, ill-health and in coffins), albeit at a price.

People needed assistance to get to South Africa, the sick had to be taken home to be cared for by relatives, the dead had to be taken home for burial, and both urban and rural households in Zimbabwe desperately needed external support. Migrants were prepared to fund the repatriation and expatriation of relatives, and *omalayisha* became central role players in these clandestine movements. Transportation contracts were usually entered into in South Africa either on "pre-paid" terms where fares were settled in advance or "pay forward" arrangements where payment was settled at the destination by the host rather than the passenger. The transport operators became something of a nouveau riche (Maphosa, 2010). An informal industry once known for its dilapidated fleet expanded as transport operators acquired modern off-road double-cabin vehicles (such as Toyota Hilux, Nissan Hardbody or Navara, and Ford Ranger) and passenger carriers like Toyota Quantums, and engaged more drivers.

RELEVANCE, RESILIENCE AND ADAPTATION

The dollarization of the Zimbabwean economy after 2008 and the restocking of retail outlets combined with the ZDP in South Africa threatened the future of the *malayisha* industry. The implications for *omalayisha* were clear and immediately evidenced by reduced traffic volumes on the N1/A7 roads to Zimbabwe. The change affected business operations and the livelihoods of the migrant operators who had invested extensively in the industry before 2009, and needed substantial capital outlays to finance vehicle bonds. The transportation of goods, particularly for those on the city routes became increasingly uneconomical as cheaper goods flooded the Zimbabwean market. At the same time, various issues of impropriety that had emerged during the expansion of the industry were affecting customer confidence. These included unreliability, unfulfilled responsibilities and exorbitant pricing (Maphosa, 2010; Thebe, 2011). Since goods were now readily available in Zimbabwe, migrants began to send more cash remittances and fewer consumer goods. As migrants interviewed by Sij Ncube of the Voice of the People radio observed:

> *It is better to send cash than groceries because grocery prices in South Africa and home (Zimbabwe) are almost similar. After all, 'omalayi[t]sha' charge exorbitant prices to transport goods especially during the festive season so why should I lose money when I can buy groceries home?* (Mthandazo Ncube, interviewed on Voice of the People, 24 December 2013).

> *Why should I lose money sending groceries home if I can just send money to my wife so that she buys groceries at home (Zimbabwe)?* (Lebani Dube, interviewed on Voice of the People, 24 December 2013).

Transport operators continued to transport funeral and wedding parties, and business was particularly healthy during public holidays when they would take as many as four consignments, often compensating for income lost during lean periods by overcharging. They also still transported the bulk of financial remittances despite the introduction of semi-formal and formal channels of remitting including Mukuru.com, Western Union and, more recently, the First National Bank money transfer and the EcoCash system. This was partly due to their lower charges (*omalayisha* charged between 3 per cent and 5 per cent, Western Union 8.7 per cent and First National Bank 18 per cent).

Despite the changes to the system, the transport operators continued to operate in rural Zimbabwe. The demand even increased with the regularization of migration. Money, consumables, furniture, outdoor appliances, water containers and building materials continued to be transported to the rural areas. The rural routes became highly contested, however, as new transport operators gained access by employing drivers from those rural communities they intended to serve. While *ukulayisha* is a business and *omalayisha* are entrepreneurs and employees, those who served their home communities faced certain constraints that militated against pure profit-making but equally presented business opportunities. As neighbours, relatives and community citizens, *omalayisha* afforded their communities a personalized service that included credits and other arrangements. The migrant, remittance recipients and *omalayisha* had a relationship that transcended monetary transactions.

Arrangements between *omalayisha* and migrants dominated transaction relationships, with the majority of migrants in the two studies having entered one or more payment arrangements with at least one transport operator. Of these, a total of 52 per cent had goods or relatives transported on credit in the 2007-2009 study and 46 per cent in the 2010-2013 study; 36 per cent had entered "pay forward" arrangements in the first study and 17 per cent in the later study; and 23 per cent had made payment instalment arrangements in the earlier study and 83 per cent in the later. Among the migrants interviewed, a total of 86 per cent had also utilized *omalayisha* for home and return journeys. While some of these held Zimbabwean and South African travel documents, others had none and relied entirely on *omalayisha* to keep in touch with families back home. If they could not afford to make the home journey, migrants trusted their *omalayisha* to deliver the goods, money or messages to their families.

Migrants from rural areas still do not have the options available to migrants from urban centres such as Bulawayo, where there is an efficient cross-border passenger service (both bus and taxi services). In many rural areas, *omalayisha* remain the only convenient means of transportation, even for documented travellers who need no assistance to cross borders. The *omalayisha* interviewed between 2007 and 2013 transported both goods and passengers including men, women and mothers with children. There were certainly occasions when the vehicles had broken down and the passengers, the trailer and the luggage were left on the roadside, sometimes for days, while the vehicle was being attended to elsewhere. Despite these risks, rural migrants preferred *omalayisha* over the formal cross-border service. This was mainly due to various logistical challenges including lodgings and connections. The formal passenger services terminate in Bulawayo and, in some parts of the countryside, local buses are unreliable and available only on certain days of the week.

In Zimbabwe's migrant labour societies, *omalayisha* are now an integral part of the landscape. Their vehicles, which have become a source of life and survival, are prominent on roads, in homes and at shopping centres. The *malayisha* system plays an indispensable role in every aspect of rural life, be it economic or social, and in the struggle of households to reconstruct livelihoods shattered by droughts, economic crisis and government neglect. *Omalayisha* have also become central agents for migrant mothers in the movement of children and infants in and out of South Africa. Moving children across borders is nothing new for *omalayisha*. Parents in South Africa would send for their children during school holidays, and this task was often entrusted to *omalayisha* who were paid ZAR300 for a child holding a passport and up to ZAR1,500 for undocumented children. For *omalayisha*, transporting children has always been good business, even before South Africa adopted new anti-trafficking measures in May 2012 and October 2014 affecting the entry of children under the age of 17. However, despite the risks involved and various highly publicized incidents of arrest and incarceration of "child smugglers", *omalayisha* have continued with these activities:

> *We are back in business and it is very good as we continue to get several people coming to us seeking our services. In fact, two days ago I managed to smuggle four children who had passports but did not have accompanying affidavits and had been denied entry by (South African) Home Affairs authorities at Beitbridge Border Post* (Chronicle, 2012).

They made light of the new regulations and emphasized instead the vulnerability of the official systems:

> *You simply negotiate the immigration procedures and then pay your way to Johannesburg. In situations where access routes are blocked through the joint deployment of officers from the Ministry of Defence and Immigration Department, you look for alternative routes* (Interview 17 August 2013).

Migrant parents also treated this as normal travel arrangements. They were prepared to pay, and understood that *omalayisha* have to pay bribes to border and other state agents to bring their children to them. They were also unconcerned about the changes in immigration regulations since they had faith in the ability of *omalayisha* to circumvent the legal hurdles.

Reliable *omalayisha* have a stable clientele and gain new clients through recommendations by people who value their services. About 74 per cent of parents in the 2010-2013 study had utilized the same transport operator for years while others had a list of trusted individuals. The relationship may be a business one but, due to its continuous nature, the transport operators, children and parents were often very close. The children were comfortable around their *malayisha* and used a variety of respectful names like *"bhuti Mandla"* (brother) or *"bab' omncane"* and *"malume"* (uncle).

The *omalayisha* are also involved in the repatriation of infants from their mothers in South Africa to grandparents in Zimbabwe. The 16 December 2013 edition of the online NewZimbabwe.com ran an article entitled *"Omalayi[t]sha* Double as 'Road Nannies.'"

According to the article, migrant mothers enlist the services of *omalayisha* "to smuggle their children back to Zimbabwe where they can be looked after by family or friends." Although this was unconventional cargo, it was good business for migrant entrepreneurs. The process was less cumbersome than reported in the media since the infants were cared for by other women passengers, including mothers or female relatives, and the role of the *omalayisha* was to negotiate border processes and deliver the children to the assigned addresses where prior arrangements had been made. This, then, is very far from the anarchic process portrayed by the media.

NEGOTIATING INFORMALITY AND PERCEPTIONS OF IMPROPRIETY

Despite its growth, the *mayalisha* industry has maintained its informal character, which in a business sense presents both business opportunities and challenges. The contemporary industry emerged as a spontaneous response to increased migration from Zimbabwe and changing trends in remitting goods and money. It developed as a loose collection of individuals without a collective or umbrella association. In South Africa, the passenger taxi (mini-bus) industry operates under certain regulations with route permits and taxi ranks, and under different taxi associations. The cross-border passenger taxi industry operates under similar conditions. However, the *malayisha* industry has remained unregulated and, despite commercialization following a surge in demand, there is still no umbrella association. Operators may create relationships among themselves but they are mostly independent operations. Any individual with access to a vehicle and trailer can engage in the transportation of goods, and equally easily cease operations if they wish. Clearly, the lack of a regulatory framework presents numerous challenges for the industry and operators, and leaves the system open to abuse by opportunists and unscrupulous individuals.

While some modern-day *omalayisha* drive around in high-end vehicles, they are generally better known for operating an unroadworthy fleet, which violates road traffic regulations and presents a danger to other road users. A consistent feature through the different phases of the industry is overloading. This has continued despite the heavy presence of traffic and police officials on the South African and Zimbabwean road network. Vehicles are regularly stopped at road checkpoints and their loading inspected. But the ability of transport operators to manipulate the system, and the propensity of officials to accept bribes, allows them to proceed with their journey with cargo intact. The industry therefore operates on the margins of the law, and depends on the connivance of corrupt officials. As a result, *omalayisha* can ship almost anything across the border at the right price.

Operating on the margins of the law means *omalayisha* lose a lot of money in transactions with officials in both South Africa and Zimbabwe. On average, *omalayisha* pay between ZAR2,000 and ZAR5,000 in bribes on a single journey. Sometimes bribes are unsolicited but still given to nurture good relations with officials. Thus, transport operators often pay a "cool drink" fee to certain officials even when they have no consignment. However, officials also prey on *omalayisha*. A letter published by online news agency ZimEye in July 2013 provides a detailed account of the extent of official extortion:

> *I boarded a cross border Toyota Quantum (popularly known as* 'omalayi[t] sha'*) on [F]riday night (13 July) in Johannesburg, on my way to Bulawayo. We arrived at the Zimbabwean border at 4am. The ZIMRA [Zimbabwe Revenue Authority] official demanded, and was paid R800 for 'quick' processing of clearance procedures. Next up was the CID officer checking Temporary Import Permits (T.I.P) for the car and trailer. He raised an issue with the trailer papers, and demanded R600 to allow us through. After negotiating with the driver, he eventually settled for R200. As we made our way towards the gate, we were stopped by two uniformed officers who demanded to see our passports. They then asked for money from the driver, who gave them R50 as some form of 'protection fee' in future. At the gate, a rude female immigration officer demanded to see our passports. She said something to me in Shona and when I told her her words were too deep for me to understand, a heated argument ensured, and the driver had to pay her R100 because she was threatening to detain us as 'punishment'. Driving down 200 metres from the gate, police officers manning a roadblock in a Ford Ranger truck demanded R200 and were paid. Still in Beitbridge, at the Masvingo turn, another roadblock, more ZRP [Zimbabwe Republic Police] officers, another R200. About 50km from Beitbridge, three ZRP officers in the middle of nowhere [and] R100 taken. Another roadblock awaited at Makhado, R200 paid. Just before West Nicholson, more policemen, and this time, the driver had no more cash, and had to borrow R100 from a female passenger. At Gwanda, yet another set of starving policemen, the same lady had to lend the driver R100 more to pay the thugs. Upon driving out of Gwanda town, yet another roadblock, the passenger again lends the driver R100 more to pay up.*

We then encountered the BMW patrol vehicle 10km from Mbalabala, and the police officer asked for a re-test certificate from the driver. Obviously, being South Africa based, he didn't have it. The corrupt officer then demanded a spot fine of $20 or a bribe of R100. The driver explained to him how dry the other officers on the route had already sucked him. The officer would have non[e] of it, got into the BMW and drove away towards Gwanda with the driver's licence and the TIP document. Now we were stranded, waited for a while hoping the BMW would return, and after an hour in the scorching heat, I decided to take over the wheel as I had my licence on me. We paid a further $10 at the Mach Binding roadblock, and after 7 long hours, we arrived in Bulawayo. After paying R2,150 and $10, we arrived in Bulawayo.

Relations between *omalayisha* and clients can involve conflict, misunderstanding and breakdown of trust due to unscrupulous behaviour by the transport operator, unfulfilled transactions and unfortunate circumstances. Attitudes towards *omalayisha* become particularly negative when they are at fault. One of the most common sources of conflict is a failure to deliver goods or a mix-up in goods. However, conflict is often mitigated by personal relationships of kinship, friendship and neighbourliness. As Thebe (2011: 655-6) argues, "conflicts were slighter in rural communities, where transporters were members of the community and of a wider kin system than in Bulawayo."

CONCLUSION

The *mayalisha* industry emerged in the late 1980s as a response to increased trans-border migration and demand for efficient channels of remittances to migrant-sending areas in south-western Matabeleland. Its popularity was based on speed of delivery, social relations (neighbourhood and kinship ties) and its similarity to earlier forms of internal migration and remitting practices. The industry expanded rapidly after 2000 alongside the massive expansion of migration to South Africa. The industry also expanded into the migrant transport business, ferrying migrants from their home communities to South Africa and back. One consequence of the expansion into the cities was the erosion of the community character that had previously defined the industry. The old fleet was also replaced by modern passenger mini-buses and 4x4 double-cabin vehicles, which are suited for the rough rural terrain but also the transportation of passengers, reflecting its adaptation to the changing operating environment.

While recent policy changes in both Zimbabwe and South Africa have changed the world that nurtured the rapid expansion of the industry, they have not rendered the notion of *ukulayisha* completely obsolete. *Omalayisha* have proven their durability, managing to negotiate and overcome the challenges associated with informality and perceptions of impropriety, while at the same time positioning themselves as central actors in the rural economy. While the industry operates on the margins of the law, it appears to manage by circumventing legal processes. With the regularization process for Zimbabwean migrants in South Africa, new business opportunities have arisen as migrants attempt to maintain contact with places of origin. One such opportunity is the movement of children to visit their parents and the return of babies and infants to the care of grandparents in Zimbabwe. The durability and flexibility of the industry suggests that the authorities in both South Africa and Zimbabwe cannot wish it away.

REFERENCES

Amit, R. (2011) The Zimbabwean Documentation Process: Lessons learned. African Centre for Migration & Society, University of the Witwatersrand, Johannesburg.

Bernstein, H. (2004) 'Changing before our very eyes': Agrarian questions and the politics of land in capitalism today. *Journal of Agrarian Change*, 4: 190–225.

Bush, R. and Cliffe, L. (1984) Agrarian policy in migrant labour societies: Reform or transformation in Zimbabwe? *Review of African Political Economy*, 29: 77–94.

Chronicle (2012) Man arrested for trying to smuggle 24 children. 17 August.

Crush, J. and Tevera, D. (eds.) (2010) *Zimbabwe's Exodus: Crisis, Migration, Survival.* Ottawa and Cape Town: IDRC and SAMP.

Derman, B. (2013) Governing the Southern African/Zimbabwean border: Immigration, criminalization and human rights. In B. Derman and R. Kaarhus (eds.), *In the Shadow of a Conflict. Crisis in Zimbabwe and Its Effects in Mozambique, South Africa and Zambia* (pp. 146-179). Harare: Weaver Press.

Duggan, W. (1980) The Native Land Husbandry Act of 1951 and the rural African middle class of Southern Rhodesia. *African Affairs*, 79: 227-340.

Maphosa, F. (2010) Transnational and undocumented migration between Zimbabwe and South Africa. In J. Crush and D. Tevera (eds.), *Zimbabwe's Exodus: Crisis, Migration, Survival* (pp. 346-360). Cape Town: SAMP.

NewZimbabwe.com (2013) Omalayisha double as road nannies. 16 December.

Ncube, S. (2013) Injiva flock back to a bleak Zim Christmas. *Voice of the People Radio*, 24 December.

Potts, D. (2000) Worker-peasants and farmer housewives in Africa: The debate about 'committed farmers', access to land and agrarian production. *Journal of Southern African Studies*, 26: 807-832.

Potts, D. and Mutambirwa, C. (1990) Rural-urban linkages in contemporary Harare: Why migrants need their land. *Journal of Southern African Studies*, 16: 677-698.

Rutherford, B. and Addison, L. (2007) Zimbabwean farm workers in northern South Africa. *Review of African Political Economy*, 34: 619-635.

Sibanda, O. (2010) Social ties and the dynamics of integration in the City of Johannesburg among Zimbabwe migrants. *Journal of Sociology and Social Anthropology*, 1: 47-57.

Solidarity Peace Trust (2009) *Gone to Egoli. Economic Survival Strategies in Matabeleland: A Preliminary Study*. Port Shepstone: Solidarity Peace Trust.

Tevera, D. and Zinyama, L. (2002) Zimbabweans who move: Perspectives on international migration in Zimbabwe. SAMP Migration Policy Series No. 25, Cape Town.

Thebe, V. (2011) From South Africa with love: The 'malayisha' system and Ndebele households' quest for livelihood reconstruction in South-western Zimbabwe. *Journal of Modern African Studies*, 49: 647-670.

Chapter Twelve

Transnational Entrepreneurship and Informal Cross-Border Trade with South Africa

Sally Peberdy, Jonathan Crush, Daniel Tevera, Eugene Campbell, Nomsa Zindela, Ines Raimundo, Thuso Green, Abel Chikanda and Godfrey Tawodzera

INTRODUCTION

Informal sector cross-border trade (ICBT) is a significant feature of regional trade flows in Southern Africa. However, moves to liberalize trade and promote development through trade have largely revolved around large-scale formal sector trade and not cross-border trade undertaken by small-scale entrepreneurs. Indeed, ICBT is often associated in the official mind with smuggling, tax evasion and illegality. The Common Market for Eastern and Southern Africa (COMESA), for example, defines ICBT as "unrecorded trade" and characterizes it as trade that "characteristically involves bypassing border posts, concealment of goods, under-reporting, false classification, under-invoicing and other similar tricks" (Njiwa, 2013: 9). Further, ICBT supposedly "deprives authorities of much needed statistics, as well as revenues." In addition to evading taxes or fees imposed by governments, "traders also try to avoid administrative formalities in areas such as health, agriculture, security and immigration" (Njiwa, 2013: 9). The World Bank, on the other hand, is more sympathetic, identifying a series of official obstacles (both legal and illegal) to freer informal trade and proposing a Charter for Cross-Border Traders to protect their rights (Brenton et al., 2014). Both COMESA and the World Bank agree, however, that ICBT should be formalized and brought under government control.

In contrast to the negative characterization of ICBT by COMESA, a series of research studies has shown that it plays a critical role in poverty alleviation, food security and livelihoods in countries of origin. One type of study has focused on monitoring aggregate informal flows of agricultural products, especially the staple cereal, maize, across borders (Ackello-Ogutu, 1996; Minde and Nakhuma, 1997, 1998; Macamo, 1998; Mwaniki, 2003; Burke and Myers, 2014). A USAID-funded project continues to track the informal food trade in maize, rice and beans at over 20 border posts across the Southern African region (FEWS NET and WFP, 2012). Only one of these monitoring sites – Beitbridge on the Zimbabwe-South African border – captures flows out of South Africa, a surprising omission given South Africa's role as a major maize exporter to neighbouring countries. A second research cluster consists of small-scale case studies focused on informal traders themselves, their profiles, activities and challenges, and their important role in poverty alleviation at the household level (Muzvidziwa, 1998, 2001, 2006, 2012; Parsley, 1998; Nethengwe, 1999; Chivani, 2008; Kachere, 2011; Jamela, 2013). A sub-set of this literature on the local impacts of ICBT characterizes it as a form of "informal entrepreneurship" and focuses on the innovative income-generating and other business strategies of traders (Peberdy, 2000a, 2000b; Peberdy and Crush, 2001; Peberdy and Rogerson, 2002; Mazengwa, 2003; Chiliva et al., 2011).

Finally, there have been attempts to join these methodological approaches by combining aggregate monitoring of flows with more in-depth information collected from individual traders at border posts. In 2008, a UNIFEM project interviewed 457 traders at three Zimbabwe border posts and 250 traders at three Swaziland border posts, the results of which have not been widely disseminated (Ndiaye, 2009). A more ambitious project was conducted by SAMP in 2006-2007, which monitored the activities of informal cross-border traders as they passed through 20 land border posts connecting 11 Southern African countries. During the course of the survey, over 205,000 people, including 85,000 traders were counted. The transactions of over 5,500 traders with customs officials were monitored and over 4,500 traders interviewed. This project led to a series of individual country studies, which provided rich insights into ICBT at the national level and analyses of destination country policy responses to the phenomenon (Campbell and Mokhomane, 2007; Green, 2007; Mulenga,

2007; Nickanor et al., 2007; Raimundo and Cau, 2007; Tevera and Tawodzera, 2007; Tsoka, 2007; Zindela, 2007).

The chapter focuses on four main questions that have been neglected in the literature on ICBT, drawing on a sub-set of data from the SAMP study; that is, informal trade between South Africa and the neighbouring countries of Botswana, Lesotho, Mozambique, Swaziland and Zimbabwe. The first issue addressed in the chapter, through the construction of a profile of traders at six different border posts, is whether informal cross-border traders can be treated as a homogenous group. The chapter argues that insufficient attention is paid to different types of trader and, further, that the idea that informal trade is undertaken exclusively by women needs to be critically examined. Second, most studies of the impacts of ICBT focus on the countries and communities from which the traders come. However, South Africa is the strongest economy in the region, the source of many products that enter informal trade networks across the region and the major trading partner of all of these countries. This chapter therefore enumerates the many economic benefits to South Africa of ICBT with neighbouring countries. Third, an assumption is often made that a firm and impenetrable line exists between the formal and informal economies. The chapter argues not only that informal cross-border traders interact with the formal economy at various points but that a variety of formal sector groups benefit from that interaction. Finally, many studies tend to assume that the kind of ICBT at one border post is duplicated at others. This leads to a tendency to aggregate the data and make generalizations. This chapter argues for the opposite approach, stressing the importance of disaggregation and understanding the nature and reasons for difference between ICBT at different borders.

METHODOLOGY

In an effort to go beyond the case study approach and compile a more general picture of ICBT in Southern Africa, the SAMP partners conducted their survey at border posts where informal cross-border trade constitutes a significant proportion of traffic. The basic aims of the study were to (a) monitor ICBT between selected countries in Southern Africa; (b) identify the types and volumes of goods carried across land borders by traders; (c) identify the values of goods carried by small entrepreneurs through land border posts; (d) record the number of traders passing through selected border posts; (e) determine the gender breakdown of ICBT; (f) record the origins and destinations of ICBT journeys; (g) record the type of transport used; (h) examine the experiences of traders at border posts; and (i) identify possibilities for policy change and streamlining at land border posts to ease congestion and promote managed movement through border posts.

Four main research activities were conducted in the umbrella project at the border posts, which took place over a 10-day period including a weekend. First, field researchers counted the number of people passing through the border post, recording whether they were traders or not. Second, they recorded the sex and nationality of traders; the type, volume and value of goods declared; and duties paid during the survey period. Third, origin and destination (O&D) surveys were conducted with a sample of 4,500 traders away from customs and immigration officials. The survey provided an in-depth profile of informal trade entrepreneurs, which included the origin and destination and purpose of their journey, the type and value of goods carried, the transport used, the type of migration permit held, the length of time taken to clear the border post, and suggestions for improvement at border posts. Fourth, key informant interviews were undertaken with government officials including from Departments of Customs and Excise/Revenue Authority, Departments of Home Affairs/Interior/Immigration and the border police services. Key interviews were also undertaken with traders and traders' associations.

For the purposes of this chapter, a sub-set of the overall data set pertaining to six border posts between South Africa and other countries was extracted for analysis (Figure 12.1). All of the border posts are the main land crossing points between the two countries (measured in terms of traffic in goods and people). An estimated 70,000 people passed through all these borders during the 10 days of the survey (Table 12.1). Of these, nearly 27,000 were informal traders (around 36 per cent of the total). In the case of Swaziland, the two border posts are both major crossing points but are very different in character: one (Lavumisa) handles north-south traffic with KwaZulu-Natal and the other (Oshoek/Ngwenya) east-west traffic with Mpumalanga and Gauteng. At Beitbridge and Lebombo, the sheer volume of traffic (foot and vehicle) made it difficult to register everyone passing through. As a result, there is likely to have been an undercount of general traffic and traders as at times the sheer volume of traffic made it difficult for the counters to register everyone. The O&D survey was administered to a total of 1,335 traders at these six border posts.

The data from the SAMP survey was augmented by Statistics South Africa (SSA) data for the period 2006-2012. SSA conducts a regular exit survey of people leaving South Africa and publishes the data on an annual basis. Respondents are asked their main reason for being in South Africa and the options include shopping for personal use and shopping for a business. While it cannot be assumed that all those shopping for businesses are in the informal economy, the SSA data does provide a general picture of the relative importance of this category of entry.

Figure 12.1: Border Posts Monitored

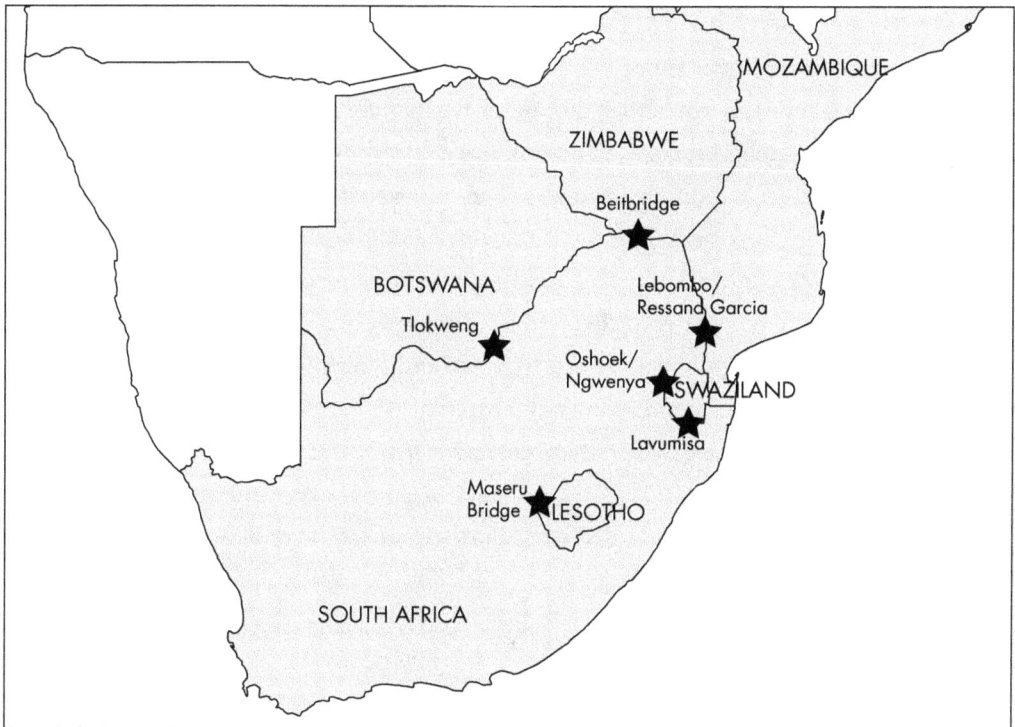

Table 12.1: Volume of Traffic and Informal Traders by Border Post

Border	Border post	No. of border crossers	No. of traders counted	Traders as % of border crossers	No. of traders interviewed
South Africa–Botswana	Tlokweng	4,223	377	8.9	162
South Africa–Lesotho	Maseru Bridge	1,922	660	34.3	67
South Africa–Swaziland	Lavumisa	8,282	258	3.1	162
South Africa–Swaziland	Oshoek/Ngwenya	9,247	532	5.8	307
South Africa–Mozambique	Lebombo/Ressano Garcia	33,948	16,795	49.5	250
South Africa–Zimbabwe	Beitbridge	16,575	8,299	50.1	387
Totals		74,197	26,921	36.3	1,335

PROFILING TRADERS

ICBT constitutes a significant proportion of cross-border traffic between South Africa and its neighbours. In the period of the SAMP survey, the proportion varied from a low of 3 per cent at Lavumisa to a high of 50 per cent at Lebombo and Beitbridge (Table 12.1). The relative importance of cross-border shopping in South Africa for business purposes can be gauged from the SSA exit survey (Table 12.2). This data shows considerable variation from country to country and over time. This does not necessarily mean that the absolute numbers of shoppers changed but rather that other reasons for travel increased or decreased in importance. Mozambique, for example, shows a fall from 45 per cent in 2006 (broadly consistent with the SAMP findings) to less than 5 per cent in 2012, while in most other countries (including Botswana, Lesotho, Zimbabwe and Swaziland through to 2011) there was a gradual increase in the importance of business shopping over this time period. Overall, the lowest numbers were recorded among Zimbabweans (less than 10 per cent each year), which may reflect the sheer volume of traffic and multiplicity of reasons for going to South Africa. On the other hand, very high numbers (45 per cent in 2013) were recorded for shopping for personal use, which may mean that the distinction between the two types of shopping is blurred in practice as respondents could only give one main purpose. The highest numbers overall were recorded by visitors from Lesotho and Swaziland.

Table 12.2: Shopping for Business as Main Purpose of Visit to South Africa, 2006–2012

	2006	2007	2008	2009	2010	2011	2012
Botswana	13.3	10.9	10.8	8.3	11.4	15.3	19.1
Lesotho	14.5	15.6	25.0	25.2	28.2	26.9	24.1
Mozambique	45.4	26.3	18.2	11.0	6.5	5.5	2.4
Swaziland	29.8	30.3	32.1	34.7	43.1	46.9	21.7
Zimbabwe	5.6	3.0	4.0	7.4	4.6	6.0	9.4
Source: SSA							

Conventional wisdom suggests that ICBT is the almost exclusive preserve of women who are forced into the sector as a survival strategy because of labour market discrimination that prevents them accessing formal employment. According to Muzvidziwa (2012: 217), for example, Zimbabwean informal traders are "a highly gendered group, as they comprise mostly women." At the same time, they are not desperate survivalists but "a highly mobile and well-connected group of entrepreneurs that has managed to establish links that cut across ethnic, class, gender and nationality" (Muzvidziwa, 2012: 232). This study suggests that the picture is more complex with larger numbers of men as actors in ICBT than previously thought. However, the ratio of male to female cross-border traders varies at different border posts (Table 12.3). Overall, women comprised 63 per cent of the informal cross-border traders crossing between South Africa and its neighbours (Table 12.3). However, the proportion varied from border to border from a high of 83 per cent at Lavumisa on the South Africa-Swaziland border to a low of 48 per cent at the Botswana and Lesotho borders with South Africa.

Table 12.3: Sex of Informal Cross-Border Traders

Border post	Male (%)	Female (%)
Tlokweng	52.0	48.0
Maseru Bridge	52.0	48.0
Lavumisa	16.5	83.5
Oshoek	32.7	67.3
Lebombo	29.0	71.0
Beitbridge	45.8	54.2
Total	37.1	62.9

At the two busiest South African borders with Mozambique and Zimbabwe, the proportion of female traders was 71 per cent and 54 per cent respectively. That men comprised almost half of the traders at Beitbridge is probably attributable to Zimbabwe's economic crisis and high unemployment rates. According to a UN Women (2009) study, men are more likely to see informal trade as a form of employment while women see it as a source of income and poverty alleviation. Regardless of their perceptions, "whenever a lucrative activity was identified men eventually moved in to compete and sometimes displaced women" (UN Women, 2009: 1). Intense gender struggles over informal trading have developed in both Mozambique and Zimbabwe (Agadjanian, 2002; Mutopo, 2010).

A second major characteristic of ICBT is its bilateral character. The vast majority of traders move backwards and forwards between two countries: their own and South Africa. They rarely venture to third countries or move across the region. Although the broader regional SAMP survey found that the major trading corridors were with South Africa, it found that other bilateral trade routes existed between other countries in the region (for instance, Zimbabwe and Zambia, and Namibia and Angola). Most traders crossing borders with South Africa were citizens of the country of origin (over 80 per cent at each border post) (Table 12.4). There were a few Zimbabweans (11 per cent) entering Lesotho but none entering Swaziland or Mozambique via South Africa. Zimbabweans entering Botswana did so through other border posts between the two countries and not via South Africa (Campbell and Mokhomane, 2007; Ama et al., 2013). There is thus little multi-lateral informal trade with ICBT entrepreneurs trading across more than one border or between more than two countries.

Table 12.4: Nationality of Traders at Border Posts

Country of citizenship of traders	Border Posts				
	Tlokweng (%)	Maseru Bridge (%)	Lebombo (%)	Oshoek & Lavumisa (%)	Beitbridge (%)
Botswana	95.5	0.0	0.0	0.0	0.0
Lesotho	2.8	87.6	0.0	0.0	0.0
Swaziland	0.0	0.0	0.4	83.4	0.5
Mozambique	0.0	0.0	99.2	4.2	0.5
Zimbabwe	0.1	11.4	0.0	0.0	89.9
South Africa	0.1	1.0	0.0	10.8	5.4
Other	0.0	0.0	0.4	1.4	3.7

ICBT between South Africa and its neighbours is not reciprocal in nature as few South Africans participate in the trade. Some were recorded entering Swaziland (11 per cent of the total), Zimbabwe (5 per cent) and Lesotho (1 per cent) but none into Botswana or Mozambique. The lack of participation by South Africans in ICBT contrasts sharply with the formal trade sector, where South African exporters dominate the cross-border movement of goods to neighbouring countries. The imbalance in ICBT, with exports from South Africa significantly outweighing imports, is also mirrored in the formal sector. In 2010, for example, South African exports to the five other countries in this study totalled over USD10.6 billion while imports were only valued at USD876 million (Table 12.5). South Africa therefore has a massive trade surplus with every one of these countries.

Another major feature of ICBT between South Africa and its neighbours is that it is largely, but not exclusively, one-way traffic (Table 12.6). The majority of traders (over 80 per cent) at the borders with Botswana, Lesotho, Mozambique and Swaziland had been to South Africa simply to buy goods for their businesses in those four countries. The activity profile of Zimbabwean traders was noticeably different from traders at the other borders. Only 32 per cent of those entering Zimbabwe had gone to South Africa exclusively to buy goods for their businesses in Zimbabwe. About 20 per cent of the traders at the Lesotho and Zimbabwe borders had also taken goods to South Africa to sell (primarily handicrafts). Zimbabwe was the only country with extensive two-way trading: 42 per cent had taken goods from Zimbabwe and brought back goods from South Africa. In effect, this means that as many as two-thirds of the Zimbabweans had taken goods to sell in South Africa.

Table 12.5: Value of Exports and Imports from South Africa, 2010

	Imports from South Africa USD million	Exports to South Africa USD million
Botswana	4,065	148
Lesotho	878	0.9
Mozambique	1,227	528
Swaziland	n/a	0.1
Zimbabwe	4,433	191
Total	10,603	868
Source: Sandrey (2013: 10)		

Table 12.6: Cross-Border Trading Activities of Informal Traders

	Tlokweng (%)	Maseru Bridge (%)	Lebombo (%)	Oshoek & Lavumisa (%)	Beitbridge (%)
Buying goods in South Africa for resale	99.0	80.6	81.0	88.5	32.0
Taking goods to sell in South Africa	1.0	19.4	1.0	7.9	20.9
Selling and buying goods in South Africa	0.0	0.0	11.6	1.3	42.4

Finally, since there is a widespread assumption in official circles in South Africa that informal traders are involved in illegal activity, the respondents were asked what kind of permits they had used to cross the border. The fact that they were allowed to cross at all indicates that they probably have some kind of valid documentation such as a passport or identity document, although corruption by officials at many border posts means that this is not guaranteed. It may also account for the fact that 16 per cent of traders at Beitbridge said they did not need South African entrance permits (Tevera and Tawodzera, 2007; Lefko-Everett, 2010). For the majority at Beitbridge, and everywhere else, two kinds of permits were used for entry to South Africa: visitor permits and local permits (commonly known as border passes).

At the time of the survey, most informal cross-border traders could enter South Africa on visitor permits. These were issued for varying periods of time and some were for multiple entry. The South African Department of Home Affairs also required all visitors to state their purpose of entry. The possible options were quite limited, however. They included "holiday" and "business" but not shopping or trading. Since there are no restrictions on what someone does on holiday or on business, there was nothing that contravened the law in buying goods in South Africa to take home. Less clear is whether visitors were able to sell imported goods without additional documentation as this could be construed as a form of work requiring a business permit. South African visitor permits were held by as many as 90 per cent of the traders at the Swaziland border and 80 per cent at the Mozambique border but as few as 10 per cent of those at the Lesotho border. Only half of the Zimbabwean traders held South African visitor permits (Table 12.7).

Table 12.7: Types of Permits Used by Traders

	Visitor permit (%)	Local permit (%)	Permanent resident (%)	Other (%)	No permit required (%)
Tlokweng	4.5	0.9	0.0	8.2	86.4
Maseru Bridge	10.4	82.1	0.0	7.5	6.0
Lebombo	80.4	0.8	0.0	18.2	0.6
Oshoek/Lavumisa	90.2	1.7	0.2	7.8	0.0
Beitbridge	50.5	26.6	2.5	1.5	16.4

The other type of permit used by traders was the border pass. These were generally issued for a period of up to six months and allowed the holder to enter and leave multiple times simply by showing the permit to border guards and without each entry and exit being officially recorded. Border passes generally have various conditions attached. In the case of Lesotho (where 80 per cent of traders held passes), they were for same-day entry to and exit from South Africa. For the 27 per cent of Zimbabweans with border passes, the restriction was geographical, allowing them to travel up to 20km from the border. However, these were phased out in 2007 following the perception among South African immigration authorities that the permits were being used as a means to enter the country for longer periods.

The overall volume of ICBT to South Africa cannot, of course, be deduced from a snap-shot of traders over a two-week period as this represents only a fraction of the total flow. The trade flow also varies throughout the year, becoming more intense in the run-up to the end-of-year holiday period and during parts of the year when there are food shortages in neighbouring countries. One proxy measure captured in the survey was how often the trad-ers entered South Africa to buy, to sell or both. Small-scale cross-border traders exhibit a complex variety of travel patterns, even through a single border post. Traders using border posts where South African border towns are in relatively close proximity travel frequently to purchase South African goods. Examples include Ladybrand near Lesotho and Polok-wane near Zimbabwe.

Nearly two-thirds (64 per cent) of the Mozambican traders at Lebombo said they went to South Africa at least once a week. At two other borders (Maseru Bridge and Oshoek) the proportion was around a third (Table 12.8). Those transiting though border posts to more distant destinations tended to travel less frequently. At most other borders, fortnightly or monthly visits to South Africa were more the norm. At Lavumisa in Swaziland, nearly 90 per cent said they travelled at least once a month to South Africa. Other borders with high numbers of fortnightly and monthly traders include Beitbridge (63 per cent), Maseru Bridge (62 per cent), Oshoek (59 per cent) and Lebombo (44 per cent). Since over 90 per cent of traders overall travel to South Africa at least once a month, the value of ICBT to the South African economy is many times the value captured in the survey.

Table 12.8: Frequency of Travel to South Africa for Business

	Once a day or more (%)	At least once a week (%)	At least once a month (%)	At least once a year (%)
Tlokweng	2.7	19.1	69.1	9.1
Maseru Bridge	4.5	28.4	62.7	1.5
Lebombo	6.0	58.2	44.6	1.2
Oshoek	3.8	28.4	58.6	9.3
Lavumisa	0.6	7.5	80.6	11.3
Beitbridge	2.3	10.3	63.3	24.0

BENEFITS OF ICBT TO SOUTH AFRICA

Most ICBT entrepreneurs purchase goods in South Africa for resale in their home countries, with clear benefits for the South African economy. ICBT is not insulated from the
formal sector and interacts with it constantly. Cross-border traders from other countries
are major patrons of South African businesses, particularly in the wholesaling, retailing and
transportation sectors. This becomes especially clear when the buying patterns of traders in
South Africa are examined. These patterns have two dimensions: economic (who benefits
from their patronage) and spatial (where they source their goods for resale).

The primary South African economic beneficiaries of ICBT are formal sector retailers.
As many as 61 per cent of the Zimbabwean traders purchase goods in South Africa from
retailers, a sector that includes supermarkets and smaller independent retailers in places
like China Mall and Oriental Plaza in Gauteng (Table 12.9). About a third of the Swazi traders and 40-50 per cent of the traders from Mozambique and Lesotho also patronize formal
retail outlets in South Africa. South African wholesalers also benefit from the custom of
informal cross-border traders from neighbouring countries. Half of the Batswana traders
and a third of the Zimbabwean traders source goods from South African wholesalers, as do
31 per cent of those crossing into Swaziland at the Oshoek border and 28 per cent crossing
into Mozambique from South Africa.

Table 12.9 Type of Outlet Where Goods Purchased

	Wholesaler (%)	Retailer (%)	Commercial farm (%)	Informal market (%)	Smallholder farm (%)	Other (%)
Tlokweng	50.9	4.6	5.6	7.4	25.0	6.5
Maseru Bridge	16.0	42.0	25.0	3.0	1.5	9.0
Lebombo	28.4	46.4	23.2	7.2	0.8	4.0
Oshoek	30.9	32.1	6.7	16.4	2.4	11.5
Lavumisa	13.4	35.4	1.8	46.5	0.3	2.8
Beitbridge	32.6	60.7	0.8	3.9	0.8	1.3

Note: Multiple response question

Patronage of the formal wholesale sector is lower in the case of Lesotho and by traders
passing through the Lavumisa border in southern Swaziland, though for different reasons.
In the case of Lesotho (as well as Mozambique), as many as a quarter of the traders obtain

their goods from commercial farms in South Africa. In both cases, there are large commercial vegetable (Lesotho) and fruit (Mozambique) farms just over the border in South Africa. South Africa's impoverished and unproductive smallholder farm sector is not a significant player in ICBT, except for traders from Botswana. However, in the case of Swaziland at least, informal markets in Durban, South Africa, are a source of goods for resale. Nearly half (46 per cent) of the traders at Lavumisa source their goods this way (Zindela, 2007).

When informal cross-border traders buy from the formal sector they also contribute to the South African tax base as they pay VAT on the goods they purchase. Traders who are carrying goods with invoices can certainly claim the VAT back when they go through border posts on their way back to their home countries. However, at most land borders, the methods for claiming VAT are complex and time-consuming and VAT refunds are not available as cash but only as cheques or deposits into bank accounts. In this study, only 6 per cent of traders passing into Lesotho, 23 per cent passing into Swaziland and 26 per cent passing into Botswana claimed VAT back at the border. Although rates were slightly higher at Beitbridge (32 per cent) and Lebombo (40 per cent), the South African fiscus clearly gains from the VAT paid by many traders.

Spatially, the major beneficiaries of ICBT are South Africa's larger cities, especially Johannesburg and Pretoria (Table 12.10). Over 80 per cent of traders at Oshoek had been to these two cities to purchase goods for their businesses in Swaziland. As many as 54 per cent of Zimbabwean traders, 51 per cent of Botswana traders and a quarter of Mozambican traders had also been to these two cities. However, they were of little importance to traders at Lavumisa (Swaziland) and Maseru Bridge (Lesotho). Traders at Lavumisa went primarily to Durban (78 per cent) while those at Maseru Bridge went to the nearby South African towns of Ladybrand, Thaba Nchu and Welkom (43 per cent). Other South African towns to benefit from proximity to neighbouring countries included Polokwane, Nelspruit and Musina. As many as a quarter of the traders at Beitbridge (Zimbabwe) had only been as far as Musina.

The value of goods carried by traders was recorded in the O&D survey. Given that most traders operate outside the formal banking system, it is fair to assume that these figures reflect direct cash injections into the South African economy. The value of goods carried by traders varied between countries of survey as well as by border post. Underpinning these variations were the types of goods carried by traders and their patterns of travel. Traders travelling longer distances and/or less frequently were likely to carry larger quantities of goods by value than those travelling frequently over short distances. In the case of Botswana and Lesotho, for example, over 80 per cent of the traders were carrying goods valued at under ZAR1,000 (Figure 12.2). On the other hand, traders entering Swaziland (at Oshoek), Mozambique and Zimbabwe, who had generally travelled much further to obtain their goods, tended to carry goods of higher total value. At Beitbridge, 84 per cent of traders had goods valued between ZAR1,000 and ZAR5,000 and 16 per cent had goods valued at over ZAR5,000. In the case of Oshoek, 42 per cent had goods valued between ZAR1,000 and ZAR5,000 and 20 per cent had goods valued at over ZAR5,000. At the Mozambique border, two-thirds of the traders had goods valued at less than ZAR1,000 but another third had goods valued at between ZAR1,000 and ZAR5,000. Clearly, ICBT does not involve large cash outlays. It is the sheer number of traders and the cumulative value of large numbers of small purchases that gives ICBT its value to the South African economy.

Table 12.10: Locations in South Africa Where Goods Purchased

	Tlokweng (%)	Maseru Bridge (%)	Lebombo (%)	Oshoek (%)	Lavumisa (%)	Beitbridge (%)
Johannesburg	51.5	13.4	23.6	74.5	0.3	44.2
Pretoria	0.0	0.0	1.1	6.7	0.3	9.6
Durban	1.0	0.0	0.3	7.4	78.0	1.3
Musina	0.0	0.0	0.0	0.0	0.0	23.8
Polokwane	0.0	0.0	0.6	0.0	16.9	5.7
Nelspruit	0.0	0.0	8.0	11.0	0.0	0.0
Komatipoort	0.0	0.0	0.0	0.0	0.3	0.0
Bloemfontein	0.0	3.0	0.3	0.0	0.0	0.0
Ladybrand	0.0	25.4	0.0	0.0	0.0	0.0
Thaba Nchu	0.0	13.4	0.0	0.0	0.0	0.0
Welkom	0.0	4.5	0.0	0.0	0.0	0.0
Other towns and farms	47.5	59.7	66.1	0.7	4.2	11.6

Cross-border informal traders do not only spend on goods for resale while they are in South Africa. There are also food, accommodation and travel costs to take into consideration. Clearly, the value of these varies with the time spent in South Africa and the distance travelled from the border. The majority of traders at some border posts said they went to

South Africa for a day or less (for example, 61 per cent of those at Maseru Bridge and 53 per cent at Lebombo). At other border posts, the proportion of day visitors was much lower, for example, only 14 per cent at Beitbridge and 24 per cent at Lavumisa (Table 12.11).

Figure 12.2: Value of Goods Carried by Informal Cross-Border Traders

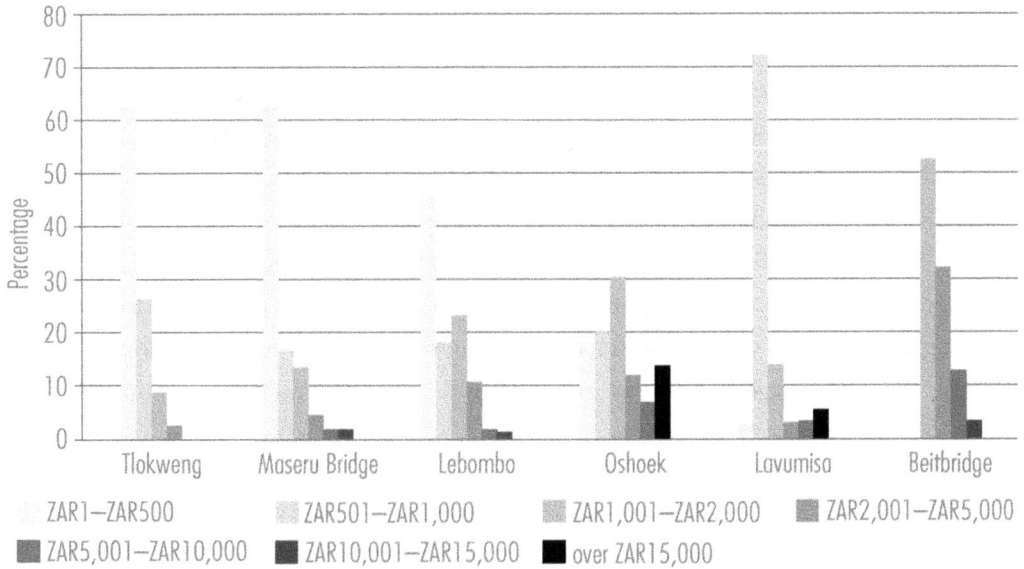

Table 12.11: Length of Stay in South Africa

Border post	Day or less (%)	2-7 days (%)	2-4 weeks (%)	>1 month (%)
Tlokweng	49.1	48.0	2.7	0.0
Maseru Bridge	61.2	28.4	9.0	1.5
Lebombo	52.8	42.4	4.4	0.5
Oshoek	44.5	47.5	7.4	0.6
Lavumisa	24.3	73.5	1.9	0.3
Beitbridge	13.9	45.7	32.8	5.5

The generally longer stays of Zimbabwean traders (with 40 per cent staying longer than a week in South Africa) are related both to the longer distances they travel from Beitbridge and the fact that the majority are going to sell as well as buy. To go to Durban from Swaziland and return within a day is also very difficult, which explains why there are relatively few day visitors passing through Lavumisa. Significant numbers of traders at all borders do stay overnight in South Africa, varying from a high of 86 per cent in the case of Zimbabwe to a low of 39 per cent in the case of Lesotho. Very few traders from any country had stayed longer than a month in South Africa.

Apart from the suppliers of accommodation and food while the traders are in South Africa, the other major South African beneficiary of their activities is the transportation industry. Over 50 per cent of traders at all of the border posts were travelling by buses and minibus taxis. At every border post (with the exception of Oshoek) this form of transportation was easily the most important conveyance used by traders (Table 12.12). At Lebombo, Beitbridge and Lavumisa, the figure was over 70 per cent. Private cars and vans (not necessarily owned by the traders themselves) were being used by over a third of the traders at two border posts (Maseru Bridge and Oshoek) and by 20 per cent at another (Beitbridge). Railway transport was only of any significance at the Lebombo border post with Mozambique. Although information was not collected on fares or other costs of transportation, the sheer volume of traders suggests that they make a significant contribution to the South African private sector transport industry.

Table 12.12: Forms of Transportation Used by Traders to Get to Borders

	Bus/taxi (%)	Car/van (%)	Truck (%)	Train (%)
Tlokweng	66.4	33.6	0.0	0.0
Maseru Bridge	64.2	35.8	0.0	0.0
Lebombo	73.5	7.6	1.4	7.4
Oshoek	50.0	39.5	4.9	0.0
Lavumisa	81.6	10.7	7.1	0.0
Beitbridge	72.6	20.2	5.9	0.0

TRADING GOODS

To understand the types of trade engaged in by informal cross-border traders, and therefore which sectors of the South African economy stand to benefit the most, the O&D survey recorded the types of goods purchased in South Africa. Food items, both fresh produce and groceries, constituted a significant proportion of the goods carried out of South Africa by traders to sell in their home countries (Table 12.13). But there were important differences among border posts and destination countries, which clearly reflect the kinds of goods in demand in those countries, the market niches identified by informal traders, and the distances travelled by traders.

Table 12.13: Types of Goods Carried by Traders

	Groceries (%)	Fresh fruit, vegetables (%)	Meat/fish/ eggs (%)	Electrical goods (%)	Furniture (%)	Household goods (%)	New clothes/ shoes (%)	Second-hand clothes/ shoes (%)	Handi-crafts/ curios (%)	Other (%)
Tlokweng	4.5	30.3	0.0	0.9	0.0	2.7	49.1	2.7	0.0	9.8
Maseru Bridge	10.4	31.3	1.5	0.0	0.0	6.0	13.4	4.5	10.4	23.9
Lebombo	75.7	21.1	74.5	0.8	0.0	0.4	5.6	0.0	0.0	5.6
Oshoek	6.1	17.0	3.9	8.8	5.2	21.8	42.2	0.7	0.7	17.4
Lavumisa	2.5	2.2	0.3	0.9	0.0	19.3	62.4	12.1	1.2	6.6
Beitbridge	71.1	2.3	0.3	14.5	1.3	3.1	4.1	1.8	0	1.6

Despite the severe shortages of fresh produce in Zimbabwe at the time of the survey, only 2 per cent of traders were carrying fresh fruit and vegetables back to the country. This is primarily because the major urban markets in Zimbabwe are too distant to guarantee that the produce would not spoil by the time they arrived at their destination. The two border posts with Swaziland also had very few fresh produce traders (2.5 per cent at Lavumisa and 17 per cent at Oshoek). Here transportation distance and the likelihood of spoilage would probably not be such an important factor. Rather, there would be little market in Swaziland for fresh produce, which is freely available to urban consumers through South African-owned supermarket chains and commercial production in Swaziland itself (Crush and Frayne, 2011). Fresh produce is most important for traders entering Botswana and Lesotho (around 30 per cent) and, to a lesser extent, Mozambique (21 per cent). The primary South African beneficiaries of fresh produce purchases by informal traders would be retail outlets (especially South Africans supermarkets) and, by extension, those who are integrated into their supply chains (especially large commercial farmers). Some commercial farmers benefit directly through sales to traders at the farm gate.

Another major category of foodstuffs crossing borders was groceries, including processed food, canned goods and packaged goods. Again, there were wide variations between borders. Informal traders carrying groceries for resale were only significant at two border posts – Beitbridge and Lebombo. In both cases, over 70 per cent were carrying groceries to sell in Zimbabwe and Mozambique. Here was an obvious market niche for informal traders. At the time of the survey, groceries were in extremely short supply throughout Zimbabwe. In Mozambique, with a minimal supermarket presence, most groceries are sold by small retail outlets at a premium. By selling into the informal economy, where most households in cities like Maputo purchase food, informal entrepreneurs are able to supply groceries that are subject to a considerable formal sector mark-up (Raimundo et al., 2014). Again because of the supermarket presence, there is little incentive for traders to sell South African-bought groceries in Swaziland, Botswana and Lesotho. Currency parity for Swaziland and Lesotho and a stronger pula in Botswana further reduce the incentives to carry groceries.

The other type of foodstuff that was only important in the case of Mozambican ICBT was meat for resale. It is unlikely that this included chicken because the Mozambican market for chicken is dominated by local production and cheap imports from Brazil (FAO, 2013; de Oliveira et al., 2014). However, the demand for beef and meat by-products such as offal has grown with the urbanization of Mozambique and a shift in urban diets. The Mozambican livestock industry is not particularly strong so meat imports from South Africa find a ready market in the informal economy of cities such as Maputo.

Clothing and shoes also comprised a significant proportion of the business of informal cross-border traders in the region. New items were more important than second-hand. Again they were more important for some countries than others. Over half of the traders entering Swaziland (42 per cent at Oshoek and 62 per cent at Lavumisa) were carrying new clothing and shoes, as were almost half of the traders entering Botswana at Tlokweng. Informal cross-border traders in the region also carry electrical and household goods as well as furniture. However, only a minority at all border posts were transporting these often bulky and expensive items. The survey uncovered a range of other goods carried by traders. These varied by country but included *chitenges* and *capulanas* (pieces of cloth worn by women in Southern and Eastern Africa) and other types of fabric, cosmetics, liquor/alcohol, car parts, construction materials and sundry goods.

CONCLUSION

This study, the largest of its kind undertaken in the Southern African region, demonstrated that informal cross-border traders comprise a significant proportion of traffic through the border posts separating South Africa from its neighbours. The study also showed that this informal cross-border trade is complex and varied, even at border posts of the same country (compare, for example, the significant differences on almost every measure between Oshoek and Lavumisa on the Swaziland-South Africa border). Informal cross-border trade is of undoubted significance to poverty alleviation, food security and livelihoods in neighbouring countries. But its benefits do not stop there as South Africa itself gains considerably from ICBT. This runs counter to the negative image in South Africa of informal trade and the informal economy.

The ICBT entrepreneurs from neighbouring countries mainly buy their goods in the South African formal sector from wholesalers, retailers, manufacturers and commercial farms. Smallholder farmers do not seem to benefit overly and nor do marketing boards. When buying from the formal sector many traders contribute to the South African tax base as the majority do not reclaim the VAT they are entitled to because the system is not user-friendly, or the traders are simply not aware of this entitlement. Another major South African beneficiary of ICBT is the private transportation industry, especially buses and minibus taxis. Others include the hospitality and food industries.

Many traders appear to act as wholesale importers of goods as they sell the goods they carry across borders to vendors in informal markets at their destinations (55 per cent in Mozambique, 31 per cent in Zimbabwe and 27 per cent in Lesotho). A smaller proportion sell to retailers and restaurants in the formal sector. However, most traders sell their goods in the informal sector, whether in their own stalls, to other vendors, door to door, or to networks of family, friends and other individuals. So, although ICBT is firmly located in the formal sector at the purchasing end, the informal sector is the primary beneficiary at the selling end.

ACKNOWLEDGEMENTS

We wish to thank the following for their assistance with the design of the SAMP survey and its implementation at border posts not covered in this chapter: Maxton Tsoka, Ndeyapo Nickanor, Chileshe Mulenga and Ntombi Msibi.

REFERENCES

Ackello-Ogutu, C. (1996) Methodologies for estimating informal cross-border trade in eastern and southern Africa. Technical Paper No. 29, USAID Africa Bureau, Washington DC.

Agadjanian, V. (2002) Men doing 'women's work': Masculinity and gender relations among street vendors in Maputo, Mozambique. *Journal of Men's Studies*, 10: 329-342.

Ama, N., Mangadi, K., Okurut, F. and Ama, H. (2013) Profitability of the informal cross-border trade: A case study of four selected borders of Botswana. *African Journal of Business Management*, 7: 4221-4232.

Brenton, P., Dihel, N., Hoppe, M. and Soprano, C. (2014) Improving behaviour at borders to promote trade formalization: The charter for cross border traders. World Bank Policy Note No. 41, World Bank, Washington DC.

Burke, W. and Myers, R. (2014) Spatial equilibrium and price transmission between southern African maize markets connected by informal trade. *Food Policy*, 49: 59-70.

Campbell, E. and Mokhomane, Z. (2007) Informal cross-border traders in Botswana. Report for SAMP, University of Botswana, Gaborone.

Chivani, C. (2008) Informal cross-border trade: A review of its impact on household poverty reduction (Zimbabwe). M.Soc.Sci. Thesis, University of Fort Hare, South Africa.

Chiliva, N., Masocha, R. and Zindiye, S. (2011) Challenges facing Zimbabwean cross border traders trading in South Africa: A review of the literature. *Chinese Business Review*, 12: 564-570.

Crush, J. and Frayne, B. (2011) Supermarket expansion and the informal food economy in Southern African Cities: Implications for urban food security. *Journal of Southern African Studies*, 37: 781-807.

de Oliveira, C., Pivoto, D. and Spanho, C. (2014) Developments and competitiveness of Mozambican chicken meat industry. Paper presented at IFAMA 2014 Symposium, Cape Town.

FAO (2013) Poultry sector Mozambique. FAO Animal Production and Health Livestock Country Reviews No. 5, FAO, Rome.

FEWSNET and WFP (2012) Informal cross-border food trade in southern Africa. Issue No. 78, Famine Early Warning Systems Network and World Food Program, Johannesburg.

Green, T. (2007) Small scale cross border trade study: Lesotho. Report for SAMP, Sechaba Consultants, Maseru.

Jamela, T. (2013) Experiences and coping strategies of women informal cross-border traders in unstable political and economic conditions: The case of Bulawayo (Zimbabwe) traders. M.Dev. Studies Thesis, University of Johannesburg, South Africa.

Kachere, W. (2011) Informal cross border trading and poverty reduction in the Southern African Development Community: The case of Zimbabwe. PhD Thesis, University of Fort Hare, South Africa.

Lefko-Everett, K. (2010) The voices of migrant Zimbabwean women in South Africa. In J. Crush and D.

Tevera (eds.), *Zimbabwe's Exodus: Crisis, Migration, Survival* (pp. 269-290). Cape Town: SAMP.

Macamo, J. (1998) Estimates of unrecorded cross-border trade between Mozambique and her neighbors: Implications for food security. USAID Africa Bureau, Washington DC.

Mazengwa, P. (2003) A business analysis of Zimbabwean cross border trading. MA Thesis, University of KwaZulu-Natal, Durban.

Minde, I. and Nakhumwa, T. (1997) Informal cross-border trade between Malawi and her neighbouring countries. Agricultural Policy Research Unit, University of Malawi, Lilongwe.

Minde, I. and Nakhumwa, T. (1998) Unrecorded cross-border trade between Malawi and neighbouring countries. Technical Paper No. 90, USAID Africa Bureau, Washington DC.

Mulenga, C. (2007) Small-scale cross border trade between Zambia, Democratic Republic of the Congo, Tanzania and Zimbabwe. Report for SAMP, Institute of Economic and Social Research, University of Zambia, Lusaka.

Mutopo, P. (2010) Women trading in food across the Zimbabwe-South Africa border: Experiences and strategies. *Gender & Development*, 18: 465-477.

Muzvidziwa, V. (1998) Cross-border trade: A Strategy for climbing out of poverty in Masvingo, Zimbabwe. *Zambezia*, 25: 29-58.

Muzvidziwa, V. (2001) Zimbabwe's cross-border women traders: Multiple identities and responses to new challenges. *Journal of Comparative African Studies*, 19: 67-80.

Muzvidziwa, V. (2006) Informal cross-border trade among women in the Southern Africa development community. OSSREA, Addis Ababa.

Muzvidziwa, V. (2012) Cross-border traders: Emerging, multiple and shifting identities. *Alternation*, 19: 217-238.

Mwaniki, J. (2003) The impact of informal cross border trade on regional integration in SADC and its implications on wealth creation. IRED, Geneva.

Ndiaye, T. (2009) Sharing the findings of the baseline studies on women in informal cross border trade in Africa. Presentation at ECA/ATPC Inception Workshop on Mainstreaming Gender into Trade Policy, Addis Ababa.

Nethengwe, N. (1999) Cross-border dynamics in southern Africa: A study of informal cross-border trade between South Africa and Zimbabwe. MA Thesis, University of the Witwatersrand, Johannesburg.

Nickanor, N., Conteh, M. and Eiseb, G. (2007) Unpacking huge quantities into smaller units: Small-scale cross border trade between Namibia and her northern neighbours. Report for SAMP, University of Namibia, Windhoek.

Njiwa, N. (2013) Tackling informal cross-border trade in southern Africa. *Bridges Africa*, 2: 9-11.

Parsley, J. (1998) Free markets, free women? Changing constructions of citizenship and gender relations among cross-border women traders in contemporary southern Africa. MA Thesis, University of the Witwatersrand, Johannesburg.

Peberdy, S. (2000a) Mobile entrepreneurship: Informal cross-border trade and street trade in South Africa. *Development Southern Africa*, 17: 201-219.

Peberdy, S. (2000b) Border crossings: Small entrepreneurs and informal sector cross border trade between South Africa and Mozambique. *Tjidschrift voor Economische en Sociale Geographie*, 91: 361-378.

Peberdy, S. and Crush, J. (2001) Invisible trade, invisible travellers: The Maputo Corridor Spatial Development Initiative and informal cross-border trading. *South African Geographical Journal*, 83: 115-123.

Peberdy, S. and Rogerson, C. (2002) Transnationalism and non-South African entrepreneurs in South Africa's small, medium and micro-enterprise economy. In J. Crush and D. McDonald (eds.), *Transnationalism and New African Immigration to South Africa* (pp. 20-40). Cape Town: SAMP.

Raimundo, I. and Cau, B. (2007) Border monitoring of cross border trade: Mozambique. Report for SAMP, University of Eduardo Mondlane, Maputo.

Raimundo, I., Crush, J. and Pendleton, W. (2014) The state of food insecurity in Maputo, Mozambique. AFSUN Series Report No. 20, Cape Town.

Sandrey, R. (2012) An analysis of the SADC Free Trade Area. Trade Law Centre, Stellenbosch.

Tevera, D. and Tawodzera, G. (2007) Cross border trade: The case of Beitbridge, Forbes, Chirundu and Nyamapanda Border Posts. Report for SAMP, University of Zimbabwe, Harare.

Tsoka, M. (2007) Cross border trade study: Malawi report. Report for SAMP, Centre for Social Research, University of Malawi, Lilongwe.

UN Women (2009) Zimbabwe. UN Women Regional Office for Southern Africa, Nairobi.

Zindela, N. (2007) Informal cross border trade in Swaziland. Report for SAMP, University of Swaziland, Kwaluseni.

Chapter Thirteen

Unpacking National Policy Towards the Urban Informal Economy

Christian M. Rogerson

INTRODUCTION

This chapter focuses on the changing policy environment towards informality and informal entrepreneurship in South Africa. More particularly, it seeks to contribute a deepened understanding of the shifting responses by national government towards informal enterprises. The chequered history of policy development by national government towards the informal economy forms the basis of the first section of discussion. Drawing upon extensive documentary analysis and a review of policy material, the key directions in national government policy towards the informal economy are unravelled. The chapter argues that over the first two decades of democracy, issues relating to policy development about and for the informal economy have moved to the forefront of the agenda of national government. One of the factors propelling the rising policy attention of national government towards the informal economy is the participation in South Africa's urban informal economies of increasing numbers of international migrants (Skinner, 2014). The chapter therefore charts the ebb and flow of policy development by national government towards the informal economy as a whole including various controversial regulatory measures that threaten substantively to undermine the livelihoods of migrant entrepreneurs.

SHIFTING POLICY

The informal economy appeared early on the policy agenda after South Africa's democratic transition. The 1995 *White Paper on the National Strategy for the Development and Promotion of Small Business* made a commitment for government legal interventions and other resources for forging an enabling environment in which small enterprises and survivalist enterprises could contribute to economic development alongside larger enterprises. The associated National Small Business Act of 1996 was a landmark in specifically including "survivalist" and micro enterprises within the umbrella terminology of small, medium and micro enterprises (SMMEs) and thus incorporating them as targets of government's small business strategy (SALGA, 2012: 22). Notwithstanding this commitment, the greatest attention by government support agencies focussed on providing assistance to medium-sized enterprises with small enterprises given reduced support and almost no attention devoted to the informal economy or survivalist enterprises.

The major achievement of the first decade of SMME support related to the establishment of a new architecture for supporting the SMME economy, which had been largely neglected throughout the apartheid era. However, few of the targeted SMMEs were growing businesses and little of the funding allocated to programme support reached the struggling communities of black-owned enterprises, which continued to be economically marginalized (Rogerson, 2004). Among the reasons for the poor performance were funding constraints, weak policy coordination and implementation, and the fact that the existing policy benefits were captured by medium-sized enterprises (often white-owned).

Among those by-passed by SMME policy implementation by national government were the enterprises of the informal economy. A critical review of the first decade of SMME policy in South Africa concluded that there was "relative neglect of policy support to micro-entrepreneurs and the informal economy where previously disadvantaged entrepreneurs are most important" (Rogerson, 2004: 773). Overall, survivalist informal enterprise was badly neglected (Rogerson, 2004). In 1999, for example, the Small Business Regulatory Review by the Department of Trade and Industry (DTI) recommended the development of a national policy for the regulation of informal trade to guide municipalities towards some consistency of approach. This recommendation was not, however, given any further attention (DTI, 2013a).

Policy debates about the informal economy were given a boost in November 2003 when President Mbeki began speaking publicly about South Africa's "first" and "second" economy

(Reynolds and Van Zyl, 2006). Mbeki's pre-occupation with the second economy elevated the policy focus and profile of a part of the SMME economy that hitherto had received little policy support from national government (Rogerson, 2007). In 2004, the ruling African National Congress (ANC) clarified the second economy as a "mainly informal, marginalized, unskilled economy, populated by the unemployed and those unemployable in the formal sector" (African National Congress, 2004: 7). Almost immediately, the concept of the second economy became part of policy discourse at all levels of government in South Africa. Skinner (2006: 125) points out that while the second economy is an "all-encompassing notion" that includes a number of different employment statuses, it "rejuvenated interest in what the state has and can do for those working in the informal economy."

One outcome was a reassessment of the existing policy framework and the workings of existing institutions. A fresh policy framework was launched in 2006, namely, the Integrated Small Business Development Strategy (DTI, 2006). This framework was rooted in three "pillars of support" for the national SMME economy: to expand access of SMMEs to credit/finance, to extend the access of SMMEs to market opportunities, and for government to engage with questions of regulatory reform (DTI, 2006). A new institutional support framework was also forged with the launch of the national Small Enterprise Development Agency (SEDA) with a mandate to ensure better coordination and integration of policy initiatives. The Integrated Small Enterprise Development Strategy made a commitment to supporting informal sector enterprises as part of South Africa's new strategy for supporting small business. More specifically, it stated that one aspect of the integrated strategy was "facilitating the transition from the informal or second-economy segment of our society to the formal sector, and their growth into small enterprises" (DTI, 2006: 19).

A progress report on the new approach was released in 2011 (Osiba Research, 2011). The key conclusion was that government programmes to support the upgrading of black-owned SMMEs (including informal enterprise) and integrate them into the mainstream economy had so far had minimal impact. The review argued that, on the whole, the continued disappointments of South African SMME policy were not so much about misguided policies but the inability of government to implement its own support programmes (Osiba Research, 2011). Certain critical policy deficiencies were still identified, however. Most important, small business development in South Africa lacked a clear champion at the highest levels of government. The absence of a small business champion resulted in government SMME support agencies not being allocated sufficient resources to execute their mandates; in their not being protected from political directives that stretched them beyond their resources and capabilities; and in a general lack of accountability in SMME policy implementation. For this reason, many called for the establishment of a national small business ministry similar to that in India.

The progress report revealed that national government recognized its own limitations in capacity to implement SMME upgrading and build competitive black-owned SMMEs able to participate in the mainstream economy. National government was even struggling to practice what it preached and apply its own procurement muscle to assist SMMEs, especially black-owned SMMEs. To achieve success, a set of integrated interventions was required encompassing finance, regulatory change and the emerging initiatives to expand market access (Osiba Research, 2011). This prompted the beginnings of a promising partnership with the private sector to promote supplier diversity, which is based on the business case for expanding linkages. One of its major contributions was a set of recommendations that catalyzed the expansion of business incubators as a vehicle for supporting entrepreneurship and improving the survival rates of start-up enterprises (Masutha and Rogerson, 2014a, 2014b). While the review by Osiba Research (2011) was primarily aimed at giving more "hitting power" to the SMME economy, it largely avoided any major policy engagement with the informal economy.

During 2012, the national government launched fresh initiatives to address the absence of specific policy around the informal economy (DTI, 2013a). The DTI stated that resources were being employed "to develop the strategy for intervening in the informal economy" (DTI, 2013b: 16). An important step was the establishment within the DTI of a new directorate, the Informal Business and Chamber Support, which was viewed as a recognition of "the vital importance of the informal business sector in broadening economic participation and creating decent employment" (DTI, 2013a: 26). This directorate was to focus among others things on the development of a National Informal Business Development Strategy (NIBDS) that would guide government intervention in the sector. The new directorate sought "to design programmes aimed at uplifting informal businesses in Townships, Rural and other Needy areas in South Africa to graduate and be part of the mainstream economy" (DTI, 2013a: 26). For the DTI, informal businesses were now "central in the drive for the development of sustainable livelihoods and jobs creation."

A reference group was established by the Broadening Economic Participation Division of DTI through the National Small Business Advisory Council (NSBAC) to provide insights into how to advance "the growth and sustainability of enterprises in the Informal Economy." The Broadening Economic Participation Division was described as "the custodian and champion towards the development of the National Informal Business Development Strategy" (Nkondo, 2012). The central aim of the NIBDS was to offer recommendations for support of the so-called "enterprising poor" (DTI, 2013a: 10). In addition, it aimed to ensure that the informal economy "becomes part of the economic mainstream of the country," a theme constantly restated in government documents (DTI, 2013a: 5). Through the planned implementation of a number of policy and programme interventions, the NIBDS would lead to "gradually unleashing the innovative potential to broaden economic participation and foster inclusive growth" (DTI, 2013a: 5).

The authors regarded the NIBDS as "a milestone" for the informal business sector (DTI, 2013a: 9). It would remove the country's informal business entrepreneurs from the economic margins and enable them "to actively and competitively contribute to the overall economic development of the country" (DTI, 2013a: 11). The proposed strategy also identified a number of challenges relating to lack of access to finance, poor access to skills training and technology, the weakness of informal business associations and their lack of "voice", problems in the legal and regulatory environment, and issues of inter-governmental coordination. These generic issues facing the SMME economy had been identified previously in other government investigations. What was distinctive about the NIBDS analysis was that they were raised in the context of the legal and regulatory environment and the need for inter-governmental coordination.

The central challenges of the legal and regulatory environment were the absence of a nationally coordinated policy and approach to dealing with the informal sector; the lack of a strategic focus by government on informal businesses; and over-regulation, which stifled the growth of the businesses (DTI, 2013a: 20). In preparing the draft NIBDS, the guiding vision was of an evolutionary rather than an involuntary perspective on the growth trajectory of informal enterprises. The strategy ostensibly aimed to create "an enabling policy, regulatory, and programming environment promoting and supporting a developmental continuum for the graduation of Informal Businesses into the mainstream of the formal economy" and more especially "with particular focus on uplifting and empowering disadvantaged informal businesses of vulnerable groups like women, youth and disabled persons" (DTI, 2013a: 27).

Key interventions proposed by the NIBDS were: to strengthen the capacity of the informal business sector by enabling access to information, markets, business development support services (including skills and technology), business infrastructure and finance; to strengthen the capacity of informal business sector organizations; and to provide policy regulatory and programmatic interventions for formalization of informal businesses. The strategy was centred overwhelmingly on the challenges facing informal retailers and devoted only cursory attention to other types of informal business, such as backyard manufacturers, construction or tourism enterprises. In its final invocation, the NIBDS significantly failed to address the need to shift radically the existing structure of informal enterprise by supporting enterprise growth in growing sectors rather than encouraging and supporting the already saturated retail sector.

In December 2013 the first public announcements were made by DTI officials in response to the NIBDS proposals for the development of assistance schemes for supporting the informal economy. The Director General of Trade and Industry, Lionel October, stated that dedicated incentive schemes for small informal businesses had been devised and would "be taken to the Cabinet shortly for approval" (Ensor, 2013a). The proposed package of incentives had, he claimed, been "extensively canvassed with municipalities and business chambers over the past six months" and would be funded out of existing budget allocations. To avert a rush of potential applications, eligibility for proposed incentives was to be confined to "only businesses which had been operating for some time."

The formal implementation of the National Informal Business Upliftment Strategy (NIBUS) commenced in January 2014 (DTI, 2014a). The mandate of NIBUS is "to uplift informal businesses and render support to local Chambers/business associations and municipal Local Economic Development offices to deliver and facilitate access to upliftment programmes" with specific attention to government's designated groups. Spatially, the emphasis in NIBUS is upon uplifting township and rural enterprises. Specifically, the strategy was evolved "to target entrepreneurs in the informal economy." According to the DTI project manager of NIBUS, "business owners will be developed to a point where they have the option to register [formalize] and thereby qualify for better opportunities" (Fredericks, 2014). The essential thinking is therefore in terms of a graduated model with DTI support at each level to open greater opportunities as supported businesses mature and grow. Service support would be channelled through local business chambers, associations and municipal structures, including offices of Local Economic Development.

In identifying the target entrepreneurs, the NIBUS recognizes that "informal business activity cuts across economic sectors" and is not simply concerned with informal trading activities. The NIBUS policy document points out that it "prioritises five economic sectors" that were identified in relation to national government's programme of action and targets specified in the National Development Plan. These include the retail sector; informal manufacturing; services (those mentioned include auto-body repairers such as panel beaters, spray painters, mechanics and car washers, hairdressers, day-care centres and "tourism"); agriculture (targeting agro-processing operations); and construction and maintenance. Five strategic intervention pillars are elaborated: namely, to foster an enabling legal and regulatory environment; upliftment through enterprise development; facilitation of intergovernmental relations for support delivery; partnerships and stakeholder management; and knowledge management for empowerment.

The second major instrument in NIBUS is what is styled as the Informal Business Upliftment Facility (IBUF). This strategy was lauded as offering support "to uplift the conditions and operations of informal businesses in the country" (DTI, 2014b). It targets informal businesses operated by designated groups and once again targets businesses based in townships, rural areas and so-called "depressed areas in towns and cities" (DTI, 2014a). Eligible activities for funding support include skills development, marketing and branding, product improvements, technology support, stock, raw materials and supplies, tools, machinery and equipment, and assistance with business compliance costs. The programme offers a maximum of ZAR60,000 worth of support per enterprise "at the lower end." According to Dambudzo and Zondo (2014: 12), the "ultimate intention is to develop informal businesses into small scale businesses, cooperatives and medium sized, with the capacity to produce high quality products and create sustainable employment opportunities."

One element of IBUF is the roll out of the Informal Traders Upliftment Project. This is described as a pilot project targeted at "developing the capacity of informal traders/retailers to increase the competitiveness of *local traders* and develop decent jobs in the sector (my emphasis)" (DTI, 2014a). Potential beneficiaries would be South African informal traders, market traders, general dealers and spaza shop operators (Dambudzo and Zondo 2014). The project is a partnership between DTI and the Wholesale and Retail Sector Education and Training Authority (DTI, 2014b). One of the aims is to train 1,000 traders in the retail sector over a period of 18 months. Beneficiaries would not have to travel from their local areas and communities to access services and support as necessary forms would be available at municipal offices and, in most cases, businesses would be visited by specialist community field workers.

THE BILL FIASCO

The NIBUS gives much attention to the making of an enabling legal and regulatory environment. The DTI's proposed Licensing of Businesses Bill represented the cornerstone of national government initiatives for dealing with this particular "strategic intervention area" (DTI, 2013b: 25). The proposed bill sought to replace the 1991 Business Act (no 71) legislation that deals with licensing and the carrying on of businesses and shop hours. A critical aspect of the passage of the 1991 Business Act was that it effectively deregulated informal trading with the consequence that municipalities across South Africa were compelled to confront policy challenges around the growing numbers of participants in the informal economy. When the release of the draft Licensing of Businesses Bill was approved in March 2013 by Cabinet, the Department of Communications (2013: 4) stated that the bill "will repeal the current Licensing of Businesses Act of 1991 and will provide a simple and enabling framework for procedures for application of businesses licences by setting standards and norms."

Under the proposed bill, every business (an estimated 6.3 million) in South Africa, whether formal or informal, would be required to register and obtain a licence from their local authority and pay an undisclosed licence fee (Holmes, 2013). For its proponents, this was a new "framework for co-operative governance and harmonisation of standard procedures and minimum requirements for application of business licences" (DTI, 2014d). The bill required each municipal authority to maintain an up-to-date registry of all licensed businesses in its area of authority. Business licences issued within the Act would be valid for five years but could be revoked in circumstances of, inter alia, licensees found guilty of selling counterfeit goods, and contravening the Customs and Excise Act, or the Foodstuffs, Cosmetics and Disinfectants Act. The implementation of the Act was to be undertaken by "inspectors" and so-termed "accredited community-based organisations" that would be given sweeping powers to assist municipal licensing authorities in monitoring and enforcement. Inspectors could include any "suitable" person appointed by the licensing authority, Customs and Excise personnel, health officers, traffic officers, or members of the South African Police Service. Such persons would have wide powers to conduct inspections, remove and confiscate goods, issue fines, enter premises, request documents and even to close a business pending investigation. Contraventions of the bill and failure to produce a licence would be punishable by fines or imprisonment of up to 10 years (Holmes, 2013).

The release of the bill for public comment unleashed an immediate storm of contro-versy. It was widely condemned across a spectrum from organized private sector business, informal sector trader organizations, NGOs, researchers and some local authorities, most notably the City of Cape Town. Among the most common criticisms was that it would increase bureaucratic processes of "red tape" and have a negative impact on business oper-ations. Ironically, this expansion of red tape was proposed at a time when the DTI was introducing, in cooperation with the Department of Cooperative Governance, a pilot pro-gramme encouraging municipalities to reduce red tape as part of its initiatives for improv-ing local business environments to encourage private investment (DTI, 2013c, 2013d). The differences between this policy and the cumbersome registration processes for licensing in the bill could not have been sharper.

A second concern related to the capacity of many municipalities faced with human resource constraints to fulfil the bill's requirements of developing a business register and of responding to applications for business licences within the defined 30-day period. As pointed out in a submission made by the City of Cape Town, "the proposed bill requires that municipalities change existing regulations within their jurisdiction and places the onus of inspection and enforcement on the municipality, without any budgetary provision made for this…the fact remains that municipalities simply do not have the resources to carry out the enforcement of the proposed bill" (Bloor, 2013). Informal traders rejected the bill as prejudicial to the poorest traders in terms of costs of licensing and to illiterate traders who were discriminated against by the application procedures (Ensor, 2013b). The South African Informal Traders Alliance issued a press statement that further highlighted that it was "very much open for corruption and abuse of power" and law enforcers and inspec-tors "have too much power" (SAITA, 2013). As Duncan (2013) pointed out, the bill "grants astonishingly sweeping authority to municipalities and to the inspectors who are tasked with monitoring business compliance" such that the "potential for abuse, corruption and harassment is clear."

The DTI Minister aggressively defended the bill as necessary to stop the importation and sale of counterfeit goods. Speaking to an audience of hundreds of informal business-persons at the Port St Johns Sports Ground, the Minister emphasized that NIBUS would "not support businesses which sell illegal and counterfeit goods" and threatened the operators of such businesses by proclaiming, "we will clamp down on you and put you in jail" (DTI, 2014c). However, organized business noted that the bill was unnecessary as provisions already existed to address compliance in terms of counterfeit goods and businesses selling illicit goods (Mail & Guardian, 2013).

A NEW MINISTRY

One indicator of continued high level policy commitment by national government to SMME development in South Africa was the announcement of the creation of a dedicated Ministry for small business. The announcement was made in President Zuma's 2014 State of the Nation Address. The rationale given for the formation of the department was the critical contributions made by SMMEs in terms of accounting for 56 per cent of employment and of the National Development Plan's vision that potentially 90 per cent of new jobs would be created by SMMEs. In early 2015, the new Department of Small Business Development (DSBD) was still in the process of being instituted formally and taking over much of the suite of responsibilities for small business development that since 1995 had been the mandate of the Department of Trade and Industry.

Press reports indicate that delays in its formal establishment relate to budgetary allocations and "turf wars" between the new Ministry and DTI. One presentation by the DSBD noted that its programmes were still structured like those of the DTI and that there had been "delays in the transfer of functions from the DTI to the Department of Small Business Development" (DSBD, 2014). It remains unclear if the final division of duties of the DSBD and the DTI will clash or overlap. Seemingly, the new Ministry will absorb the programmes falling under the Broadening Participation Division of DTI, which relate to small business development under the relevant legislation of the National Small Business Act (Mohoto, 2014). A presentation made by the DSBD to the Parliamentary Portfolio Committee in August 2014 confirmed that its operations were fundamentally structured by the National Small Business Act, which provided guidelines for state promotion of small businesses and authorized the establishment of the national Small Enterprise Development Agency as well as the National Small Business Advisory Council (Parliamentary Monitoring Group, 2014).

One statement of the potential division of responsibilities between the DSBD and the DTI stressed that although the two departments shared similar goals they would have different mandates. The DSBD would prioritize "entrepreneurship and the advancement of small, medium and micro-enterprises as the catalyst to achieving economic growth and development, whereas the DTI provides financial support to qualifying companies in various sectors of the economy" (Dludla, 2014). Put another way, the DSBD would "plant entrepreneurial seeds and DTI will provide funding and support to grow the enterprise" (Dludla, 2014). An address by Lindiwe Zulu, the appointed Minister for Small Business Development, highlighted that "innovation, entrepreneurship and small business development are areas where we need to focus with every ounce of our collective energy."

The DSBD will clearly assume responsibility for the implementation and rollout of NIBUS (DSBD, 2014). The operations of a group of informal sector programmes are part of the DSBD's objective of facilitating "broad-based economic participation through targeted interventions to achieve more inclusive growth." The rollout of NIBUS is to move beyond the pilot projects undertaken in the Eastern Cape. Among "action plans" that have been flagged are, inter alia, a chamber support agreement that has been signed with SEDA to support the leadership and members of chambers, partnership guidelines for funding between DTI/DSBD and municipalities, and a draft implementation agreement between the DTI, the Department of Higher Education and Training (DHET) and the German Federal Enterprise for International Cooperation (GIZ) on the rollout of support for a basic entrepreneurial skills development programme, which will fall under NIBUS.

EXCLUDING MIGRANT ENTREPRENEURS

Implicit at first, and now increasingly explicit, is the fact that government support for the informal economy is conditional and exclusionary in nature along lines of citizenship and immigration status in South Africa. Government programmes are to be targeted at and support South Africans rather than everyone in the informal economy. This means that refugees, asylum-seekers and other migrants are not the intended beneficiaries of government programmes. Indeed, the new policies are explicitly designed to improve the competitive position of South Africans against non-citizens.

One of the most striking aspects of the NIBDS is the detailed focus given to "foreigners" under the legal and regulatory environment and what was styled at one DTI presentation as the "foreign trader invasion" (DTI, 2013b: 20). The strategy document observed that "there are no regulatory restrictions in controlling the influx of foreigners", "no synergy between the DTI and Home Affairs in devising strategies and policies to control foreign business activities" and no data "to confirm the expressed challenge on foreigner trading" (DTI, 2013b: 20). It further argued that "the Immigration and Refugee Status Act (sic) is still perceived by majority citizens (sic) to be too lenient to foreigners; giving them an unfair advantage over nationals" (DTI, 2013a: 29). The report also selectively applauds policy initiatives that have been introduced in Ghana, India and Malaysia restricting certain segments of the informal economy to locals and excluding non-citizens from trading in certain areas.

Under the heading of inter-governmental coordination, the report highlights the lack of alignment between local government and national and provincial tiers of government in supporting the informal economy and that national legislation "has not been able to empower municipalities in addressing informal business issues" (DTI, 2013b: 21). That said, the discussion again turns into an anti-migrant discourse with the statement: "informal businesses feel strongly that there is no synergy or institutional linkages between the DTI and COGTA…on one hand and the DTI and Department of Home Affairs on the other, on synchronizing legal and regulatory elements dealing with informal sector, *especially the one involving foreigner trading* (my emphasis)" (DTI, 2013a: 20).

Several aspects of the 2013 Licensing of Businesses Bill are explicitly aimed at migrant entrepreneurs. The strategy stresses the imperative for registering informal entrepreneurial activities on a national registration database built from a municipal base and the need to crack down on counterfeit goods, which is associated with immigrant-run businesses. In addition, in terms of responses to the so-called foreign trader challenge, it proposes upliftment of local traders, the need for clear policy and regulations on foreign traders such that there could be "no trading without being legal in the country, and partnership promotion between local and foreign traders" (DTI, 2013b: 25). Further, "there is no indication given in the Bill as to what the criteria will be for issuing a licence" (Dadoo, 2013). Officials of the Department of Home Affairs considered "that foreigners whose status is not confirmed (6 months) should not be granted licences" and requested that the Bill "be aligned to the provisions of Immigration and Refugees Acts" (DTI, 2014d).

In addition, the obligation of licensing authorities to involve community-based organizations and business associations in monitoring and implementation "sounds suspiciously like an attempt to get South Africans on board to assist the police in identifying and rooting out foreign traders" (Crush, 2013). Among its provisions for application for licences in relation to migrant entrepreneurs was the stipulation that they must hold a valid business permit in terms of the 2002 Immigration Act and any other documentation that might be required "to verify the status of such a foreigner" (DTI, 2014d). Segatti (2013) argues that the bill "scapegoats" foreign business operators. Crush (2013) points out that one of its less subtle objectives "is to make it so difficult for non-citizens to operate small businesses in the country that they will go home."

In particular, licences would be granted only to non-citizens who have first acquired a business permit under the Immigration Act or a refugee permit under the Refugees Act. Effectively this means that all non-South African cross-border traders and entrepreneurs would "first have to apply for a business permit in their country of origin and guarantee that they have R2.5m to invest in South Africa before they can get a licence to trade" (Crush, 2013). Without such business permits, "foreigners" would not be granted licences to trade in terms of the bill (Skinner, 2014). Arguably, as Duncan (2013) points out, this proposal "is meant to give police a good excuse to harass Somali street hawkers and immigrant spaza owners, and to be a sop to South Africans who feel they face 'unfair competition' from foreigners."

Representatives of street trader groups such as StreetNet Association reiterated that the "bill took no account of informal cross-border traders who had no way of getting a work permit as the Immigration Act made no provision for them" thus opening them up to extended harassment by officialdom (Ensor, 2013b). For Segatti (2013), the bill simply threatened an "immediate blow" to an already fragile sector, that of regional cross-border trade. As a whole, the poorly-conceived draft of the Licensing of Businesses Bill exhibits "the major intent to circumscribe informal entrepreneurship as well as to stop foreign nationals" (SAMP, 2014: 3). Moreover, Skinner (2014) maintains that the xenophobic sentiments in the bill underscore the pressing need for greater and more nuanced appreciation of the contributions made by foreigners to the informal economy in South Africa.

Finally, other critics railed against the bill which "stands as a testament to political short-sightedness and dysfunctional government coordination" and suggested that "the real motive behind the Bill was more to respond swiftly to mounting lobbying pressure than to legislate responsibly" (Segatti, 2013). The growth of such lobbying pressures had been building since 2008. An important landmark, however, was in 2011 when an organization termed the Greater Gauteng Business Forum was formed and threatened "drastic measures" against asylum-seekers and refugees who had opened retail stores in Eldorado Park, Johannesburg. Leaders of this grouping issued statements such as this:

> *We want them to leave. Before, we said let them remain here because they are also human beings and they're supposed to stay somewhere. Now we're saying:*

Just close your shops and leave the area. We don't like them, we don't want them to be around townships any more. The government is supposed to take them to a camp somewhere, not allow them to come inside our townships (Misago and Wilhelm-Solomon, 2011).

In 2012, an ANC "peace and stability policy document" proposed that non-South Africans should not run spaza shops without adhering to certain legislation "which may or may not apply to South Africans" and called for a strengthening of laws against "foreigners" running spaza shops (Mail & Guardian, 2012). Although the proposal was shelved, it was reported in 2014 as again "being raised by party structures and going to be a major issue at the national general council next year [2015]" (Zwane, 2014a). The refugee rights group, People Against Suffering, Oppression and Poverty, describes the anti-migrant proposals as "unconstitutional" and "foolish" in that they take no cognisance of the reliance of many South African poor communities on the cheap goods made available through Somali, Bangladeshi or Pakistani operated stores. Arguably, "the ANC seems to be more concerned about the businessmen and elites in the townships and not the poor families who depend on the foreign-owned shops for cheaper loaves of bread and cups of rice" (Zwane, 2014b).

Overall, the anti-foreign proposals of the DTI indicated that it was "giving in to the pressure of small but powerful groups of business operators":

Calls for evictions of foreign traders, caps on numbers of foreigners authorised to operate in designated areas, and a toughening of immigration and border control, by organisations such as the Greater Gauteng Business Forum, often related by ANC local representatives, have clearly made their way up the government machinery. First in ANC policy documents discussed throughout 2012 culminating in the Mangaung regulations. Then in Cabinet and down to DTI... Instead of taking into consideration the complexities coming with the regulation of trade in volatile and vulnerable communities, and adopting a prudent and inclusive approach, the DTI has preferred to expedite an inconvenient matter in a crude manner. And to surrender to the pressure exerted by a small but powerful constituency of politically connected entrepreneurs (Segatti, 2013).

In response to the outcry surrounding the bill, DTI officials initially sought to suggest that its proposals had "won strong support from some municipalities and small business people in townships who saw registration as a way of gaining access to government support programmes" (Ensor, 2013c). Further, the value was reiterated of developing a central database of all businesses, particularly in terms of regulating businesses. DTI officials defended the bill as never having the intention of introducing an onerous registration process and that instead the department wanted a "negative" database containing those found to be involved in illegal activities with transgressors to be excluded from operating in South Africa (Ensor, 2013d; McLaughlin, 2013). Moreover, the Minister claimed that in his view "there was no provision in the Bill that targeted foreigners" and at its core it was designed to combat the trade in substandard products and "the significant illicit economy that was operating in South Africa's urban and peri-urban areas, and which posed a serious threat to small businesses in the country" (McLaughlin, 2013).

Eventually, during May 2013, DTI officials conceded that the bill was "too blunt" and in need of re-drafting before going back to Cabinet (Ensor, 2013d). As part of the process of rethinking the bill, the DTI appointed a task team to re-examine and make recommendations in areas of its shortcomings. The team was informed that general agreement exists that the bill would assist greatly in curbing xenophobic tendencies and promoting a regulated approach regarding refugees and immigrants who were in the country lawfully. Indeed, one of the task team's terms of reference was to assess how the Refugees Act and Immigration Act could be enforced uniformly without inciting xenophobia (Davies, 2013).

In support of the work of the task team, several workshops were hosted by the DTI as part of its programme of provincial consultations on the Licensing of Businesses Bill. At one of the workshops, however, it was evident that "the DTI was not able to clearly articulate the policy objectives behind the Bill or what gap in the current legislation this new formula is supposed to remedy" (Dadoo, 2013). The consultation process about the revised bill was concluded by mid-2014, albeit it appears the task team met only a few times. However, by February 2015 the promised revision of the bill had still not appeared and it was unclear whether the proposed legislation would be tinkered with or dropped altogether.

A xenophobic streak is also evidenced at the highest level of the DTI with statements from the former deputy trade and industry minister about "foreign-owned businesses hampering rural growth." At a national SMME summit held in White River, Mpumalanga, the deputy small business development minister is reported to have said: "You still find many spaza shops with African names, but when you go in to buy you find your Mohammeds and most of them are not even registered" (City Press, 2013). In terms of the controversies surrounding competition from migrant businesses, the new Small Business Development Minister Lindiwe Zulu made several forthright statements. She said that South African spaza owners should learn from the business practices of their foreign counterparts who were described as "better at running shops than the local owners – they have a great network system" (Zwane, 2014b):

> They must ask themselves how can they [foreigners] be successful in the same communities [where] others [locals] claim they can't succeed. I'm not talking about illegal immigrants or foreigners who trade without proper licences; I'm talking about legitimate foreign traders. How are they able to make it when our people can't. It is because they know business. It is in their blood...We can bury our heads in the sand and not want to learn. We can say, but they don't pay taxes, they are here illegally and are being successful, you must ask yourself why and how. This is a global world and South Africa is no longer cut off from it... Let us wake up to the reality of today to say how the wide world is operating. You have foreigners – how are they more successful when they operate in the same communities in which we fail? (Zwane 2014b).

Finally, the Minister made another clear statement on potential proposals that foreign entrepreneurs not be allowed to own spaza shops in townships as local traders could not compete:

> I think we need a conversation as South Africans around that issue. What are you going to do with the ones that are already here [legally]? Throw them in camps and say don't make a living? They must make a living. The more they make a living, the more they contribute to the economy. They pay taxes and are active participants in the economy. By allowing them to be immigrants you have given them a right to make a living. It's a human right (Zwane, 2014b).

The "us" and "them" framing of the issues is a constant refrain in the Minister's world. Indeed, on another occasion she urged all migrant entrepreneurs to "share their secrets" with South Africans, a prescription that has been criticised by commentators (Skinner and Crush, 2015).

CONCLUSION

Looking back over the past 20 years of South African national government policy towards the informal economy, a number of critical points emerge. From 1994 to as recently as 2011 the government made a set of rhetorical commitments to support informal enterprises as part of the SMME economy. However, few initiatives were actually launched in terms of implementation of support measures towards the informal economy. Instead, informal enterprises were marginal to the activities of the DTI, which gave preference to supporting the upgrading challenges of more established enterprises. It was not until 2012 that the first national initiatives were made to design a policy specifically to support elements of the informal economy.

The new policy framework that has emerged is encapsulated in the National Informal Business Development Strategy and subsequent roll out of support programmes as well as proposals for a changing of the regulatory environment. Regrettably, the new policy has been drawn up against the backdrop of only a limited empirical knowledge base about the actual size, structure and dynamics of informal economy development in the country. In addition, the proposed policy framework essentially seeks to bring support interventions into play to bolster the existing forms of informal economic enterprise, which is massively dominated by survivalist informal retailing. The policy documentation offers little analysis and focus to support the imperative for transforming the complexion of South Africa's informal economy from its dominance by survivalist informal retailing towards a greater contribution by other kinds of informal enterprise that might offer greater opportunities for sustainable enterprise development.

In the development of a new national informal business development strategy and the shifting regulatory environment, much policy attention has been directed at the activities and role of international migrant entrepreneurs. In particular, the perceived threats to South Africans posed by competition from migrant retail businesses have been an important stimulus for new, and so far incomplete, regulations about business licensing. The proposed Licensing of Businesses Bill has been severely criticized in many respects, not least for being unworkable given the existing capacity constraints of South African local municipalities and for potentially discouraging informal entrepreneurship. The greatest threat to entrepreneurship is that posed to migrant entrepreneurs in South Africa whose operations would be endangered by many of the provisions contained in the bill. It has been argued that the xenophobic content in the proposals of the Licensing of Businesses Bill represents a rejection of an inclusive policy approach to the informal economy and has been introduced under the pressures of small but influential groups of politically connected entrepreneurs.

The analysis presented in this chapter highlights a number of immediate policy directions that might be considered in respect of migrant entrepreneurship. First, to achieve the objective of an inclusive informal economy, there is an urgent need for facilitating partnerships, cultural dialogue and skills transfers between South African and migrant entrepreneurs. Second, as refugee and migrant flows appear likely to continue, there is a requirement for national and local governments to offer integration programmes that seek to increase the local embeddedness of migrants, particularly in cities. Third, the policy lens must be re-directed away from xenophobia per se to produce spaces of integration where locals and migrants can interact and coexist in more meaningful ways. Above all, there can be no progress towards inclusive informal cities without accepting that migrants are an inevitable feature of South African life. The collection of a base of new knowledge, such as that presented in this volume, across a range of empirical investigations potentially can inform and strengthen the vision for building policies to achieve inclusive growth for South Africa's informal economy.

ACKNOWLEDGEMENTS

Thanks are due to Vanya Gastrow who undertook the interviews in Cape Town, to Tanya Zack for critical documentation inputs on Johannesburg, and most importantly to Teddy and Skye Norfolk for compelling contributions to this report as a whole.

REFERENCES

ANC (African National Congress) (2004) Approaches to poverty eradication and economic development VII: Transform the second economy. *ANC Today*, 4.

Bloor, G. (2013) Cape Town opposed to licensing of business bill. *Politicsweb*.

City Press (2013) Foreign-owned businesses hampering rural growth: DTI. 10 October.

Crush, J. (2013) Proposed law will hammer informal economy. *Business Day*, 15 April.

Dadoo, R. (2013) Department of Trade and Industry (DTI) organizes a workshop on Business Licensing Bill in the Western Cape Province. *CORMSA News*, October.

Dambudzo, J. and Zondo, B. (2014) The role of policy and legislation in promoting township enterprise competitiveness. Paper presented at 5th Annual Soweto Conference on Entrepreneurship and Small Business Development, University of Johannesburg, Soweto.

Davies, R. (2013) Letter of appointment to serve on the Task Team: Licensing of Businesses Bill, 12 August.

Department of Communications (2013) Statement of Cabinet Meeting of 13 March 2013. Pretoria.

DSBD (Department of Small Business Development) (2014) Presentation on the APP for Quarter 1 and Quarter 2 of 2014/2015. Pretoria.

DTI (Department of Trade and Industry) (2006) Integrated small-enterprise development strategy: Unlocking the potential of South African entrepreneurs. Pretoria.

DTI (2013a) The National Informal Business Development Strategy (NIBDS). DTI Broadening Participation Division, Pretoria.

DTI (2013b) National Informal Business Development Strategic Framework. Presentation to ESEC by Informal Business and Chamber Support Directorate, 9 October.

DTI (2013c) Guidelines for reducing municipal red tape: how municipalities can improve service delivery that supports small business. DTI and Department of Cooperative Governance and Traditional Affairs, Pretoria.

DTI (2013d) Red tape is an unnecessary burden to SMMEs: Davies. Media Statement, Pretoria.

DTI (2014a) The National Informal Business Upliftment Strategy (NIBUS). Pretoria.

DTI (2014b) Minister Davies to unveil the National Upliftment Strategy for informal traders. Media Statement, Pretoria.

DTI (2014c) The National Informal Business Upliftment Strategy will not support Illegal Businesses: Davies. Media Statement, Pretoria.

DTI (2014d) Businesses Act Review. Presentation by the Consumer & Corporate Regulation Division of DTI. Pretoria.

Dludla, S. (2014) Intro to the Small Business Development Ministry. *SME South Africa*, 29 September.

Duncan, F. (2013) Why you should really worry about the Business Licensing Bill. *Moneyweb*, 9 August.

Ensor, L. (2013a) Department devises incentive scheme for informal sector. *Business Day Live*, 3 December.

Ensor, L. (2013b) Informal traders criticise licensing bill. *Business Day Live*, 29 April.

Ensor, L. (2013c) Business licences 'not socialism just normal practice.' *Business Day Live*, 26 April.

Ensor, L. (2013d) Licensing Bill to be redrafted after avalanche of disapproval. *Business Day Live*, 16 May.

Fredericks, N. (2014) Informal businesses to get help. *Small Business Connect*, 16 February.

Holmes, T. (2013) Half-hatched law lays hawkers low. *Mail & Guardian*, 3 May.

Mail & Guardian (2012) Stricter laws mooted for foreigner owned spaza shops. 10 March.

Mail & Guardian (2013) SACCI rejects Bill intended to ease licensing process. 24 April.

Masutha, M. and Rogerson, C. (2014a) Small business incubators: An emerging phenomenon in South Africa's SMME economy. *Urbani Izziv*, 25: S48-S63.

Masutha, M. and Rogerson, C. (2014b) Small enterprise development in South Africa: The role of business incubators. *Bulletin of Geography: Socio-Economic Series*, 26: 141-155.

McLaughlin, P. (2013) Minister Davies withdraws Licensing of Businesses Bill, *Parlyreportsa*, 22 May.

Misago, J-P and Wilhelm-Solomon, M. (2011) Foreign traders are fair game. *Mail & Guardian*, 20 May.

Mohoto, M., (2014) Briefing on the Broadening Participation Division of the DTI and the National

Empowerment Fund (NEF) to the Portfolio Committee on Trade and Industry, Cape Town, 11 July.

Nkondo, G. (2012) Invitation to participate on the Reference Group – National Informal Business Development Strategy, 23 August 2012.

Osiba Research (2011) Rethinking small business support in South Africa. Report for Department of Trade and Industry, Pretoria.

Parliamentary Monitoring Group (2014) Legislation supporting small medium and micro enterprises & cooperatives: Department and Minister of Small Business Development Briefings Meeting 20 August.

Reynolds, N. and van Zyl, J. (2006) South Africa's misunderstood 'dual economy'. *SANE Views*, 6(14).

Rogerson, C. (2004) The impact of the South African government's SMME programmes: A ten year review, *Development Southern Africa*, 21: 765-784.

Rogerson, C. (2007) Second economy versus informal economy: A South African affair, *Geoforum*, 38: 1053-1057.

Segatti, A. (2013) Business Bill: Target trade policies not people. *New Age*, 10 May.

Skinner, C. (2006) Falling through the policy gaps? Evidence from the informal economy in Durban, South Africa. *Urban Forum*, 17: 125-148.

Skinner, C. (2014) Setting the scene: The South African informal sector. Paper for Workshop on Urban Informality and Migrant Entrepreneurship in Southern Africa, Cape Town.

Skinner, C. and Crush, J. (2015) Forget the myths about foreigners. *Sunday Times: Business Times*, 1 March.

SAITA (South African Informal Traders Alliance) (2013) Statement: Press conference held to discuss the Licensing Bill. Soweto.

SALGA (South African Local Government Association) (2012) Making the informal economy visible: Guidelines for municipalities in respect of adopting a more developmental approach towards the informal economy. Pretoria.

SAMP (2014) Urban informality and migrant entrepreneurship in Southern African cities. Conference Report, African Centre for Cities and SAMP, University of Cape Town, Cape Town.

Zwane, T. (2014a) Spazas: Talking shop is good for business. *Mail & Guardian*, 6 November.

Zwane, T. (2014b) Price is king in clash of the spazas. *Mail & Guardian*, 6 November.

Index

Note: Page numbers in italics refer to tables and figures.

www.ingramcontent.com/pod-product-compliance
Lightning Source LLC
Chambersburg PA
CBHW080356030426
42334CB00024B/2890